P9-ECP-975

CULTURAL POLITICS

Medieval literary politics

CULTURAL POLITICS

Further titles in preparation

Medieval literary politics:
shapes of ideology

Sheila Delany

MANCHESTER UNIVERSITY PRESS
MANCHESTER and NEW YORK

distributed exclusively in the USA and Canada by ST. MARTIN'S PRESS

Copyright © Sheila Delany 1990

Published by Manchester University Press
Oxford Road, Manchester M13 9PL, UK
and Room 400, 175 Fifth Avenue,
New York, NY 10010, USA

Distributed exclusively in the USA and Canada
by St. Martin's Press, Inc.
175 Fifth Avenue, New York, NY 10010, USA

British Library cataloguing in publication data
Delany, Sheila
  Medieval literary politics: shapes of ideology. –
  (Cultural politics).
  1. English literature, 1066–1400 – Critical studies
  I. Title   II. Series
  820.9'001

Library of Congress cataloging in publication data
Delany, Sheila.
    Medieval literary politics: shapes of ideology/Sheila Delany.
      p. cm.—(Cultural politics)
    Bibliography: p.
    ISBN 0–7190–3045–5. — ISBN 0–7190–3046–3 (pbk.)
    1. Literature, Medieval—History and criticism. 2. Civilization,
  Medieval. I. Title. II. Series.
  PN681.D45   1990   89–12636
    809'.02—dc20

ISBN 0 7190 3045 5 hardback
    0 7190 3046 3 paperback

Photoset in Linotron Joanna
by Northern Phototypesetting Company, Bolton

Printed in Great Britain
by Bell & Bain Limited, Glasgow

Contents

This book is dedicated to my father and mother,

William and Mina Winnick

of New Haven, Connecticut

Acknowledgements

In conversation, correspondence and commentary on earlier versions of material included here, friends and colleagues have helped me to take things further. I want especially to thank David Aers, Francis Barker, Louise Fradenburg, Bernard Ezuma Igwe, and Stephen Knight. Thanks also to my undergraduate research assistants – Caroline Raderecht, Rufus Polson, Arlene Cook and Derrick Pohl – for their energy in ransacking libraries and catalogues over the last few semesters, and Sharon Vanderhook and Anita Mahoney of Simon Fraser University for their skillful help in preparing this manuscript.

Portions of the material, or versions of it, have been presented as talks before groups that include the Australia and New Zealand Association for Medieval and Renaissance Studies, the University of British Columbia Medieval Symposium, the Simon Fraser University History Colloquium, the New England Modern Language Association, the New Chaucer Society, the Medieval Association of the Pacific, the University of California at Berkeley, Stanford University, Wellesley College and the University of Notre Dame, as well as at independent conferences. I want to express my warm appreciation to those who invited me for the opportunity and the stimulus they made possible, particularly to Stephanie Trigg, Tom Hahn, Charles Muscatine, Dolores Frese, Ed Vasta, Peter Beidler and Kathryn Lynch, and to James Herman for hospitality and his back file of 'politics'. I have elsewhere publicly acknowledged the influence of my former comrades of the Spartacist tendency, and if that influence has been supplemented now with others less polemical, it remains nonetheless a perceptible factor in some of the essays included here.

Some of the historical reading that informs these essays was done during a sabbatical year supported by a Canada Council Leave Fellowship in 1976. The writing of the two most recent pieces was completed in Berkeley on a year's release-time grant from the Social Sciences and Humanities Research Council of Canada in 1987-88.

All Chaucer quotations are from F.N. Robinson's second edition of *Works* (Boston: Houghton Mifflin, 1957).

The following essays were previously printed, some in slightly different form: 'Clerks and Quiting in *The Reeve's Tale*', *Mediaeval Studies* 29 (1967); 'Undoing Substantial Connection', *Mosaic* (1972); 'Substructure and Superstructure: the Politics of Allegory in the Fourteenth Century', *Science and Society* 38 (1974); 'Theocratic and Contractual Kingship in *Havelok the Dane*', *Zeitschrift für Anglistik und Amerikanistik* 22 (1974); 'Politics and the Paralysis of Poetic Imagination in *The Physician's Tale*', *Studies in the Age of Chaucer* 3 (1981); 'Mulier est hominis confusio', *Mosaic* 17 (1984); 'Rewriting woman good' in *Chaucer in the Eighties*, ed. J. Wasserman (Syracuse, 1986); 'Mothers to think back through' in *Medieval Texts and Contemporary Readers*, ed. Laurie Finke (Ithaca, 1987).

Preface

These essays, written over a period of two and a half decades, share the premise that the production of literature and of criticism is a social act. I hope that they convey the multiplicity of ways in which this can be true, whether the extra-literary social fact they focus on be class structure, kingship, rebellion, religion, gender relations or language. That listing itself will suggest the evolution of my interests (though the work is not arranged in chronological order), and I've been glad to note, in preparing and revising the essays for publication here, their consistency over time.

What I mean by consistency perhaps deserves some comment, since the methods and theoretical frameworks used in these essays are heterogeneous. There is a fairly classic Marxian substructure-superstructure study (Chapter 3). There is straightforward historicist contextualisation assisting in the definition of the social thrust of a romance (Chapter 4) or in the question of literary 'sisterhood' in gender-oriented criticism (Chapter 6). Other essays concentrate on the determinative force of authorial gender (Chapter 5), on tactics of feminist reading and medieval cultural attitudes (Chapter 8), on treatment of source (Chapter 10) or tradition (Chapter 9) as expressive of authorial social attitudes, on the relevance of language theory and the exchange of women to the Chaucerian representation of women (Chapter 11).

Such diversity of approach is inherent in the project of one who is known as a 'Marxist medievalist' and who has already published a collection of essays entitled *Writing Woman* (1983). This is not only because Marxism addresses itself to the broad field of cultural practices, but also because the left today is a diverse enterprise. It was in Marx's lifetime too, and has been since. The range of methods and theories represented here can be seen as paradigmatic of historical and theoretical developments within the left that have resulted in expansions of Marxist theory, particularly in the areas of language, ideology, bureaucracy, subjectivity, power and gender.

Moreover, if we draw from contemporary critical theory and its modern antecedents the principle that a theoretical approach is a means of generating meaning which itself is chosen and fabricated rather than absolutely immanent, then a given approach is useful to the extent it helps the writer produce the kind of meaning he or she wishes to produce. To this end – the production of social meaning, the meaning I wish to produce – I have found Vladimir Propp appropriate at a certain point; at other points Barthes, Foucault, Althusser, Macherey, Brecht, Trotsky, Virginia Woolf or others have enabled me to generate the picture as I see it or choose to represent it.

If an essay is an attempt or experiment, than a collection of essays, especially one written over a period of time, can fairly be expected to reveal shifts in emphasis which the reader may interpret as fissures or contradictions. One of these, in the present volume, may be my orientation toward gender and its role in literary representation. I continue to believe, as I write in 'Rewriting woman good' and 'Mothers to think back through', that a narrowly feminist approach to culture, which consistently privileges gender over history and class, cannot answer the most important questions we may ask about past or present. At the same time, I have become far more aware in recent years of the importance of gender to our interrogation of history. If I give gender a prominent role in representation – as I do in 'Strategies of silence' and 'Women, nature and language' – it is not in order to deny but rather to expand a historicist rejoinder to a narrower feminism.

Something similar can be said for the movement from substructure-superstructure study in 'Undoing substantial connection' and 'The politics of allegory' to the concern with language and gender in other essays. For some problems or texts, a simpler and more schematic approach can effectively elicit the patterns I wish to emphasise. For access to other patterns, a more nuanced and layered analysis is required, but this doesn't invalidate the former approach. If I refuse a sectarian stance, preferring a more effective tactical flexibility, it is because culture is not monolithic: why should our methods be?

Having said this, I need now to bend the stick the other way, in order to indicate my differences with various other left critics and tendencies, whether Marxist or not. I didn't begin to write socially-oriented criticism out of a desire to be politically effective. On the contrary, I was already politicised. I admired the Russian revolution. In 1964, the Schwerner-Cheney-Goodman case (the kidnap/murder/mutilation of three young civil-rights workers) cut through my lingering indecision whether capitalism could be reformed. I concluded that a system which could perpetrate and legally exonerate such atrocity – admittedly little different from hundreds of other, less famous, racist atrocities over the generations – had to be replaced. This decision led me to work with a revolutionary organisation, to read the classic authors in revolutionary literature, and eventually to join an organisation whose programme seemed best to incorporate a revolutionary will. To write as a Marxist was an extension into scholarship of my beliefs and of my non-academic work, an effort of integration. As Louis Althusser put it, 'I was already a Communist, and I was therefore trying to be a Marxist as well' ('Is it Simple to be a Marxist in Philosophy?'). Organisational life – public life – remained the arena of political effectiveness. And the distinctively Marxian difference from other 'engaged' criticism was – is – neither class nor the value of labour nor social relations of production but rather – as Lenin stressed in *State and Revolution* – the perspective of proletarian revolution leading to destruction of the bourgeois state and to the establishment of a workers' state, eventually and hopefully to evolve ('wither') into full socialism. That it hasn't yet done so doesn't, in my view, invalidate the model.

Unlike many left intellectuals, I didn't believe then, and I don't now (when I am no longer affiliated with an organisation), that intellectuals will change the world through their scholarship. They will change it as everyone else does: through participation in the public life around them. Class struggle manifests itself in cultural representations – hence my sub-title – but it isn't resolved there. (If this were a medieval manuscript I would draw a little pointing hand in the margin here for the benefit of those who like to have the 'message' of a book explicitly defined. On the other hand, I know that assorted 'messages' will be taken, some intended, some not.) This collection becomes, then, what Stanley Fish has called a 'self-consuming artifact', with all that that phrase implies about a relation to its premises and its audience. Any Marxist criticism must 'unbuild its own structures' in hoping for its own obsolescence in the wake of – and as the consequence of – the very social transformation it demands. Indeed it's my ardent hope that a self-consuming artefact is what this will have been – 'along with', as Leon Trotsky commented, 'the programme of our party'.

Why continue, then? For myself, it's in order to participate in some small way in the process of demystification that for many people, especially in the university milieu, is the necessary beginning of radicalisation. This movement in turn can have positive, i.e., socially progressive, effects at a moment of social crisis whether intensely local (as in Berkeley's Free Speech Movement of 1964) or international (such as the issue of support to the Nicaraguan Contras) or anything in between: a strike, an election, etc. It isn't a new idea. It goes back well before February 1944, when Dwight MacDonald, launching his new cultural journal *politics*, wrote:

'We are very well off as to politics', says old Hammond in William Morris's *News From Nowhere*, 'because we have none'. The essence of reactionary politics is to try to get people to behave in a class society as though it were a classless society, i.e., to stop 'playing politics'. ('Why *politics*?')

That the journal's third-campist waffling soon resolved itself into flat post-war anti-communism was predictable. This fact invalidates neither the statement above (limited and fragmentary as it is), nor the many incisive and courageous essays the journal published. (I have in mind particularly the late Robert Duncan's 1946 'The Homosexual in Society'.) Indeed, MacDonald's inadequacy to the task of demystification and radicalisation suggests what I note above about the limits of our chosen arena of work. It remains as true now as it did in 1910 that 'if the actual conquest of the apparatus of society depended on the *previous* coming over of the intelligentsia to the party of the . . . proletariat, then the prospects of collectivism would be wretched indeed' (Leon Trotsky, 'The Intelligentsia and Socialism'). Some leftists concur that those prospects are wretched; I don't.

If, as Terry Eagleton argues, the category of 'aesthetic' has developed over the last two centuries not simply nor even primarily as discourse about art but rather as discourse about structures of feeling, mediating between the rational and the sensual to produce an ideologically laden social practice whose coercive quality is concealed in its appeal to 'universals' of taste, manners, feeling and desire – if this is the case, then to help demystify the aesthetic is a socially useful act. To do so seems especially desirable in the arena of English-speaking medieval studies, a field notoriously resistant to new critical development and one whose father-figures still consider Marxist or gender-conscious work 'marginal' or 'special-interest pleading', believe that the nineteenth century rightly viewed wordplay as 'the lowest form of humour', and could dub as 'historicist' the anti-historical thesis that all medieval vernacular literature re-enacts the Augustinian doctrine of charity. Welcome inroads are being made, on both sides of the Atlantic and in Australia as well, into this consensus: one thinks of the recent work of David Aers, Eugene Vance, Howard Bloch, Stephen Knight, David Lawton, Laura Kendrick, David Wallace, Judith Ferster and others. I know that some of the previously published essays offered here and in *Writing Woman* have helped to form the new consensus, and I hope that this volume will continue to contribute to it.

I don't, I repeat, see such a contribution as the equivalent of direct involvement in the workers' movement or the organised left, but as a supplement and perhaps in some cases a prelude. It isn't, I believe, within the discourse of academic life that a scholar's politics are most importantly tested, but it can be a place to start from.

Run silent, run deep: Heresy and alchemy as medieval versions of utopia

From the decline of the Middle Ages until recent decades, utopian thought has flourished in modern western culture, evident both in writing and in social practise. Every period over the last half-millenium has nourished the utopian impulse, but not, apparently, the Middle Ages: an absence producing, in most histories of utopia, an embarrassing blank between ancient Greece and the sixteenth century. The Renaissance whether humanistic or scientific, the Enlightenment, the industrial nineteenth century, and the first third of the twentieth century: all are rich in texts and some in communities. The recent efflorescence of feminist utopian writing allows us to include our own time in this plenitude, after a short interruption tthat might be called the dystopian interlude. Whether there is a future for utopia is a question that continues to occupy theorists of the mode.[1]

My interest here, though, is not the future of utopia but its prehistory, before it emerged as a distinct subgenre of imaginative literature or political speculation. I am interested in those missing pages in the histories of utopian thought, the moment when the current ran underground: in short, utopianism in the Middle Ages. My working premise for this paper is that the desire to live better was not among the discoveries of the Renaissance, and that what the Manuels call 'the utopian propensity' did indeed exist in the Middle Ages.

Does it matter? That depends on the kind of history we want. I don't wish to revive or recommend utopianism as a political strategy, nor, on the other hand, to render the spectre of revolution less frightening by displaying its tamer 'antecedents'. Yet if we want what Marc Bloch in *The Historian's Craft* called 'a wider and more human history', if we do not merely read history but use it, if we wish to intervene in history to change it, then we are helped – if only in imagining Difference – by a history that includes what was dialectical and materialist and different: the Other, we might say, of that 'historical fable' Francis Barker writes of, the alternatives to that 'conjunction of themes and powers which it is still ours to live, and if enough time remains, undo, today' (p. 116).

Where, then, to look for medieval utopianism? And why the absence of explicit texts? I shall propose two possible sites for exploration, one fairly obvious, the other less so. They are popular heresy and alchemy. Before showing how these two discourses served as channels to the utopian impulse, I want to offer a general account of the lack of specifically utopian material as a corollary to the dominant Catholic ideology of that epoch. That I do not speak of economics here should be taken neither as evasive of the Church's economic role in medieval society (landlord, merchant, financier and consumer); nor as denial of the evolution of Catholic doctrine as an aspect of concrete social practice over many centuries. What I want to focus on here is rather the importance of ideology as a mechanism for social control, a theme announced by Frederick Engels (letter to J. Bloch, 21 September 1890) and taken up more recently by Louis Althusser.

According to orthodox theological doctrine, the ills we confront are a necessary part of the human condition. Poverty, social classes, exploited labour, the concentration of wealth in a few hands, the subordination of women to men, the nuclear family, illness, disease, death and cold weather are seen as necessary consequences of Adam's fall. They constitute the essential human condition, and they are implicit in the curse God laid on Adam and Eve in expelling them from the garden of Eden:

To the woman he said, 'I will greatly multiply your pain in childbearing; in pain you shall bring forth children, yet your desire shall be for your husband, and he shall rule over you.' And to Adam he said . . . 'Cursed is the ground because of you; in toil you shall eat of it all the days of your life; thorns and thistles it shall bring forth to you; and you shall eat the plants of the field. In the sweat of your face you shall eat bread till you return to the ground, for out of it you were taken; you are dust and to dust you shall return.' Genesis 3: 16–19.

In this view of things, life must be a continual expiation for original sin. True happiness is not possible on earth but only in the life after death.

To such an ideology, utopian speculation can only be taboo, for its basic premise implicitly cancels out the effects of Adam's fall. The utopian premise is that human happiness can be achieved by human effort, and it can be achieved during our present historical lifetimes. 'Paradise NOW!' – the title of a famous Living Theatre performance – is the utopian slogan par excellence. The demand for 'paradise now' is what makes

Chaucer's January, in *The Merchant's Tale*, implicitly a heretical utopian when he seeks to recreate the condition of primal sexual innocence with his young wife May in an Edenic garden of his own construction. Dorigen, in *The Franklin's Tale*, takes a step in the same direction when she wishes away the dangerous rocks on Brittany's coast. This wish is of a piece with her earlier effort to create an egalitarian marriage by denying the principle of husbandly lordship. Her refusal to accept the consequences of original sin, whether in marriage or in nature, is Dorigen's central flaw; it is potentially a heretical position precisely because of its utopian content. We recall that, in *The Franklin's Tale*, the correct balance is restored when, in crisis, Arviragus reasserts a correct dominant and authoritative husbandly role.

A modern student of the philosophy of St. Thomas Aquinas explains the Catholic attitude toward utopia as it has survived over the centuries: 'Utopians as a group refuse to believe that the Garden of Eden has been definitely closed. Each apparently considers himself a new Jacob – quite capable of overcoming the angel with the flaming sword guarding the gate.'[2] Another Catholic scholar, Thomas Molnar, claims that utopian thought 'is itself evil and leads to evil' because it is 'an ontological condemnation of the existence of evil . . . a belief in unspoiled beginning and attainable perfection' (pp. 5-7). If these still orthodox views commanded the physical power now that they did in the Middle Ages, there would be no modern history of utopian writing, and certainly that anthem of the 1960's, Bob Dylan's 'Gates of Eden', would have been burnt in public, probably along with its composer.

I don't want to leave it at this, though, for the ideological suppression of utopia is only half the story. The material axis can be approached through an apparent paradox: if the Catholic suppression of utopian heresy, or heretical utopianism, was successful, why does the utopian impulse surface in less explicit forms of heresy? Or, from the other side, if suppression was unsuccessful, if numerous individuals were not afraid to take the sometimes fatal risk of acquiring the heretic label, why did they not go all the way to produce fully-developed speculative social models? The absent necessary, I suspect, is the science of statecraft, which – until the era of fullblown national centralisation in the Renaissance – was not sufficiently defined and diffused as a cultural goal to produce an imaginative literature. If utopia is the imaginative projection of the idea (and the reality) of statecraft, then its development would have to take account of such factors as the spread of literacy and education, the proliferation of national lay bureaucracies, the Tudor revival

of the old Platonic/medieval metaphor of the body politic, and a variety
of other superstructural phenomena linked to the development of bourgeois society in its pre-industrial phase. This is why Louis Marin lists, as
number 3 in his 'Theses on Ideology and Utopia', the following: 'Utopic
discourse makes its appearance historically only when a mode of capi-
talistic production is formed.'[3]

The absence of a distinct medieval genre has sent scholars gleaning bits of
the utopian spirit – what Ernst Bloch calls 'the hope principle' – from
other discourses. It is what I propose to do here, and what one has to do.
However, some of these gleanings strike me as having little to do with
utopia. I shall define utopian thought or writing as that which offers
alternatives to the way we live now, whether these alternatives be collective or individual, mass or elite, political or psychological. Utopia
offers other models, and it is infused with the conviction of genuine
possibility. The lack of such historical present possibility has been my
criterion for excluding from my discussion millenial and apocalyptic
literature, fairytale and myth (including paradisal or golden-age myth),
and the topos of the *locus amoenus*. These modes usually have other
purposes than the utopian: they aim to account for the status quo, to
reconcile us to it, to teach us about it or to transcend it: anything but to
change it. Let me illustrate with two typical and apparent candidates for
inclusion in medieval utopianism: Cokaygne and Joachism.

Cokaygne[4] is that 'big rock candy mountain' land where rivers flow of
milk, honey, oil and wine; where cooked geese walk about; and where
'he who sleeps most earns most'. It is a land of plenitude where even
time runs overfull, for the month has five weeks, and Christmas comes
four times a year. The Cokaygne material was especially popular in Italy,
though single works appear elsewhere: in France (a thirteenth-century
fabliau), England (a fourteenth-century verse satire) and Holland (an
imitation of the French poem). Rabelais echoes the Cokaygne *fabliau* in
Chapter 32 of *Pantagruel*. There, in 'the world in Pantagruel's mouth', the
narrator Alcofribas finds work 'A dormir: car l'on loue des gens à journée
pour dormir et gaignent cinq et six solz par jour; mais ceux qui ronflent
bien gaignent bien sept solz et demy.' So we have Utopia squared, utopia
within Utopia, for Pantagruel and his servant Alcofribas are, at this
moment, already in Utopia, Pantagruel's native land which he has come
to defend against the invasion of the Dipsode King Anarch. Thus Rabelais
goes Sir Thomas More one better, not simply borrowing a place-name
from More but fleshing out his own evangelical vision by locating utopia

within, giving it the dimensions of subjectivity.

In Italy, the Coccagna material seems already to have been present in the popular oral tradition by Boccaccio's time, for the *Decameron* refers to a Cokaygne-like Bengodiland (VIII: 3); but there are no extant printed texts about Coccagna until the fifteenth century. An interesting aspect of an eighteenth-century Italian broadsheet combining pictures and text about Coccagna is its concern to mitigate the labours of human reproduction and socialisation. Women are said to give birth in song and dance, and children are born already walking. This particular text is noteworthy also for its technological orientation: it includes large buildings and a self-propelled vehicle.

But I am getting ahead of the period I've chosen to discuss. Despite its potentially subversive features, and its undeniable expression of the aspirations of ordinary people, I would define Cokaygne as fantasy rather than as utopia. It is not the imagination of the possible that motivates Cokaygne, but rather of the impossible. Its literary affiliations are not with alternate visions of real life, but rather with visions of the afterlife: the New Jerusalem, the Elysian fields, the earthly paradise. This is why the Cokaygne material is so co-optible, even by the clergy itself, custodian of the very ideology that Cokaygne traditionally challenges. This co-optation we see in the English verse satire about Cokaygne, which is not (as A.L. Morton would have it) a 'folk utopia' but patently a clerical production and in fact the product of rivalry between Franciscans and Cistercians in fourteenth-century England (Garbaty).

The same standard of possibility accounts for my exclusion of Joachism,[5] an apocalyptic schematisation of history based on Scriptural exegesis. Joachism offers a peculiar version of millenial/eschatological speculation. It might be characterised as a utopian frame of mind devoid of actual utopian content; or perhaps it might be seen as a utopianism too timid – or too doctrinally orthodox (Joachim of Fiore was, after all, a Cistercian abbot) – to make the leap into possibilism. Although the net effect of Joachim's system may have been to help create some of the subjective conditions for utopian thought, and though he claimed that the 'third kingdom' (or Ideal Era, or final phase) would occur within history, i.e., before the Second Coming of Christ, nonetheless the vision remains ahistorical and essentially mythic. Joachim desires and predicts a spiritual *renovatio* as the last phase in a divinely determined pattern of history. It will be a new world whose inhabitants will be resurrected persons with spiritual bodies. These beings will have no remaining human weaknesses, and therefore no need for social coercion. Since this vision is not imagined of real people in real time, it is not pertinent to my discussion.

Where we locate utopia, then, is already the first stage in our relation to the concept: do we understand the utopian 'no place' as 'never', as 'impossible', or (in Bloch's term) as 'not-yet-achieved' in whatever register? In bringing forward heresy and alchemy as sites of medieval utopian thought, I suggest that both of these discourses did offer alternatives to certain aspects of the late-medieval status quo, alternatives that they considered historically or materially feasible. This was the case not least with respect to women. It was a nineteenth-century utopian, Charles Fourier, who observed that the position of women is an index to the level of any society – or, we might add, any social theory, design or reform. In this sense it is no coincidence that the two discourses I have chosen to discuss did maintain distinctive attitudes on *die Frauenfrage*. The heresies did so practically and directly, alchemy conceptually and indirectly, the subversive potential of the latter always curtailed by its hermetic and elitist form. In their respective areas – social organisation on one hand, natural science on the other – the animating vision is that of reform. It is a vision we may at times be tempted to deride for its naiveté or its rigidity; yet we do it and ourselves an injustice if we will not perceive – as Frederick Engels perceived in the utopianism of a later era – 'the stupendously grand germs of thought that everywhere break through their phantastic covering'.

Utopia is the art of the possible taken to its limits, and therefore it is programmatic: it lays out a plan of action. If anything in the medieval heretical sects represents a conceptual advance beyond the earlier Gnostic groups with which, ideologically, some of them share so much, it is precisely the component of social programme. This was accompanied by an aggressiveness, a proselytising zeal, that brought heresies definitively onto the public scene, and not necessarily in a marginal role. It should be clear that not every and all medieval heresy is relevant to my subject. I am not concerned with intellectual heresy on one or another doctrinal point, such as might be expounded by a university professor like William of Ockham and discussed in a scholarly milieu. Only partly germane is the poverty movement – spiritual Franciscans, Waldenses, Beguines – which rarely had doctrinal differences with orthodoxy but which, often unjustly, incurred the heretic label because it denied the legitimacy of ecclesiastical wealth and power.

The heresies I shall discuss here were aggressively public in their orientation. Some actually had, like the Cathars, or hoped to have, like the Guglielmites, their own hierarchy. They preached widely. Some – Cathars, Fraticelli and various independent heresiarchs – staged public debates against Catholic opponents. Occasionally they expelled or assassinated the Inquisitors sent to investigate them. In 1208 the papal legate against the Cathars was murdered in Toulouse, a stronghold of heresy; the fanatical inquisitor Conrad of Marburg died in 1233 at the hands of heretics; the inquisitors of Toulouse, with their retinue, were murdered in 1242 at the chateau of the Count of Toulouse; and in 1252 the famous preacher and inquisitor Peter of Verona was assassinated on the road from Como to Milan. That the latter was known henceforth as Peter the Martyr tells the story of class monopolisation of cultural production.

Heretics held property and wielded political power in towns and territories of southern France and northern Italy. Florence was especially important for Cathars and Fraticelli as a missionary centre and seat of a heretical bishopric. Lucca, Rome, Ancona and numerous other cities counted among their adherents men and women of wealth and power, as well as the less exalted levels of the population. In short, the Catholics were by no means wrong to worry about the competing influence of heretical groups and organisations. Few of the medieval heresies evolved anything like a coherent social programme, nor was it their primary intention to do so. Nonetheless, religious principle did often manifest itself in social theory or practice; and even if – as scholars tirelessly reiterate – much of our information on heresy comes from the testimony of its Catholic opponents, such cautions may temper but need not suppress speculation. I believe that the data are adequate to a compilation of a schematic social programme synthesised from numerous texts. In such a synthetic programme, some points are shared by several sects but none is common to all. We have, in short, what Wittgenstein called an open concept: a category which – as with 'game', 'art', or 'language' – does not exhibit a perfect exemplar. With heresy as well, no single exemplar possesses every feature of the category-definition, but all of them display similarities and overlaps.

What would a synthetic heretical social programme look like?[6] For many sects it included removal of spiritual authority from ecclesiastical hands and its restoration to the lay believer: the right of laymen to preach was upheld by Paulicians, Pataria, Waldenses, Humiliati and Lollards; the Bogomils added the right of laymen to hear confession. For some groups this democratisation of spiritual authority extended to women, for

Cathar women could become *perfectae*, or leaders of the sect; they could
also preach, as could Waldensian and Lollard women; some Lollards
argued the right of women to priesthood (though there is no evidence
of woman priests among them).

Numerous sectlets crystallised around the figure of a saintly or charis-
matic woman. The thirteenth-century Guglielmites believed in salvation
through a specific woman, Guglielma of Milan, who claimed to be the
female incarnation of the Holy Spirit and who planned to establish a
new, all-female ecclesiastical hierarchy with the help of her female assistants (Wessley). A similar claim to incarnate the Holy Spirit was made by
the heresiarch Prous Boneta, an unlettered woman of visionary and
ecstatic tendencies who was arrested in Montpellier in 1325, confessed
to the Inquisition and was presumably executed (May). In Belgium there
was the beguine and mystic Margaret Porete, who had a significant
following and whose book *The Mirror of Simple Souls* was widely read after
the author's death at the stake in 1310.[7] One of Margaret's followers,
Bloemardinne of Brussels, wrote and taught during the next two
decades. Such documented personalities doubtless constitute only the
tip of the iceberg. They suggest that many women, whether independent or affiliated with a known group, played a leadership role in medieval society via heresy.

Orthodox marriage theory and the very concept of gender were challenged by the more important dualist sects such as Bogomils and Cathars. Gender, merely an accident of physicality, is irrelevant to the
spiritual life. These groups defined procreation as the perpetuation of an
inferior reality, hence they opposed it. All physical matter is corrupt:
why produce more of it? Such a principle might be expected to encourage a general asceticism among adherents of the sect, and occasionally it
did. More often, though, it had opposite effects, among them sexual
libertinage and contraception. The idea was that since all physicality is
equally corrupt, therefore sexual indulgence is no worse than any other
physical activity (such as eating) or physical condition (such as chastity):
'Since everything is forbidden, everything is allowed.'[8] Such a challenge
to marriage, based as it is in a thoroughly idealist depreciation of the
physical world, can scarcely recommend itself to us. Yet the practical
consequence was nonetheless genuinely subversive of hegemonic and
oppressive sexual codes that the Catholic Church had for centuries
fought to control and to define as virtuous.

That channels for leadership, on one hand, and pleasure, on the other,
were opened to women in a variety of sects large and small is doubtless

one reason why women joined heretical sects in surprisingly large proportions. It is certainly why Jacques LeGoff characterised the history of
heresies as 'in many respects, a history of woman in society and religion';
why Georges Duby has referred to some heretical theory as 'a radical
contestation of marriage ... perceived by its contemporaries as a
feminist movement', and why Brian Stock describes heresies as 'labora-
tories of social organisation, attempting both to improve their own
communities and to offer a model of betterment to society at large'.[9]

Other important points in our synthetic utopian-heretical programme
would include the following. Item: communal property, though not a
widespread idea, was practised by the eleventh-century dualist ascetics
of Monforte near Milan. Item: the withholding of taxes or tithes was
preached by the tenth-century Bulgarian Bogomils, the eleventh-century
French peasant leader Leutard, the twelfth-centry German heresiarch
Tanchelm and the thirteenth-century Waldenses. Item: withholding
labour and obedience from civil authorities was recommended by Bogomils. As for outright rebellion, the twelfth-century heretical preacher
Henry brought the entire town of Lemans to revolt against its bishop;
Arnold of Brescia, executed in 1155, twice mobilised the citizens of
Rome to expel the Pope; the Cathars conducted civil war in southern
France against Church and northern barons for over three decades
during the first half of the thirteenth century; the Dolcinists waged armed
struggle for three years in the Italian Alps; and two abortive rebellion-
conspiracies in England (1414 and 1431) were probably inspired by
Lollard theories of dominion. The fourteenth-century heresy of the Free
Spirit (with which some scholars believe Margaret Porete was connected) is said to have taught that spiritual enlightenment brings freedom from all servitude, release from labour and release of the
enlightened woman from her husband's authority – this last anticipating
some domestic interventions of later enthusiastic sects.

In concluding these remarks on heresy, I want to stress that I am not
attempting to revive a classic nineteenth-century sociological explanation of heresy. We know that at different times and in different places,
men and women from every social rank were attracted to heretical
groups. It was not, in short, simply a means of protest by the oppressed
or labouring classes. Moreover, it is important to note that the strong
presence of female members in the heretical sects does not correspond
to a period when women were more drastically oppressed than they had
been in preceding periods. On the contrary, the high Middle Ages, with
its development of mercantile capital and urban industrial life, opened

new opportunities for women such as had not existed much before 1100 and would not exist after 1500. If women had a Renaissance, it was surely during the high Middle Ages, and it is not merely provocative to suggest that fourteenth-century London or Paris might have been as good a place to be a middle-class woman as any other in the western world before the present century. One would have had the right to own property and business, to work in virtually any occupation, and to attend public elementary school. One could rely on full (even overfull) acknowledgement of one's sexuality – especially by the Catholic Church, as any confessional manual will confirm. Prostitution was legal and municipally controlled (this citation of fact should not be construed as my position on prostitution). Freedom of choice in marriage was not legally constrained by consideration of race, colour, servitude, illegitimacy or hereditary status; forced marriage could be annulled. As John Noonan writes, 'greater range of choice was recognised in the canon law than had ever existed in the Roman empire or was to exist in the United States until *Loving vs. Virginia* in 1967 invalidated the state statutes on miscegenation' ('Power to Choose').

So that it would be both mechanical and inaccurate to see heresy as simply an alternative to worsening oppression. I interpret its attraction rather as the expression of newly elevated aspirations, of hopes and expectations not without their genuine social foundation. I see it less as escape, less as negation of contemporary society, than as a utopian effort to develop, extend and complete historical tendencies already evident in the late medieval world.

My second candidate for utopian discourse, alchemy, was invented long before the Middle Ages, and its popularity peaked well afterward. Unlike heresy, alchemy was never more than a marginal social phenomenon. The discipline came from Iron Age Egypt as a metaphysical/symbolic narrative of recently discovered metallurgical processes: a technical guide presented as myth. It entered western Europe in the twelfth century along with other ancient scholarship and lore that had been preserved in Arabia. By the Middle Ages, the original artisanal function had been deeply submerged, and what remained was a pictorial or hieroglyphic narrative to which additional meanings could be attached. The system became a kind of floating language, a set of visual and verbal signifiers to which modern scholars and artists have continued to supply a signified. Many psychologists, including Carl Jung, have credited the alchemists with discovering the unconscious and with representing the processes of psychic integration. André Breton, following the suggestion of Rimbaud, saw in alchemy a genuine forerunner of surrealism, both discourses enabling 'the human imagination to take a brilliant revenge on everything'.[10]

If one were looking for medieval versions of dialectical materialism, s/he might locate its theoretical articulation in the work of the fourteenth-century English Franciscan William of Ockham – Lenin thought so too[11] – and its experimental arm in the discipline of alchemy. (This is not to imply any explicit links among Ockham, alchemy and popular heresy, only contemporaneity and a subversive orientation.) Where heresy aimed to reform social life to one degree or another, alchemy aimed to re-form nature in the most literal and material way: by transmuting physical matter from a lower to a higher form. The system of alchemy displays the classic utopian premises: first, the possibility of perfection here and now; second, the efficacy of human intervention.[12] Thus, despite the hermeticism that renders alchemy an elitist discipline, the system is founded in essentially humanistic assumptions – perhaps one ought to say, assumptions which at a later date would find their fuller humanistic expression.

At the time, however, the progressive sub-text of medieval alchemy was framed in the language of an archaic myth-system: the theory of correspondences or cosmic similitudes that constituted its intellectual structure. We might call this a theory of economy of form, since it replicates similar form at numerous levels of being, and that form is the organic body. Macrocosm is isomorphic with microcosm, for the universe, planet, and our bodies are composed of the same elements and subject to the same laws. In the words of Hermes Trismegistus, 'That which is below is like that which is above; and that which is above is like that which is below, to work the miracles of one thing.' The *New Pearl of Great Price*, an Italian text of the fourteenth century, teaches that the creation of an embryo from menstrual blood, of a chicken from an egg, or of gold from sulphur and mercury are analogous processes. Alchemy sees nature as constantly in flux: the transmutations of foetus into child, rain into flowers, food into muscle, ice into water into steam show that change is inherent in nature. Moreover, the telos of this change is perfection. Some parts of the universe have already achieved the perfection inherent in their natures – gold, for example, is the perfection of metal – but other parts are still developing toward that end. All metals are gradually changing toward gold; the human soul is developing toward renewal of its original prelapsarian innocence and nobility. We might see alchemy, therefore, as a medicinal intervention into earth, its aim to cure the disease or imperfection of metals by hastening the natural process. Or we might see it, as Mircea Eliade has done, as an obstetric based in the conviction that 'man can take upon himself the work of time' to actively assist nature in its slow ripening. We do this today in agriculture with cross-breeding and hothouses; we do it in biology with artificial insemination or in vitro fertilisation; the alchemist intended to do it for and with minerals. So that the transmutation of metal into gold became an effort by one part of nature to help another to become its best self. It was seen as a charitable and redemptive act whose successful performance also required the transmutation of human nature into its refined and perfected Possible: a moral as well as a scientific discipline, whose interior laboratory was the practitioner's soul.

Although alchemy has no social programme as such, it does have social implications. I've stated already its utopian premises, and my sketch suggests two further and equally subversive notions. These are the complementary democratising notions of common essence in all created nature, and the fluidity of categories. Conservative social philosophies have always depended on fixed, impermeable and inherently different categories. Human nature is not only imperfectible but permanently definable by category (class, race and gender are commonly-used categories). So we find it in Plato's Republic, so in many fairy tales and romances, so in Thomas Carlyle's 'Shooting Niagara', and in other texts too numerous to mention. The idea is that people born into a given category possess a nature specific to it, which they cannot and ought not try to change. Thus one of Andreas's noblewomen reproves her suitor, in the twelfth-century chaplain's De Arte Honesti Amandi: 'Even if a falcon should sometimes be put to flight by a buzzard, still the falcon is classed with falcons and the buzzard with buzzards – the one being called a worthless falcon, the other a very good buzzard' (p. 52).

That I am able to cite, in this connection, a treatise on courtly love, should demonstrate how very widely discussed during the Middle Ages was the question of social class, and how widespread the fact of social mobility. Indeed, social mobility whether horizontal or vertical – that is, as travel or as altered social status – was the less dramatic form of social aspiration. Other, more violent, forms included not only rebellion and revolt, but what we would today call strikes, lock-outs, occupation of premises, urban and rural civil war. The democratising implications of alchemical theory might well have stoked the already quite healthy fires of revolt, had the texts been readily accessible. This is perhaps one reason why the material was transmitted in the highly coded language of arcane symbolism, a form curiously at odds with its theoretical content.

Several comparable cases suggest themselves, the most famous being More's *Utopia* (1516). The Renaissance text offers a revolutionary social critique and social programme; but it is published in Latin, the language of a bureaucratic cultural elite with no interest in radical change and every interest in maintaining the status quo. Not until 1553 did an English translation appear. That More lets Hythloday begin his recital with a reminiscence set during the great Cornish revolts of 1497 (that is, only twenty years before first publication of *Utopia*) shows how fully conscious the author was of the incendiary potential of his work and of conditions generally. Indeed the episode carries much of the urgency of More's vision, the threat of real possibility that legitimates his graceful demand for change from above. In such a time, with such a population, a work intended strictly as propaganda might well become agitation in spite of itself. To publish in Latin was not only to address those who held power and could initiate much-needed reform, but equally to avoid addressing those who might attempt to get state power by transforming utopia from witty humanistic reprimand into bloody social practice. Martin Luther learned this lesson to his chagrin, only a decade after More's text appeared. The 1525 Peasant Revolts in Germany explicitly acknowledged their debt to the Lutheran doctrines and reforms that for years had been widely preached in the vernacular. Luther was quick to disclaim responsibility; this was not what he had meant at all, he said, and the peasants would have to wait for heaven to find their justice. No utopian he! Closer to home is the case of John Wyclif, whose unorthodox doctrines leaped the university wall by way of vernacular literature and preaching to achieve popularity as Lollardy, called by Anne Hudson 'the heresy of the vernacular'. One suspects, then, that the alchemists' constantly reiterated fear that their message could be misused, had a realistic social motive; for what if perfectibility, common essence, human intervention and natural development toward the highest class or form were given a social rather than simply a mineralogical reading? There would be a transmutation indeed!

The theory of correspondences that underpins alchemy is not without special interest for its representation of women and the female principle. Eliade's Chapter 3 is entitled 'The World Sexualised', and if in this set of allegories God is the father, then earth is the mother, the great womb in which metals grow. A seventeenth-century text shows Alchymia as a naked woman urinating in two streams over the earth. The Latin inscription reads in part: 'I am alchemy, hostile to fools but illumination to philosophers. Open your eyes. I feed your sons and nurse you. I am the beginning, the middle and the end. I nurture with my milk . . .' etc. (Burland, p. 131). The imagery of marriage, coitus, conception, gestation, birth and family is central to the alchemical code, signifying various chemical reactions. Strong acids are king and queen, their mixing 'the Royal Marriage'. The coagulation of mercury into its fixed and volatile components is described this way: 'The male is under the female and has no wings; the female has wings, and desires to fly, but the male holds her back. Hence the philosophers say: make the woman rise over the man, and the man rise over the woman' (New Pearl, p. 280). This myth-system knows no inherent subordination of female to male. The stone itself which accomplishes transmutation is hermaphroditic. In short, the female principle is half the dialectic of nature, represented as such in the theory and the symbols of the alchemical discipline. Modern psychologists take this even further with their claim that the art required the integration of male and female components of the practitioner's personality.

Was there a place for women in the practice as well? We read of a third-century A.D. Coptic papyrus called *Cleopatra's Chrysopoeia* (Goldmaking), cast in the form of dialogue between 'Cleopatra' and the philosophers. Some scholars take this as evidence of an actual woman alchemist calling herself Cleopatra, and in the worldly Alexandrian milieu this is not unlikely. Burland makes a similar assumption for the woman referred to in Alexandrian texts as Maria Prophetissa, who is credited with the invention of a special form of still.[13] Eighteenth-century alchemy developed the notion of the *Soror Mystica*, a female companion or assistant, neither wife nor mistress, who, as part of the production process, represented the hermaphroditic balance sought in the work itself. Though I have found no evidence that a woman's presence was required for the work in medieval times, it is nonetheless interesting that the most famous of European alchemists, the fourteenth-century Parisian notary and scribe Nicolas Flamel,[14] seems to have worked in close partnership with his wife, Peronelle, 'whom', writes Flamel, 'I love as myself'. Peronelle, middle-aged and twice a widow when she married Flamel, is portrayed as a paragon of intelligence, sympathy and discretion; moreover, 'without doubt, if she would have enterprised to have done [the alchemical work] alone, she had attained to the end and perfection thereof.'

The trouble with these touching testimonies to connubial partnership

is that the book in which they appear, the Livre des Figures, is evidently a
forgery by its seventeenth-century publisher. To this author, the notion
of an egalitarian marriage and work-relation was not alien, and their
connection with alchemy seemed appropriate. Unfortunately for my
hypothesis, this was a Renaissance and not a medieval author. Indeed
Claude Gagnon, who makes a strong case for the Livre as forgery, remarks
of Flamel's last will and testament (1416) that its legal history over the
years suggests that 'l'harmonie ne régnait pas toujours au foyer philo-
sophique' (p. 146).

Flamel's career reminds us of what it is easy to forget in reading the
mythic discourse: that alchemy was, after all, an entrepreneurial activity.
This was not, however, forgotten by medieval authorities. Royalty who
interested themselves in the work did so in the hope of expanding their
treasuries, and the 1317 bull of Pope John XXII condemns the 'souffleurs'
not for their ideology but for their potentially disruptive financial activity:
coinage must remain the prerogative of kings, counterfeiting money is a
civil crime. In fact numerous clerics and priests were fairly soft on
alchemy and even practised it. They justified their interest on the
grounds that God created nature, and they atttributed their powers to
God. This was acceptable in canon law; even such authorities as St.
Thomas Aquinas and St. Albert considered transmutation theoretically
possible. Those who did offer a critique of alchemy did so in a curiously
moderated way, treating it as pseudo-science rather than as a seriously
competing or subversive ideology. The attitude has remained consistent
on this as on much else: the New Catholic Encyclopedia tolerantly says, 'The
story of alchemy is the history of a mistake' – but nowhere is alchemy
denounced as a heresy.

Far more trenchant critiques came from the poets. Dante placed the
alchemist Capocchio in the lowest circle of hell (Canto 29), the circle of
falsifiers and counterfeiters, because he dared to try to duplicate the
creativity of nature. Chaucer gives a devastating ideological attack in The
Canon's Yeoman's Tale which, along with The Second Nun's Tale of St. Cecelia,
constitutes Fragment VIII of The Canterbury Tales. The saint's life is a paean
to simple, humble orthodox faith and to high philosophical idealism.
The CYT, a contrasting companion piece, makes the same propaganda
but from the other side. Chaucer treats alchemy as a real scandal – a
skandalon, obstacle to faith – using it to exemplify the misuse of intellect, a
traditional Christian topos:

> For whan a man hath over-greet a wit,
> Ful oft hym happeth to misusen it. (648-9)

Chaucer's version of the theme is absolutely obsessed with the materialism of alchemy: the chemicals, the processes, the exotic equipment, the devastating effects on health, the heat, odour, sweat and filth that constitute Part I of the Yeoman's recital. Despite the Church's relatively moderate views on the topic, Chaucer sees alchemy as specifically anti-Christian, connecting it with diabolism and, in general, the forces of evil. A passage of eleven lines is devoted to the traitor Judas; the words 'fiend' and 'devil' are used at least 13 times; there are at least 26 mentions of and variations on the words 'false' and 'cursed'. We are warned that alchemy is a 'science' (form of knowledge) that 'Cristes peple . . . may to meschief brynge' (1072) and that can 'brynge folk to hir destruccioun' (1387), a destruction clearly by no means only economic. Thus Chaucer produces a vitriolic attack that far exceeds what the Church itself had to say about alchemy. It may be (as Manly long ago suggested) that this tone emanates from Chaucer's personal experience with an actual alchemist. But whether or not there is a biographical source for the material, it is clear that Chaucer did – and in some sense correctly – perceive the genuinely subversive thrust of alchemy as rival, albeit unsuccessful rival, to the Pauline-Augustinian orthodoxy that the poet so pointedly emphasises, especially in this latter section of *The Canterbury Tales*. Here he gives us, as in the preceding saint's life, an irreproachable Christian quietism, the idea – familiar from the heyday of scholasticism in the previous century – of intellect as handmaiden to faith:

> I rede, as for the beste, lete it goon.
> For whoso maketh God his adversarie,
> As for to werken any thyng in contrarie
> Of his wil, certes, never shal he thryve . . . (1475-8)

To return to Flamel, the contemporary of Chaucer: if the *Livre des Figures* is a forgery, then there is no evidence whatever that Flamel was an alchemist at all. He was simply a notary who became very rich, and a well-known philanthropist in his day. His wealth, doubtless puzzling to many (and in reality far beyond what one would expect a notary to have) might have been made though usury or investment or graft. There is evidence that Flamel speculated in mortgages, and we may recall that through his brother Jehan Flamel – a painter in the service of the Duc de Berry – Nicolas Flamel had a connection with the incredibly wealthy and incredibly corrupt court of Charles VI. Flamel's secret is less likely to be alchemy, than Parisian political economics in a very turbulent period.

It is easy enough to forget all this because alchemy is a discourse whose overt statements tend to neutralise or repress the activity of literally making money – to submerge it in the quest for moral and physical perfection. Clearly alchemy did not participate in the current of 'peasant radicalism' that Carlo Ginzberg writes of (p. 143), nor in the 'diffused popular materialism' documented by Walter Wakefield. It was radical and materialist enough, but far from popular. What it tells us, therefore, as does heresy, is that the utopian impulse is precisely not limited to society's poorest and most oppressed, but is rather a transclass phenomenon, and perhaps even more the luxury of those who can afford to dream rather than to act. In a sense the real utopians of the Middle Ages were those peasants, workers and artisans who took power briefly in Florence in 1357 and in Paris in 1413, and who nearly did so in London in 1381 demanding an end to feudal social relations. Their demands, like the possibilism of alchemy or heresy, would not seem so utopian a few generations later when history caught up with them.

Bronislaw Baczko ends his illuminating volume on utopia with a chapter called 'L'homme volant': the title refers to an engraving by Goya in which two men, flying toward a distant mountain-top city, are shot down by those below. I too would like to end with a flying man who is, as it were, shot down; but one whose story, as told by Bertolt Brecht, offers a rather more balanced or dialectical vision of human effort:

Bishop, I can fly
Said the Tailor to the Bishop.
Just watch what I do!
And he climbed with things
That looked like broad wings
On the great, great church roof.
The Bishop walked on.
That's nothing but lies
Man is no bird
Never will a man fly
Said the Bishop of the Tailor.

The Tailor is dead
Said the People to the Bishop.
It was a slaughter!
His wings were split
And he lay smashed
On the hard, hard church square.
The bells shall be rung
It was nothing but lies
Man is no bird
Never will a man fly
Said the Bishop to the People. ('Kinderlieder, Ulm 1592'; my transl.)

Knowing that men do fly, and that Albert Einstein, father of relativity-theory, was born in Ulm, we find it easy enough to judge the Bishop ultimately wrong. It may be more difficult to make a similar judgment of the nay-sayers of our own day, particularly if the vision of the new is offered in another mode of discourse than poetry, even one so lyrical as the one below, distilled from the conclusion to Leon Trotsky's *Literature and Revolution*:

The wall will fall not only between art and industry, but simultaneously between art and nature also. Communist life will not be formed blindly, like coral islands, but will be built consciously. The shell of life will hardly have time to form before it will burst open again under the pressure of new technical and cultural inventions and achievements. Life in the future will not be monotonous. More than that. Man at last will begin to harmonise himself in earnest. Man will make it his purpose to master his own feelings, to raise his instincts to the heights of consciousness, to make them transparent, to extend the wires of his will into hidden recesses, and thereby to raise himself to a new plane, to create a higher social biological type, or, if you please, a superman. The forms of life will become dynamically dramatic. The average human type will rise to the heights of an Aristotle, a Goethe, or a Marx. And above this ridge new peaks will rise.

Events subsequent to the 1924 publication of this text have made us justifiably suspicious of talk of supermen and human types. Yet if we are not to succumb to the formalism and passivity that let the Nazi horror grow, we need to remain open to the premise that 'human nature' or 'personality' is constructed, a social fabrication and changeable. Rather than assent to the privileged, elite status of 'an Aristotle, a Goethe, or a Marx', the text looks forward to the extension of education and social opportunity that will dissolve the special status of these names, reinscribe them as norms. Further, Trotsky's anticipation of the new is based on a program that can accomplish that aim. That Brecht compromised his vision in supporting Stalin[15] is less to the point than the claims made on us by such a passage as the one above: no-place as the impossible, or no-place as the not present yet?

2

Undoing substantial connection: The late medieval attack on analogical thought

'Many similarities, when closely examined, prove not to be explicable in terms of imitation. I would freely admit that these are the most interesting ones to observe, for they allow us to take a real step forward in the exciting search for causes' (Bloch, *Land and Work*, p. 54). The similarities documented in this chapter are of the order described by Marc Bloch. They are not explicable in terms of imitation, nor is it possible to establish a direct causal relation between, say, late-medieval political theory and poetic practice, or between scientific method and political theory. Still there is a relation among these phenomena. Historical simultaneity is a mediated relation which we sometimes designate by the term 'culture'. That we speak of 'a culture' implies some readiness to suspend the notion of strictly causal relations among various kinds of creative thought; indeed, the etymology of 'culture' itself carries the image of organic growth, of parallel growths in a common field. If the inquiry after causes is pursued far enough, that common field will be discovered in the economic basis of society, in the social development and changing class structure which it is the business of historians to describe. Here I want simply to notice certain similarities among various intellectual disciplines in the fourteenth century.

Chaucer's dream-vision *The House of Fame* first brought to my attention the related questions of poetic allegory and analogical thought. That curious work tells of Geffrey's eagle-borne journey through the cosmos to Fame's palace, where he observes the fickle goddess distributing judgments that will determine the good or ill fame of various petitioners. The judgment scene is less interesting than significant, for while it only repeats a point that has already been made many times in the poem (that tradition, or fame is unreliable as a source of absolute truth), it does represent Chaucer's only original use of fully-developed personification allegory. Why had Chaucer made so little use of a literary mode that had dominated the European mind for nearly a thousand years? It was a mode, moreover, with which Chaucer was quite familiar. He translated two of the most famous and influential of all medieval allegories, the *De Consolatione Philosophiae* of Boethius, and part of the *Roman de la Rose* of Guillaume de Lorris. From the French Chaucer also translated a personification allegory of virtue and vice which appears in *The Canterbury Tales* as *The Tale of Melibee*. And *The Clerk's Tale* of patient Griselda is interpreted by its teller according to the traditional method of literal, moral, and doctrinal levels of meaning. Chaucer knew very well the traditional uses of allegory as a creative mode and as an exegetical tool. Yet for the greater part of his own work, he chose other modes of expression.[1] It is the purpose of this paper to explore some uses of the allegorical mode, and to propose some reasons why that mode was not suited to Chaucer's poetic vision.

Allegory and analogy

Like its close relatives simile and metaphor, allegory is a form of analogy: it establishes a proportional relation among things otherwise unlike. It establishes an analogy, or proportion, between the relation of parts in a narrative, and the relation of parts in another system. By virtue of that analogy, the narrative structure can be said to 'correspond' to the other system. Because proportional analogy is the statement of a constant relation, we can – in mathematics, at least – derive unknown terms from known; we can extract general truths from particular. This mathematical process is supposed to hold true in literature as well; indeed the didactic function of allegory apparently depends on our performing that inductive operation.

These principles can be illustrated with some well-known literary texts. The earliest extant Christian allegory is the fourth-century *epyllion* of Prudentius, the *Psychomachia*. Here, narrative action – the battle of virtues and vices – represents the moral struggle in each individual soul, and also the perpetual cosmic struggle of good and evil in the universe. The narrative image of battle imposes a particular structure upon our moral experience: we infer that the function of Christian virtue is constantly to struggle against vice, and that life consists of a series of confrontations. Battle is to the field what moral conflict is to life. The image also suggests a particular structure of mind and behaviour, for the reader learns specific manifestations of vice (Libido, Superbia, Luxuria) and the qualities of mind and character required to defeat them (Pudicitia, Mens Humilis, Sobrietas). On this level, battle is to the field what moral struggle is to man's soul. So that the *Psychomachia* is educational in the strictest etymological sense: its purpose is to lead the reader forth from entertaining literal narrative to didactic, 'higher' or more abstract levels of meaning.

Guillaume de Guilleville's *Pelerinage de la Vie Humaine*, the anonymous morality play *Everyman*, and John Bunyan's *The Pilgrim's Progress* have the same purpose as the *Psychomachia*, though they use a different central metaphor – that of journey – to represent the process of becoming virtuous. Each of these Christian allegories establishes a proportional analogy between narrative structure and a metaphysical structure: the Christian scheme of salvation. In all four, the purpose of the narrative is to transcend itself by directing the reader's attention to theological truth: 'God makes base things usher in divine' (Bunyan).

Nor is this process of transcendence limited to religious allegory, for the system to which allegorical narrative 'corresponds' may be any structure of ideas. In the *Roman de la Rose* of Guillaume de Lorris, the conceptual structures are social and psychological. The Narrator enters a garden which represents courtly society: Oiseuse lets him in, just as leisure permits a man to enter such society. Within he meets figures representing different qualities of the aristocratic life-style: Cortoisie, Leesce, Richesse. He chooses a love-object from among many attractive rosebuds in the garden. The Narrator's efforts to pluck his rose bring him into contact with figures who represent aspects of a lady's mind (Pitié, Venus), of the Narrator's own mind (Reson, Amors) and of society (Male Boche, Jalosie). The interrelation of these personifications tells the story of a young man's initiation into courtly life and courtly love. In fact Guillaume's *Roman* is an instructional manual in the form of an allegorical romance. 'Qui amer veut, or i entende', Guillaume exhorts his readers:

Qui dou songe la fin ora	Whoever hears the end of the dream
je vos di bien que il porra	I promise you that he will
des jeus d'Amors asses apprende . . .	learn plenty about the game of love . . .
(2065-7)	

As Judson Allen shows, many texts were read by their medieval audiences as manuals of ethical or behavioural instruction, though our own critical (and ethical) apparatus no longer permits such an engagement with most fictional texts. The *Roman*, though, is didactic in its own terms, albeit secular. Its hero is a wealthy, ambitious young 'everyman', his conduct is prescribed by the God of Love, the salvation he hopes for is strictly earthly. And the world of the *Roman* is as rigidly defined as that of theological allegory, its virtues and vices as sharply delineated, its

22 MEDIEVAL LITERARY POLITICS

episodes requiring translation into social or psychological terms.
Historical time offers another possibility for allegorical meaning. The
past may be thought of as an abstract system with a particular structure. In
George Orwell's fable *Animal Farm*, the animals' rebellion parodies the
Russian Revolution of 1917, the relation between the pigs Napoleon and
Snowball resembles Stalin's persecution of Trotsky, and Napoleon's
policies for managing the farm remind us of Stalin's increasingly revisionist rapprochement with the capitalist world. As with other kinds of
allegory, we have to recognise in the narrative the structure of an analogous system. Or epistemology may provide the system, as it does in
Plato's allegory of the Cave (*Republic*, VII, 514A), in which a man's progress
from darkness to full sunlight represents the movement of the mind
from ignorance to enlightenment. In body-allegory such as Spenser's
House of Alma (*Faerie Queene*, II, ix) or Phineas Fletcher's *The Purple Island*,
the system is the structure of the human body. So that the allegorical
narrative may refer to a concrete or an abstract structure, its meaning may
be social, historical, psychological, philosophical or theological. Only
the method is constant: it requires the reader to bear in mind a structure
different from that of the narrative but proportional to it, and to interpret
the narrative in terms of that other system.[2]

In a general way, all literature must be read inductively, insofar as it
represents any larger or other truth beyond itself. In this sense, all
literature might be considered '*állos a'goría*': other-speaking. But there is a
crucial difference between allegory and other literary modes, and that is
the nature of the 'other' it implies. Non-allegorical literature usually
refers the reader back to the world s/he inhabits, so that the proportion it
establishes is between two known systems. The world beyond the narrative can be verified. Most allegories, however (excepting, of course,
biological and historical), refer us to a realm of abstract moral or religious
ideas which are not only unknown but unknowable. Its 'truth' (if it refers
us to an abstract system) is unverifiable. Non-allegorical literature shows
us proud persons who are very like other proud persons whom we can
actually meet, or it chronicles a love affair such as we can experience if we
wish; it describes the society in which we live, or one which we know
others to have inhabited. But allegory shows us Pride herself, whom we
will never meet, or a psyche whose parts walk before us, or a heavenly
city which we will never physically see.

In fact, the allegory of abstraction can produce no new knowledge. Its
method is circular, for the general truth to which allegory claims to lead
must first be accepted if the narrative is to have a didactic effect.

Prudentius's battle is the image of what Christian doctrine teaches about virtue, and Prudentius's reader must already believe that doctrine if he is to benefit morally from the poem. Plato's allegory of the cave is used only when the epistemological system it represents has been carefully laid out in discursive argument: 'Every feature in this parable', says Socrates, 'is meant to fit our earlier analysis'. A materialist will find the parable no more convincing than the earlier analysis. The instructive value of Guillaume's garden depends on the reader accepting the aristocratic life-style it enshrines. When this is questioned – as it was by Jean de Meun, the continuator of Guillaume's unfinished work – then the action, symbols and iconography appropriate to Guillaume can no longer convince. That is why Jean substituted his own. In *Animal Farm*, Orwell's use of animal fable already reveals the author's political judgment, and the reader must have a grossly distorted notion of communism if he can accept the symbol of pigs for revolutionaries.

Allegory speaks, then, to the already convinced. It speaks to Christians that they may be saved, to wealthy men that they may succeed in love, to intellectuals that they may be philosopher kings. Far from persuading his audience to accept a particular conceptual structure, the allegorist must expect that that structure has already been accepted. Meaning precedes narrative in allegory. Meaning generates symbols and provides in advance the correct interpretation of those symbols. In this way allegory perfectly illustrates in another register Augustine's experience of learning that a certain Latin word is a sign only when he learns what it is a sign of (i.e., its meaning or translation): 'And that reality I got to know not from [its] being signified to me, but by seeing it (*non significatu sed aspectu didiceram*). Therefore, it is the sign that is learnt from the thing rather than the thing from the sign given' (*De Magistro* x, 33; in Markus, pp. 69-70). The rose of Guillaume's *Roman* is for this reason far easier to understand than the rose of Blake's lyric 'The Sick Rose', which refers to no single system.

As a form of analogy, poetic allegory shares the fortunes of analogical thought. I want to suggest that analogy and allegory do express a way of perceiving reality, but that they are not adequate to express all perceptions of reality. During the fourteenth century, scholars in fields as varied as physics and cosmology, political theory and logic, began to question received theories based on analogy. Such simultaneity, rooted in history and therefore far from coincidental, testifies to the emergence of new social needs which generated new ways of looking at man, the universe, and society. It is a cultural phenomenon which may help us to understand Chaucer's curious neglect of the allegorical mode.

Analogy and science

The theoretical basis for analogical science is what Mircea Eliade has called 'archaic ontology'. For archaic man, 'neither the objects of the external world nor human acts . . . have any autonomous intrinsic value. Objects or acts acquire a value, and in so doing become real, because they participate . . . in a reality that transcends them' (Eliade, *Cosmos*, p. 3). This transcendent reality provides models which the phenomenal world imitates: 'for archaic man, reality is a function of the imitation of the celestial archetype.' The world itself participates in a cosmic analogy with supraterrestrial reality. It is misleading to label such a world-view 'primitive', for societies and individuals at an advanced stage of intellectual sophistication have held it.

Plato's theory of Forms provided the metaphysical basis for much medieval scientific speculation. Plato's *Timaeus* was the only work of classical science (if such it can be called)[3] that was known throughout the Middle Ages, for most of Aristotle's work was translated from Greek and Arabic only in the twelfth century. The premise of *Timaeus* is that 'Our world must necessarily be a likeness of something' (29B). The world is framed in the likeness of a living creature (30C), which is 'the unchanging Form, ungenerated and indestructible' (51E-52).

With the adaptation of Platonic theory to Christian doctrine, the Forms became Ideas in the divine mind (John Scotus Erigena, St. Anselm, Albertus Magnus, Duns Scotus, Roger Bacon) or pre-existent effects in an infinite Intelligence (Aquinas's formulation). This provides several possible bases for analogy, among them cause and effect. The effect (the created world) both represents its cause (God) and strives to resemble or rejoin it; indeed the creature 'is called a being only insofar as it imitates the First Being'.[4] The analogy between supraterrestrial 'reality' and our own world becomes an analogy between God and the world. In the words of Aquinas's contemporary, St. Bonaventura:

> All creatures of this sensible world . . . are shadows, echoes, and pictures, the traces, simulacra, and reflection of that First Principle . . . They are signs divinely bestowed which, I say, are exemplars or rather exemplifications set before our yet untrained minds, limited to sensible things, so that through the sensibles which they see they may be carried forward to the intelligibles which they do not see, as if by signs to the signified. (*Mind's Road*, 2:11)

The world itself is allegory, and we the exegetes.

Some scientific implications of archaic ontology can be observed in Plato's cosmology, and in that of later theorists as well. Plato considered the universe a living creature composed of matter and form, body and soul, capable of 'ceaseless and intelligent life for all time' (Timaeus, 36D-E). Each planet, Plato asserts, is also a creature endowed with a special kind of life; each has a material body and a soul which guides its motion and enables it to learn its appointed task (38E).

While Aristotle denied the theory of Forms – the mythic embodiment of archaic ontology – he did not exorcise every vestige of analogical cosmology from his own scientific speculation.[5] The Platonic planetary souls appear in Aristotle, hardly altered, as a set of celestial intelligences. They are posited, of course, from premises different from Plato's, namely from Aristotle's concept of motion as the effect of a continually imparted cause. Since all that moves must be moved by some internal or external force, and since an effect must cease when its cause ceases to operate, then the natural and eternal movement of the celestial spheres must be caused by certain eternal and innate principles of motion, which are analogous in function to the human soul. So Aristotle urges us to think of the stars not as inanimate bodies, but rather 'as enjoying life and action . . . similar to that of animals and plants' (De Caelo, 292A-B). He writes of the heaven that it must have, like any other living creature, an absolute directional orientation – above, below, right, left (De Caelo, 285A). And since each of the spheres will have its own 'soul', the total number of such celestial intelligences will be fifty-five (Metaphysica, 107A).

Although the theory of celestial intelligences became a central doctrine in Hellenic, Arabic and scholastic cosmology, it was attacked during the fourteenth century by several scholars, and most incisively in the work of Jean Buridan (died c. 1358) and his pupil Nicole Oresme (1320-1382).

Buridan, logician and rector of the University of Paris, was perhaps the most influential of fourteenth-century scientists. His ideas were brought by his pupils to the new universities of central Europe; in western Europe they were known to Leonardo da Vinci and Galileo. Buridan refused to consider the planets as animate creatures. He saw them as mere objects and accounted for their motion by the same principle with which he explained impetus:[6] motion need not be continually imparted to the moved object by way of the medium (air or water), but once imparted will simply continue until it is overcome by resistance. The planets, like any moving thing, need not be moved by God or by any celestial intelligence:

Since the creation of the world, God has moved the heavens with movements identical to those with which they move at present: he imprinted in them forces

by which they continue to be uniformly moved. These forces, meeting no
contrary resistance, are never destroyed or weakened. . . . It is not necessary to
assume the existence of intelligences which move the celestial bodies. . . . Moreover it is not necessary that God move them continually, except through that
general influence by which we say that he operates in all that is.[7]

Following Buridan's theory, Oresme noted in his own vernacular
commentary on Aristotle's *De Caelo* that

excepting violent interference, it is similar to what happens when a man has made
a watch and allows it to work and be moved by itself. In this way God allows the
heavens to be moved continually according to the relation of motive force to
resistance, and according to the established order. (*Livre*, 71E; my transl. from
Menut)

The image is startling, anticipating as it does the mechanistic world-view
of later centuries. With it we have moved from analogy to simile, a very
long step away from the allegorical world-view. Oresme also anticipated
Renaissance astronomers in arguing that the earth moves about the sun,
rather than the reverse.[8] In addition, he denied Aristotle's proposition
that the universe is a being with an innate principle of movement, or
soul. As corollary, he added that the absolute universal left, right, up
and down posited by Aristotle are only relational concepts existing
'par similitude' (86D) – clearly, for Oresme, an unsatisfactory basis for
scientific hypothesis.

Another consequence of analogical speculation was the scholastic
concept of natural place which, as Chaucer's Eagle remarks,

> ys knowen kouth
> Of every philosophers mouth,
> As Aristotle and daun Platon,
> And other clerkys many oon. (*House of Fame*, 757-60)

Plato's theory of natural place derives from the analogy between this and
the supraterrestrial order: physical processes imitate the prototypical
movement of like to like by which the four elements – earth, air, fire,
water – divided themselves into four main masses (*Timaeus*, 53 A-B).
Vision (45 B-C), digestion (81D) and the weight of all natural objects
(62C-63E) are also explained by 'the travelling of each kind towards its
kindred' (63E).

Aristotle's theory of weight does not, of course, rely on the existence of
a world of archetypal Forms. It does retain some aspects of analogy in
assuming, first, the existence of elemental spheres which surround the
earth and, second, the analogical principle of like to like. To its proper

sphere each thing will naturally, by virtue of its innate principle of motion, attempt to go: 'For a single clod moves to the same place as the whole mass of earth, and a spark to the same place as the whole mass of fire' (De Caelo, 276A). Weight and lightness, then, were intrinsic relations between physical objects and the primal mass from which they came. This notion was attacked by Buridan, among others, on the grounds of observation.[9] He argued that if place is the cause of upward or downward motion, then the attractive force must be greater when the object is nearer its natural place; this, however, is contradicted by experience, for if two stones are dropped from different heights, the one that was higher has a greater velocity than the other when both are a foot from the ground. Moreover, one can lift a stone near the earth as easily as a stone in a tower, which disproves the theory that heaviness increases with closeness to 'natural place'. Buridan's pupil Albert of Saxony (1316-1390), rector of the University of Vienna and Bishop of Halberstadt, rejected the Aristotelian hypothesis for similar reasons.

Buridan's critique of analogical cosmology extended to the rhetorical consequences of that cosmology: he objected strongly to Aristotle's use of anthropomorphic metaphor. In writing, for example, of celestial movement, Aristotle had used such terms as 'fatigue' and 'labour'. Buridan administers a tart reprimand for this practice:

It must be remarked briefly that these words fatigue, perturbation, labour and difficulty are only synonyms. It is necessary to see whether they are appropriately given, and why they are given. It seems to me that fatigue and labour are not appropriately attributed to purely passive virtues. . . . Moreover it seems to me that these words cannot adequately describe inanimate things. It would be inaccurate to call a stone tired or perturbed because you had dragged it along for some time. And likewise if we say that the earth is disturbed when it is not fertile as usual, this is inaccurate: it is only a figurative locution, that is, it assumes a similarity to us, who do become perturbed when we cannot function as well as usual. (Quaest, 2:1; my transl. from Moody)

What Buridan requires is a new scientific language, a new discourse properly expressive of the new episteme – and properly suppressive of the old one. For the most advanced late-medieval scientists analogy no longer gave an accurate picture of reality. It could no longer serve as the basis for logical argument, or as a stylistic feature of scientific discourse.

Analogy and political theory

Like all myth, the analogical world-view is, among its other dimensions, profoundly a social phenomenon. This social level of meaning makes the myth of another world useful to societies as different as the pre-literate tribes described by Mircea Eliade, imperialist Athens of the fifth century B.C., and urbanised late-medieval Europe. It is a perennially useful myth, for its primary function is social cohesion.

In a classless society such as the tribe, myth is political theory, for 'political' life is not separated from the general life of the group: every activity is 'political' in conducing to the survival and well-being of the tribe. To plant, cultivate and harvest, to hunt, to raise children, make tools and wage war are necessary to the tribe as a whole (even though these activities are performed by one or another segment of the tribe). But these activities are not, after all, instinctive, as they are with animals; were individuals left to their instincts, the social group could disintegrate. Even in a classless and so-called 'primitive' society, some form of social control is required. This makes its appearance as a body of myth which provides the rationale for all socially necessary activities, so that such activities become rituals modelled on a divine archetype.

In a class-structured society, myth also serves as a means of social control. But since the interests of a ruling class nearly always oppose those of the ruled, myth can no longer represent the needs of society as a whole. It can represent only the needs of a particular class.

An especially versatile myth, hence an especially durable one, is that of the 'body politic': the image of society as an organic creature with a precise and necessary formal structure. The treatment of this analogy in late-medieval political theory constitutes an important aspect of the general critique of analogical thought.

The versatility of the organic analogy is demonstrated in its use by Plato to prove the necessary dominance of an aristocracy (Rep. 427C-445B), by Aristotle to support the claims of the upper middle class (Pol. I, 5), and by St. Paul to impose unity upon the scattered communities of the early Christian Church (Romans 12:5, I Cor 12:12). The image, along with several other analogies, came into its own again with the revival of political theory that attended the papal controversies of the late-eleventh to thirteenth centuries. It made effective propaganda for the proponents of papal power in their struggle against the Holy Roman Emperor and other kings.[10] By far the most detailed statement of the organic analogy is found in the Policraticus (1155) of John of Salisbury. Supporting the superiority of ecclesiastical power (sacerdotium) over state power (regnum), John compares each member of the body politic to a physical counterpart. The prince is the head, the senate heart, judges and provincial governors eyes, ears and tongue, financial officers digestive organs, soldiers hands, and peasants feet, 'which always cleave to the soil'. As for the Church: 'Those things which establish and implant in us the practice of religion, and transmit to us the worship of God . . . fill the place of the soul in the body of the commonwealth. And therefore those who preside over the practice of religion should be looked up to and venerated as the soul of the body' (5:2).

Thomas Aquinas (1225-74) makes constant use of organic analogy whether discussing the structure of the Church itself, or its relation to the state: 'In the Church the Pope holds the place of the head and the major prelates hold the place of the principal limbs'; 'Mankind is considered like one body, which is called the mystic body, whose head is Christ both as to soul and as to body.' In relation to the state, however, the Pope becomes not head but soul, so that 'Secular power is subject to the spiritual power as the body is subject to the soul, and therefore it is not a usurpation of authority if the spiritual prelate interferes in temporal things. . . . (In Bigongiari, pp. xxxiv-xxxv). Elsewhere Aquinas constructs multiple analogies between macrocosm and microcosm, between cosmic, social, physical, psychological orders: as God is to the universe, so the ruler is to society, the soul is to the body, and reason is to the soul (De Reg. Princ. in Dawson).

Indeed, analogy was the conceptual stock-in-trade of the supporters of papal power, and their repertoire was varied. Besides the organic analogy, they used the allegory to the sun and moon, according to which papal and royal power correspond to the greater and lesser luminaries, the former conferring power upon the latter. There were the Biblical examples of Samuel and Saul, Jacob and Esau, Isaac and Ishmael, all of them hierarchal pairs demonstrating the superiority of priestly to royal power. The allegory of the two swords, a particular favourite, was taken from Luke 22:38, where Jesus declares the two swords to be 'enough, not too much' in the hands of his disciples. In 1302 it appeared in the famous bull 'Unam Sanctam' of Boniface VIII, which proclaimed the redemptive necessity for every creature to be subject to the Roman pontiff. The bull is a high point in the history of papal ambition, and virtually a compendium of analogical arguments for papal power. Expounding the two swords, it concludes:

Both the swords, spiritual and material, therefore, are in the power of the Church: the one, indeed, to be wielded for the church, the other by the church: the one by the hand of the priest, the other by the hand of kings and knights, but at the will and sufferance of the priest. One sword, moreover, ought to be under the other, and the temporal authority to be subjected to the spiritual. (Henderson, 435-7)

The medieval conflict between church and state was one between two ruling classes. Each aristocracy, the lay and the ecclesiastical, had its king, owned land, levied taxes, raised armies and waged war, made and executed laws and held trials in its own courts of law. We should not expect, therefore, to find among the opponents of papal power a thorough rejection of the epistemological bases of analogical thought, for the propagandists of royal authority could scarcely afford to dispense with every abstract justification of power. Their aim was not to destroy the metaphysical basis of authority, but to adjust it as necessary to effect its transfer from pope to king. Moreover, the imperialists were not as homogeneous a group as their opponents: their positions ranged from the simple limitation of papal power, or the exclusion of ecclesiastics from temporal power, to the complete subjection of church to state. Rather than systematic destruction of the basic principles, then, we find an eclectic process of rejection and revision. Many of the papalists' key arguments are demolished on logical grounds; some are set aside as inconsistent with experience or observation; still others are only re-interpreted. For their own arguments, the secular theorists usually avoided analogy as a logical premise, though they might refer to it for purposes of illustrative comparison. Analogy would survive, of course, in political theory, and the myth of the body politic would maintain some relevance to the problem of social control. The tradition continues for instance, in the work of the fifteenth-century jurist Sir John Fortescue. It is revived fairly massively during the later Tudor period – in widely-circulated homilies and in the plays of Shakespeare, among many other texts – in service of the centralised Tudor state. It surfaces in Hobbes's Leviathan, and even in some political writing of our own time.[11] But analogy would survive in a very diminished way, unable in the long run to withstand the impact of bourgeois pragmatism whose first efforts can be discerned in the work of the political theorists cited below.

Master of Theology at the University of Paris and a prominent controversialist on behalf of Philippe le Bel, Jean Quidort (also known as Jean de Paris, 1241-1306) presents a very thorough case against papalist analogical theories. The bulk of his tract De Potestate Regia et Papali demonstrates the different and mutually exclusive natures of regnum and sacerdotium. This amounts to a long series of careful distinctions between the two with respect to origin, purpose, and actual function. The concept of unity, on which the papalists depended so heavily, is thus attacked, as it would be again and again during this period by the partisans of royal power. Toward the end of his work, Jean adduces and refutes forty-two specific papalist positions, including the old allegorical favourites drawn from Scripture. Among them is the allegory of sun and moon, and Jean begins by stating his own principles of allegorical exegesis of Scripture: 'The [papal] position is mystical ('mystica'). But mystical theology, according to Dionysius, cannot be argued unless it can be proved from another part of Scripture, because mystical theology is no valid argument' (Cap. XIV, Leclerq). Jean then proceeds to demonstrate the arbitrariness of allegorical exegesis by mentioning several other interpretations, from the patristic tradition, of the same parable. He points out further that the moon has its powers ultimately from God, and concludes that what the prince receives from the Pope is information about faith, while his power he receives immediately from God. Jean refutes with Aristotle's help the papalist analogical position that corporalia are ruled by spiritualia. If, as Aristotle claims, the function of the state is to help its members live a virtuous and happy life, then the state has a moral and spiritual function as well as a physical one; it cannot be relegated to mere corporalia (Cap. XVII). The analogy of head and body is adjusted but not rejected out of hand: Christ is true head of the mystical body of the Church, the Roman church is head of all other instituted churches, and the king is head of his kingdom. As for the two swords, Jean repeats his strictures on allegorical exegesis. The papal argument is merely an allegorical interpretation (quaedam adaptatio allegorica), and even Augustine does not accept allegory (allegoria) without some other manifest authority (Cap. XVIII).

Dante Alighieri argues in his short treatise De Monarchia (c. 1310) for a single universal and temporal government – a world-empire. It is not for Dante to reject analogical argument out of hand; his thesis that mankind should be ruled by a single authority resorts to analogy with the household and the cosmos. Nonetheless, Dante does not hesitate systematically to refute the analogical arguments with which the papacy had supported its claims to temporal power. This is done in Book 3 of the treatise, which examines the question whether the temporal ruler holds power directly from God, or indirectly through the Pope's mediation.

The analogy of sun and moon is rejected on both logical and theological grounds, for it contains both logical fallacies and mistaken appeals to 'mystic interpretation'. First, if the two luminaries represent types of government, God could not have created figures of government – an

accidental property of human existence and the remedy to sin – before
he had created human life itself. Further, 'this falsehood can also be
destroyed by using the gentler method of exposing a material fallacy, and
instead of calling the opponent an out-and-out liar, we can make a
distinction which he overlooked.' That distinction is between the being
of the moon, and its power, and its functioning; for the moon in its being
in no way depends on the sun. The final and most trenchant criticism is
this:

Lastly, there is a formal fallacy in their argument, for the predicate of the conclusion is not identical with that of the major premise, as it should be. . . . In the
major premise it is light that the moon receives, and in the conclusion it is
authority, which are two quite different things, both as to their substance and
their meaning, as I have explained. (3:4)

It is, of course, precisely the purpose of allegory to bring together 'two
quite different things', and we may note that for his own great work,
Dante found a poetic mode which operates quite differently from ordinary allegory.[12]

Dante proceeds to treat, in similar terms, several other analogies, most
of them drawn from the Bible: Levi and Judah, Samuel and Saul, the gold
and incense offered to Christ, the power of binding and loosing. 'I could
simply', notes Dante, 'deny their symbolism, and with equal reason'
(3:5). He does not, however, confine himself to simple denial but rejects
these allegories on various grounds, pointing out formal fallacies and
theological errors. The theory of two swords is treated as a mistaken
reading which can only be corrected by close analysis of the literary
context, which Dante provides at some length (3:9); as with Jean, the
principle of allegorical exegesis of Scripture is given rational limits but its
validity is not finally denied.

Although De Monarchia was ordered burnt in 1329 and was placed on
the Index in 1554, Dante's dream of a world-empire was still-born, a
historical anomaly in its own time and destined to be without significant
influence. Quite different was the role of the Defensor Pacis (1324) of
Marsilius of Padua (Marsiglio dei Mainardini), the impact of which
'reverberated during the following centuries both from hearsay descriptions of its conclusions and from actual reading of it' (Gewirth, vol. 2, p.
xix). It seems at first that Marsilius can turn analogy to his own purpose
when, imitating Aristotle, he compares the state to a living creature, (I, ii,
3 and I, xvii, 8). Yet such comparisons evidently make Marsilius uncomfortable, opportunistic as they are: 'But let us omit these points', he

remarks, 'since they pertain rather to natural science' (I, xvii, 8). And shortly we find him refuting the very analogy of body politic which he has just used: for while the king may be compared to the human heart with respect to importance, he differs from it in other obvious ways which invalidate the analogy as a logical premise (I, xviii, 2-3).

Like Dante, Marsilius employs several kinds of argument against the traditional papalist analogies. He refutes, with remarkable amplitude, analogies (what he calls 'quasi-political arguments') drawn from Scripture and from philosophy. With regard to the allegorical interpretation of Scripture, Marsilius clearly sets out his own critical assumptions and states the limits of the method:

> Those authorities of the sacred canon or Scripture which do not need a mystical exposition, we shall follow entirely in their manifest literal sense: but with regard to those which do need mystical exposition, we shall adhere to the more probable views of the saints. Those views which the saints have uttered by their own authority, apart from Scripture, and which are in harmony with the Scripture or canon, I shall accept; those which are not in harmony I shall respectfully reject, but only by the authority of Scripture, on which I shall always rely. (II, xxviii, 1)

Thus the papal interpretation of the two swords is rejected as inconsistent with Christ's other teachings (II, xxviii, 24). But Marsilius can in this case only combat allegory with allegory. For the papal analogy he substitutes another, more congenial, reading – St. Ambrose's – that the two swords are really the Old and New Testaments.

More scrupulous in method is Marsilius's treatment of claims to power based on philosophical arguments, and these he combats with the weapons of experience, dialectics, and logic. The principle of unity of rule was often used by the papalists to support their claim that, just as there is one ruler of the cosmos, so must there be only one supreme ruler (the Pope) of the Church or of any social group. Marsilius shoots this down with the concise observation that 'Even if we grant the analogy with regard to the similarity or proportion which it initially assumes, yet to the added assertion, that the primary ruler or government is one, we can reply that this is true by human establishment, and not by any ordainment or degree made immediately by God or divine law' (II, xxviii, 14). Thus the formal similarity is granted but the causal nexus is denied, and with it the whole coercive intention of the analogy.

Finally, Marsilius treats the central papal argument that 'as the body is to the soul, so is the ruler of the body to the ruler of the soul'. Again it will be futile to look for an examination of the epistemological basis of such an argument, but Marsilius does provide a close analysis of the argument itself. As Jean had done, he first replaces Augustinian dualism with the Aristotelian notion of soul as the body's principle of motion, change and appetite. In this way, soul and body are not subject to two separate types of government, but temporal government itself may properly be said to concern itself with soul. The argument is rejected on the evidence of simple experience and observation:

For between the soul and the body, and again between the rational and the irrational faculties, there are many differences which do not exist between those persons who are teachers or caretakers of the one and those who are teachers or caretakers of the other. For the rational faculty, in the image of the Trinity, composes syllogisms, while the irrational does not; but there is no such difference between the teachers or caretakers of these respective faculties; and so on with the rest. (II, xxx, 1)

If experts in more perfect disciplines were to exercise temporal power over experts in less perfect disciplines, then mathematicians would rule over physicians, 'and very many would be the manifest evils which would follow from this'. The argument is extended into dialectic, for the judge of spiritual things judges differently than does the judge of temporal matters, and the papal claim to universal judgment 'is fallacious because of the equivocal use of the word "judge" '.

On logical grounds too the soul/body analogy is refuted: 'And when it is assumed in the minor premise that the body is subordinate to the soul ... then, even if we unqualifiedly grant that the body is subordinate with respect to perfection, it does not follow that the body is subordinate with respect to jurisdiction: for to argue in this way would be to draw an invalid inference.' Marsilius provides many more arguments to the same effect, for this and other papalist analogies; but they do not, I think, add a great deal more to our understanding of his method than those already cited.

Unlike Marsilius, William of Ockham treats analogy with terse impatience. True to the principle of 'Ockham's razor', he provides the minimum sufficient refutation, usually the tellingly simple refutation from experience. The papal arguments are taken up in Ockham's tract *Octo Quaestiones de Potestate Papae* (c. 1340). Biblical exegesis is discussed in terms similar to those of Jean Quidort: *sensus mysticus* – in this case of the two swords – is to be avoided unless absolutely necessary, and is acceptable only when supported by other Scriptural authority (Q. II, cap. xiii). Typical *comparationes* of papal to imperial power (e.g. father/son, teacher/

pupil, gold/lead, sun/moon) are summarily dismissed on the ground that the emperor bears no such relation to any man on the basis of physical power, but only of spiritual power, in which he is admittedly subject to the Pope (II, xiv). The important analogy to soul and body is also treated with disappointing brevity: Ockham simply asserts that in actual fact the rational or spiritual power does not always control the physical: there are several physical operations not under rational control (I, xiv). It is not, therefore, in his political works that Ockham investigates the fundamental assumptions of analogical thought. That task is accomplished in his logic, to which we must now turn.

Analogy and experience

During the early fourteenth century, advances in scientific theory had furnished the means of criticising traditional cosmology, and political necessity had been the motive for the revision of traditional political theory. Neither among the scientists nor among the political theorists have we found any systematic critique of the general epistemological basis of analogy. The work of the English Franciscan William of Ockham (1290-1349) provides that critique. Ockham's importance in the history of philosophy has never been disputed, though the nature of his contribution has been variously estimated. Though in his own day Ockham was known by the titles 'Invincible Doctor' and 'Venerable Inceptor', his reputation had degenerated by the seventeenth century to that of a sophistical malcontent. In Fuller's *Worthies*, the life of Ockham ends with these words:

For his soul of opposition it will serve to close his epitaph, what was made on a great paradox-monger, possessed with a like contradicting spirit:
> Sed iam est mortuus, ut apparet,
> Quod si viveret, id negaret.

Despite Dr. Fuller's sniping, the nominalist[13] attack on traditional thought is more than an exercise in logic. It offers, and comes from, a radically new approach to reality, an approach which has its parallel in the other disciplines already discussed, and in literature as well.

I have already documented the analogical basis of neo-Platonic Christian thought. As Eliade points out, the tribal society sees its planting, harvesting and love-making as versions of the archetypal creation. In a more sophisticated version of the same impulse, the person who experiences limitations on freedom may construct a universal scheme of predestination in order to account for the human condition as s/he perceives it. Such was the effort of Gottschalk (c. 805–869),[14] whose poignant story remains a powerful human tragedy as well as a useful philosophical anecdote. Dedicated at birth by noble parents to the religious life, the young man by the age of sixteen had realised that his own wishes lay elsewhere: in music, poetry and the secular life. Despite this reluctance, his teacher at the monastery of Fulda – the formidable theologian and later Archbishop of Mainz, Hrabanus Maurus – compelled Gottschalk to take ecclesiastical vows. Some years afterward, in 829, Gottschalk obtained release from these vows, pleading compulsion; but Hrabanus appealed this decision to a higher synod and obtained its reversal. Gottschalk began to compose poetry – among the best surviving from the Carolingian period and including the famous *o cur jubes canere?* Beside poetry, he began to study Augustine, particularly the question of free will and predestination, and to evolve his own theological positions. He fled his monastery to Italy, where Hrabanus pursued him and obtained his expulsion. On his return to Germany, Gottschalk was convicted of heresy and imprisoned in a monastery. His treatise was burnt; he composed it again from memory. Thereafter Gottschalk essentially committed suicide by starvation. On his deathbed the struggle of his lifetime was reenacted: requesting absolution, he was denied it by Hrabanus unless he signed a confession of orthodox faith. Gottschalk refused, and died without the last sacrament. The work for which he had suffered was a rigorous demonstration of predestination, a denial of the efficacy of free will.

For Ockham, such an effort to organise experience in abstract patterns would be logically impermissible (however necessary it might be emotionally). From the nominalist point of view, the condition of being free or unfree, for example, corresponds to no actual entity 'freedom' or 'slavery', nor to any cosmic pattern or 'meaning'. 'Freedom', like 'whiteness', 'beauty', 'justice' or 'mankind', is a universal. It is not a real thing in any sense; it has no objective existence outside the mind and no psychological existence in the mind. It is not the same thing as an idea, for an idea is the image of something, while the universal is not the image of any actual thing. The universal 'has only a logical being in the soul and is a sort of fiction existing in the logical realm. . . . In the same way, propositions, syllogisms, and such other things as philosophy treats, have no psychological being, but have a logical being only: so their being is their being understood.'[15] Another form of universal is the relation-concept: similarity, difference, paternity, causality, etc. These relation-concepts also have no being, but are only an act of the intellect. Like other universals, the relation-concept is a kind of shorthand, a convenient way to express several separate perceptions at once. We may say than an egg is white, and we may say that paper is white; or we may say, using a relational concept, that the egg is similar in colour to paper: 'Just so, the concept "every" is relational in the soul. And although without this concept every man is capable of laughter, still we can only express this through a relational concept' (*Sent*. I in Hyman, p. 641). Many abstract concepts which we use for the sake of convenience are neither provable nor logically necessary to account for the facts. Such concepts are, strictly speaking, dispensable ('Ockham's razor').[16]

Especially in a Christian society, such a theory of universals and relations has enormous implications. One might ask how, if the abstract class 'mankind' has no real existence, mankind can be said to have sinned in Adam or to be redeemed in Christ. If there are no real abstract essences, in what sense can bread and wine be said to 'be' the body and blood of Christ? How can Christ be considered both man and god at once, or god to have three distinct essences in one?[17]

What relevance to poetry has the attack on analogical thought – especially to the poetry of a man like Chaucer, who knew little, if anything, of the work of the scholars I have mentioned in this paper? Despite the lack of direct influence, the questions that scholars were asking during the fourteenth century were not unlike the questions that laymen were asking at the same time. What impelled laypeople was not logic or science or the struggle for political power, but experience and observation; and the historical experience of the late thirteenth and fourteenth centuries was such as to undercut the authority of institutions and values that had once been regarded as unimpeachable. The historical events which had most effect on the ordinary person's experience were the failure of the crusade movement and its degeneration into a purely political tool; internal dissension in the Church, which culminated in the Great Schism of 1378 and generated the heresies of Wyclif and Hus; the plague that periodically swept Europe after 1348; and numerous rebellions such as those of the Jacquerie in France (1357), English peasants and artisans (1381) and the Parisian middle and working classes (1413).

What would these events mean to a moderately well-educated middle-class person of the fourteenth century? The evidence, drawn from sermons, anecdotes, university disputations and vernacular poetry, suggests that such a person could not avoid noticing that the feudal social order was being called into question by those who formed its base. Nor could s/he help observing that the sacred notion of retributive justice did not operate with the Black Death, for many good people died, many evil people survived, and neither virtue nor prayer was efficacious. The military failure of the Crusades had done much to undermine the earlier medieval conviction – so confidently expressed in the *Chanson de Roland* – that 'God is on our side.' And with the perversion of crusade rhetoric and ideals to political ends, it became painfully obvious that the interests served were no longer spiritual, if they ever had been. The same conclusion must have been obvious when all Europe was treated during several decades to the spectacle of two opposing popes, each claiming ultimate authority.

For these reasons the fourteenth century was a period of unusual complexity: unusual in that so many institutions and assumptions were challenged simultaneously. It is precisely this sense of the ambiguity of life that allegory is not suited to convey. I want now to return to the question of allegory and to consider it in the light of the nominalist critique of analogical thought.

The writing of allegory requires that qualities be abstracted from the entities which display them in real life, and that these qualities be granted an independent literary existence. Our own perceptions and experiences are not, of course, fragmented in this way, and if we assent to the literary portrayal of Lust or Humility it is because we know people who are lustful or humble. The advantage of such fragmentation is that it allows us at our leisure to examine and analyse certain phenomena, to isolate certain elements of experience, to judge. Ernst Cassirer notes this phenomenon when he writes:

> The dividing lines which the symbolism of language and the abstract concept introduce into reality may seem necessary and inevitable: however they are necessary not from the standpoint of pure knowledge but from the standpoint of action. Man can act upon the world only by breaking it into pieces – by dissecting it into separate spheres of action and objects of action. (vol. 3, p. 36)

Similar observations, by no means pejorative in intent, have been made more recently. Jean-Charles Payen, for example, writing of the fundamentally utopian and optimistic character of allegory, notes that

> L'allégorie exprime un univers rêvé, rectifié, corrigé par une intention de moraliste qui aspire à l'exemplarité. . . . L'allégorie est d'autant plus suggestive qu'elle se présente comme une révélation. Mais c'est une révélation tronquée qui, dans la mesure où elle exclut le malheur irréversible, ampute de sa dimension tragique la réalité qu'elle prétend transcender. Elle participe donc d'une littérature d'évasion en détournant l'individu du monde où il vit pour lui imposer la

valorisation fabuleuse d'un absolu fantastique. A cet égard, elle est un inestimable instrument pour toute idéologie aliénante.

Michel Zink, affirming the link of allegory with subjectivity, is compelled to remark that

> In personifying ... the forces which confront each other within consciousness, allegory renders them independent of the subject who is the theater for their struggle, and it perceives in this struggle the application of permanent and nontemporal laws much more than it sets forth the particular accidents, the circumstances, the immersion in the present of a subjectivity, which experiences this struggle each time as if it were unique.

Allegory, like Ockham's relation-concept, helps us to communicate and in turn to act: allegory is well-suited, therefore, to didactic purposes. In fact, the allegorical persona is usually a personified universal, and the nominalist might argue (much as I have argued in the first part of this essay) that the allegorical persona corresponds to nothing knowable; he might inquire, as Ockham did, how we can recognise any similitude unless first we know the reality it resembles.

Naturally, a writer will not approach this problem as the professional philosopher does. Instead, s/he will think of its aesthetic manifestations: does a particular mode render experience and meaning as fully as s/he would like? The limitation of allegory becomes apparent, I suggest, when the experiences and attitudes to be portrayed pass a certain degree of complexity. I do not mean complexity of plot, which may certainly exist in allegory, but rather the simultaneity of motive and implication which exists at any given point in the story: a vertical, not a horizontal, complexity. Allegory simplifies experience by systematising it. If one wishes to know why a lady is receptive, then it is merely tautological to say, as the *Roman de la Rose* says, 'Because she is under the influence of Belacueil.' If one wants to be sober, it is pointless to reply, as the *Psychomachia* does, 'Sobriety always conquers Luxury.' Our sense of choice and possibility is more involved than that, and so, I think, was Chaucer's. The ambivalence of human will is his constant theme.

The nominalist theory of will expresses the same consciousness. Ockham considered will to dominate other mental powers, including intellect: we do not learn to will, but will to learn; we understand only when we wish to do so. Because will is not subordinate to other mental operations, the human soul does not necessarily desire what is good for it, as Aquinas and others had taught. It is ambivalent, and Ockham denies that everything has a natural inclination toward its own perfection.

The will may like happiness and not like it; may desire happiness and may not. This is evident from the fact that many believers, with faith in future life, just as well as unbelievers without faith in any future life, have killed themselves with the full use of their reason; have thrown themselves into the arms of death; even these have not wanted to exist. . . . Some of the faithful are convinced that they cannot attain happiness without a good life, and still they do not cultivate a good and saintly life. Therefore they do not desire happiness efficiently, and, consequently, with the same reason, they may not want it. (Sent. I)

As for being influenced by God's intention, 'There is no proof that whatever God intends is done by God, or is done by somebody else' (Sent. I in Tornay, p. 179). The will is entirely free from internal and external compulsion.

If the writer should interest him or herself in the infinite and infinitely subtle behavioural possibilities that free will implies, then s/he will not, I think, be drawn to allegory. Allegory cannot do justice to the capricious aspect of personality, for the composite allegorical personality is circumscribed from the beginning by the self-evident functions of its parts. In The Allegory of Love, Lewis notes a similarity between the so-called heroine of the Roman de la Rose, and Chaucer's Criseyde. 'We see', Lewis goes on, 'how little the allegorical form hampers the novelist in Guillaume by the fact that when we have finished his poem we have an intimate knowledge of his heroine, though his heroine as such has never appeared. (p. 135). With this I disagree: surely Guillaume's heroine and Chaucer's Criseyde are more profitably contrasted. We know no one in the fragmented manner that we know Guillaume's heroine. Criseyde's hesitations and impulses are not separated and named, nor do we know her precise will – 'entente' and 'entencioun' are words Chaucer constantly uses in the poem, not only about Criseyde but about Troilus and Pandarus also. That obscurity makes Criseyde more 'real' than the composite non-entity of the Roman, for the mystery of will, which allegory dispels by fragmentation, is what we know in reality.

For the nominalist, not only human will but God's will too is perfectly free. God's actions cannot be constrained by what he has already done, or by what he has promised to do. Since God is not bound by any principle or precedent, he could theoretically will other worlds like ours, or the reversal of present moral values, or the opposite of present physical laws.[18] This vision of a pervasively contingent universe is one of the most important contributions of nominalist theory, for it points to a radical revision of traditional relations between humanity and the world, humanity and God.

Ockham was fully aware of these implications. Summarising arguments against himself, Ockham notes that his opponents will say that those who deny the reality of relations 'undo the substantial connection of the universe' (*Sent.* I in Hyman, p. 636). Ockham's opponents would have been correct in saying so, for although much more was to happen before that process was complete, precisely the undoing of substantial connection was at issue in nominalist theory. It was the undoing of connections metaphysical, scientific and literary that John Donne was to regret in 'The First Anniversary', where, mourning the death of a young woman, he wrote:

> What Artist now dares boast that he can bring
> Heaven hither, or constellate any thing,
> So as the influence of those starres may bee
> Imprison'd in a Herbe, or Charme or Tree,
> And doe by touch, all which those stars could do?
> The art is lost, and correspondence too.
> For heaven gives little, and the earthe takes lesse,
> And man least knows their trade and purposes.
> If this commerce twixt heaven and earth were not
> Embarr'd, and all this traffique quite forgot,
> She, for whose losse we have lamented thus,
> Would work more fully, more pow'rfully on us . . . (II. 391-402)

I think it no coincidence that an ex-Catholic wrote this, whose own personal experience of conversion to Anglicanism embodies, figures, that of his nation and eventually of his culture: of Europe as a whole. The saintlike 'she' lamented here is after all more than a single individual. It is a biological mother, a childhood, a way of life, a disappearing *episteme* and the feudal civilisation that accompanied it. All are irrevocably distanced by events both personal and historical, so that the story of Donne – like that of Gottschalk before him – attains an emblematic resonance.

This sketch of one feature of fourteenth-century learned discourse suggests the importance of its attack on analogical thought. In this tendency I believe Chaucer participated, turning intuitively from allegory to other modes of representation in order to express his vision of a profoundly contingent world. In doing so he participated as well, however ambiguously, in creating the discourse of a new power, a bourgeois and nationalist, and therefore (at this early stage of its development) a secular, empirical and rationalist one. Sixteenth-century religious and political reformers who enlisted Chaucer in their cause were 'wrong' in the narrowest sense, but taken more broadly their misprision opens a passage to what was most fertile in late-medieval culture.

The politics of allegory in the fourteenth century

'Surely anyone who professes to think that the question of art and cultivation must go before that of the knife and fork . . . does not understand what art means.' So wrote the poet and craftsman, the Marxist medievalist William Morris (p. 659). Though Morris was speaking mainly about leisure – or, as he put it, 'a thriving and unanxious life' – as prerequisite for the production of art, he was also calling attention in a more general way to the economic foundation of culture. Morris implies that economic conditions affect or even enable social and aesthetic life. Morris's own experience taught him this approach to art, and he found it confirmed in the writings of Karl Marx and Frederick Engels, his contemporaries and fellow residents in London. A more elaborate statement of the premises of Morris's views on art, and of those of the present essay as well, comes from Marx:

In the social production which men carry on they enter into definite relations that are indispensable and independent of their will. . . . The sum total of these relations of production constitutes the economic structure of society – the real foundation, on which rises a legal and political superstructure and to which correspond definite forms of social consciousness. The mode of production in material life determines the social, political and intellectual life processes in general. It is not the consciousness of men that determines their being, but, on the contrary, their social being that determines their consciousness. . . . With the change of the economic foundation the entire immense superstructure is . . . transformed. In considering such transformations a distinction should always be made between the material transformation of the economic conditions of production which can be determined with the precision of natural science, and the legal, political, religious, aesthetic, or philosophical – in short ideological – forms in which men become conscious of this conflict and fight it out.[1]

This essay will follow a cultural phenomenon of the fourteenth century to its 'knife-and-fork' basis; that is, it will trace the relation between one feature of the late medieval superstructure and its economic foundation. 'Base' and 'superstructure' constitute a spatial metaphor, indeed an architectural metaphor. It was particularly helpful

to Marx and Engels in their polemic against proletarian political tendencies that underestimated the importance of economic factors to a
social analysis ('utopian' socialism) or to a political programme (anar-
chism). To locate this trope in its time and its rhetorical kind doesn't
invalidate the concept it represents. What it represents is not mechanistic
reduction of all cultural phenomena to a single economic 'cause' – a
vulgarity, as Engels notes, imposed by polemical urgency – but rather a
constant necessary reminder of what revolutionary change requires if it
is to succeed, endure, and evolve: alteration in the economic structure of
social relations.

The phenomenon I want to look at is the rejection of analogical
argument and allegorical representation by a significant portion of the
intelligentsia in fields as varied as cosmology and logic, physics and
poetry, political theory and the visual arts. The problem is worth our
attention for other reasons than that, like Mount Everest, it is there.
Because the allegorical mode has appeared in many genres (lyric, epic,
romance, drama and novel) and in many historical periods (Old and
New Testament, Greek, Roman, medieval, Renaissance and modern),
writers on allegory have tended to generalise about 'the allegorical tradition' or about the 'universality' of the allegorical impulse. This tendency
characterises some of the most distinguished contributions to the study
of allegory, from C.S. Lewis to D.W. Robertson and beyond. Though the
tendency to universalise does not necessarily invalidate these contributions, it is reductive in permitting or encouraging us to ignore the
social origin and social function of cultural forms. In fact the uses of
allegory vary; neither the allegorical tradition nor the medieval approach
to allegory is monolithic. Insofar as any cultural form reflects the attitudes
of one or another social class, so does allegory. In short, the dialectics of
history creates a dialectics in art, an ebb and flow which most writing on
allegory seems to minimise or omit.[2] In discussing the fortunes of
allegory in the fourteenth century I hope to provide some sense of that
dialectic. It is an effort whose implications do not end with the Middle
Ages.

My purpose is first to summarise the allegorical tradition and the anti-
analogical trend of the fourteenth century, as documented in the preceding essay and with some further evidence. I shall also draw out some
social implications of these positions and of the late-medieval confrontation between them. The next section of this paper describes the major
economic and historical changes relevant to the new approach to

analogical thought.

a. *Science.* Until the fourteenth century, medieval cosmology, founded mainly on Platonic and Aristolelian principles, supported several hypotheses based on the analogical perception of nature. The universe was thought to be round, like the earth at its centre. Geocentricity itself was an analogical notion, duplicating the fundamental human condition of perceptual egocentricity, each of us at the centre of her or his own perpetual world. This interpretation of geocentricity is supported by the notion (present in somewhat different forms in both Plato and Aristotle, as well as their predecessors) that the cosmos itself was a living organism. Like any other creature it had a body: the physical universe. Like any other creature it had a soul: a nature, or innate principle of movement and learning. Aristotle thought that each celestial sphere or body had its own particular intelligence, and he was able to calculate a total of 55 celestial intelligences. Like other living creatures the universe also had an absolute directional orientation: a universally valid up, down, left and right.

In physics, theories of weight and motion also reflected analogical perceptions. They were accounted for by the principle of natural place, or like to like. Fire rises to the empyrean, rivers flow to the sea, stones fall to the earth, in an effort to rejoin the primal element from which they came. Each object or element tries to unite with the divine or universal model of which the object is part, copy or analogue. Underlying this physics is a profoundly analogical notion of causality, which would be resurrected by Thomas Aquinas. It is that an effect resembles or participates in the essence of its cause, hence strives to imitate or join its cause. So fire to the empyean, so the child to its parent, so (according to St. Thomas) the mind of man to God.

Though the social function of such ideas in classical Greece does not concern us here, their effect in the Middle Ages was to provide scientific support for a particular social arrangement. The corruption and degradation of the sublunary sphere, its distance from divine goodness, could be adduced as proof of the Christian (and ruling class) virtues of humility and subordination: pride, together with its offshoots, ambition and rebellion, could be treated as unnatural.[3] The existence of celestial intelligences demonstrated the universality of the elitist principle, and the principle of like to like would be used as an argument against social mobility.

Ideas based on analogy survived in Hellenic, Arabic, scholastic and even Renaissance theory, though they were refuted by the most

advanced fourteenth-century scientists, among them V
ham (d. 1349), Jean Buridan (d. 1358) and Buridan's
Oresme (1320–1982). In Buridan's work, cosmic soul
intelligence became simply irrelevant as causes of motion, r
theory of impetus. The theory of natural place was rejected c   ɔasis
of observation and experiment, and the probability of a heliocentric
universe was logically and mathematically demonstrated by Oresme.
The spherical universe was denied, with Ockham and Oresme asserting
the likelihood of an infinite universe. A natural corollary of this
hypothesis was relative direction, and absence of any single centre in the
universe. Buridan's critique of analogical thought extended even to style
when he attacked Aristotle's use of anthropomorphic metaphor: 'It is
only,' Buridan writes scornfully, 'a figurative locution'.

It is true that many of the new ideas were held 'by logic only' and were
not asserted to be absolutely true. Oresme, for instance, retreated from
his demonstration of heliocentricity into fideistic reassertion of the
Biblical statement that *Deus enim firmavit orbem*. For its lasting advances,
cosmological theology would have to wait for Copernicus's commitment to the physical basis of hypotheses, and for the seventeenth-
century technology of telescopic lenses, used by Galileo. Nonetheless,
fourteenth-century logic helped to prepare the way for the later
developments.

b. *Political theory.* The late medieval conflict between papal and
secular powers generated, in the fourteenth century, a thorough
polemical attack on the repertoire of analogical and allegorical arguments with which the papacy had traditionally supported its claims to
temporal power. Among the papal arguments was the venerable
metaphor of the body politic, given its fullest development by John of
Salisbury. All of society is like a human body, with the papacy as supreme
power, or soul, and other social groups ranged below, down to the feet
which, like the peasantry they represent, cling firmly to the soil. Again,
the allegory of sun and moon represented the papal and royal powers as
the greater and lesser lights, the latter dependent on the former. The
allegory of the two swords was another papal favourite, based on the
interpretation of a Biblical locus and purporting to prove the validity of
papal power. It was the notion of 'representation', with its double
meaning, that united allegorical interpretation with the historical transmission of power: as Lagarde notes, contemporary ecclesiastics were
said to 'represent' Biblical figures both because they were their image,
and because they occupied their position by succession ('L'Idée . . .).

Hence the Pope 'represented' the entire Christian community in both imagistic and political senses.

A variety of arguments was used to refute these claims. Jean (Quidort) de Paris (1241–1306), a prominent polemicist in the service of Philippe le Bel, denied the validity of 'mystical' or analogical argument, and, like Marsilius of Padua after him, conceded only very limited use of allegorical interpretation of Scripture. Both Marsilius in *Defensor Pacis* (1324) and Dante Alighieri in *De Monarchia* (c. 1317) relied heavily on the logical analysis of papal analogies, and also on arguments drawn from Aristotle. By contrast, William of Ockham, writing under protection of King Ludwig of Bavaria, used simple observation, foregoing the pyrotechnical display of the others in favour of minimum effective refutation: Ockham's razor.

Ockham also argued against representation as a logical reality, for although one person or group might delegate its power to another, there could be no real transmission of essence. The so-called 'representative' body – the Church, a Church council, a city, a kingdom – remains nothing more than a group of individuals, a collective noun, a plurality which no legal fiction can reduce to true unity. The same is true for representation as image, symbol or allegory: similarity in one respect is not identity, hence it confers no special powers. That the Pope inherits Jesus's power does not entitle him to claim Jesus's infallibility.

For these fourteenth-century theorists, the immediate requirements of partisan politics dictated the attack on older modes of argument. This was of course no death-blow to allegory, for the old body-politic metaphor would reappear in the work of Sir John Fortescue, the fifteenth-century jurist, and it flourished mightily under the Tudors, who adapted wholesale the venerable methods of their enemy in Rome. Analogical argument is admirably suited to the needs of any ruling class which feels itself threatened by change; while those who desire change will tend to be as wary of allegory as was the Protestant reformer William Tyndale when he wrote: 'Beware of allegories; for there is not a more handsome or apt thing to beguile withal than an allegory; nor a more subtle and pestilent thing in the world to persuade a false matter, than an allegory' ('Prologue to Leviticus').

c. *Logic.* It was William of Ockham who in the realm of pure logic contributed most to the anti-analogical campaign, a contribution centring in his theory of universals. Basically Ockham denied the epistemological grounds for analogical thought in denying the real existence of abstract entities: universals such as 'whiteness', 'beauty', 'justice', 'paternity', 'similarity', 'motion', 'time', or any other such noun that corresponds to no physical object. Plato's ideal Forms are universals, so are St. Thomas's ideas in the mind of God; and the characters in personification allegory are nothing more than universals personified: *Amor, Natura, Mens Humilis*. Christian theology depended heavily on the reality of abstract essences in order to support such dogmas as the triune nature of deity, the transsubstantiation of wine and wafer, original sin, and salvation. The allegorist also accepts at some level, implicitly at least, the reality of the abstract essences he bodies forth; otherwise the persuasive force of his work is lost. He must also accept that those essences are knowable, and that there is some reliable connection between them and our own world – a connection enabling the reader to transfer meaning from literal to figurative levels and to reason from known to unknown.

As Lovejoy reminds us, this sort of otherworldly or idealistic world view has been 'the dominant official philosophy of the larger part of civilised mankind throughout most of its history'. Lovejoy further remarks, with some naiveté, that 'by a familiar paradox . . . the chief power in the affairs of this world is not unlikely to fall . . . into the hands of those who have withdrawn from it' (p. 27). The fact becomes rather less paradoxical, however, when we observe that the theory of correspondence between this and a supernatural reality forms the ontological basis of the theory of isomorphic structure. In this theory we are invited to see the cosmos, political society, the family and the individual mind as analogue structures, with God, king or pope, father or husband, and the rational faculty supreme in their respective hierarchies. The theory is fundamental to conservative political theory in the Middle Ages, constantly used not only in papal polemics but also in the more general writings of Thomas Aquinas and others. There is in this world view no relationship that cannot be assimilated into an isomorphic scheme.

All this Ockham's philosophy would refute. The universal, he proposed, has no existence, either in the world or in the mind. It is not an idea, since it is not the idea of any thing. It is, simply, a piece of logical shorthand, 'whose being is its being understood'. If there were such essences, they would not be knowable in themselves, nor could we legitimately infer any relation between them and the physical world, whether that relation be similarity, causality or imitation. The entire process of reasoning from known to unknown becomes extremely precarious, and some scholars, such as Nicholas of Autrecourt, deny that it is possible at all. Ockham and Buridan agree that in many cases of natural law, probability suffices; still, there is in fact no way of knowing absolutely what God's will is, or that it won't change tomorrow. We cannot argue that God's behaviour up to the present is any guarantee of His future behaviour, or that His qualities as we now define them will not alter. Since God is bound by neither natural law nor His own promises, the universe becomes profoundly contingent and, in the absolute sense, unpredictable. Neither nature, society, nor the human mind are necessarily permanent or static in their structure; all are open to change and plurality, none can be fully understood by reference to an abstract *a priori* scheme.

In its time Ockham's logic was known as the *via moderna*. Its dominance in European universities, especially those of central Europe, helped pave the way for the Reformation, in rupturing that hard-won connection between this world and the next which had been the pride of medieval ecclesiastical philosophy.

d. *Poetry.* I am using two criteria in my definition of literary allegory: that it is a sustained narrative, and that it requires translation from literal to figurative levels of meaning. According to these criteria, the poetry of the fourteenth century shows a marked tendency away from the allegorical mode as it is represented by the fourth century *Psychomachia* of Prudentius, the *De Planctu Naturae* of Alain de Lille, or Guillaume de Lorris's *Roman de la Rose*. Of course this tendency did not mean the end of allegory. Like any obsolescent cultural form it would decline gradually, and in the late-medieval period one can still point to Guillaume de Guilleville's monumental tripartite work, or to the anonymous early fifteenth century *Assembly of Gods* with its miniature *psychomachia*. Nonetheless allegory did change, and in its classic form was rarely practised.

The directions taken by the two major poets of the fourteenth century, Chaucer and Dante, indicate a movement away from the rigid allegories of the earlier Middle Ages, though with neither poet was the break complete. In using what Erich Auerbach has called the figural mode, Dante in the *Divine Comedy* retains all the complexity of history and personality which traditional allegory is incapable of. His characters are not personifications, nor do they participate in any action whose meaning differs from that of real life. Chaucer translated three allegories: two appear as *Melibee's Tale* and *The Clerk's Tale*; the other is part of the *Roman de la Rose*. The judgment scene in *The House of Fame* is his only original piece of personification allegory; elsewhere there are scattered allegorical or symbolic motifs (e.g., the pilgrimage through life, the cosmic intellectual flight in *The House of Fame*) or purely decorative personified abstractions (*The Parliament of Fowls*). For the most part, though, Chaucer turned to realistic representation. The meaning that his characters achieve is not separate from their physical and social being, for, as with Dante, normal life itself is charged with meaning. Even such late-medieval works as are generally called allegories, are allegorical only in an incomplete and diffuse way. The major type is the instructional dialogue modeled on Boethius' *Consolation of Philosophy*. A personified abstraction may interrogate or instruct the central character, as in Gower's *Confessio Amantis* or Usk's *Testament of Love*. Minor allegories may be embedded in the treatise, like the beast fable in Gower's *Vox Clamantis*. There may be a symbolic or allegorical framework, as in *Pearl*, though Pearl herself is a figural character, with biological and social existence within the poem. Indeed she can function as divine messenger precisely because she was a real person who has died and been saved. *Piers Plowman* can be considered, with *Confessio Amantis*, an example of the 'estates of the world' genre. Its opening allegory of the field of folk soon becomes indistinguishable from realistic satire, and the poem shifts rapidly among various modes of representation. In none of these works do we find a sustained metaphorical narrative; none requires translation; there is no difference between vehicle and tenor, but only a single level of meaning straightforwardly expressed.

e. *Painting and sculpture.* Some important developments in the visual arts parallel those noted above. Earlier medieval painting, like Egyptian and Byzantine painting, practises conceptual rather than optical representation,[4] making relatively little effort to reproduce a naturalistic image. It displays, therefore, little foreshortening or perspective; space is two-dimensional; side-views and front-views are combined. We find rigid, immobile body postures and unrealistic proportions, stereotyped faces devoid of emotion, and hierarchal scaling in which the size of figures is determined not by their distance from the viewer's eye, but by their social or religious importance. Indeed the viewer's eye is not an important element in conceptual representation, because the figures portrayed are little more than personified abstractions. They are not people at all, but subordinate parts of a developed abstract, theological system, which depreciates the importance of the physical world. Conceptual art expresses an otherworldly religion in which the 'real' form of a thing is not its visual form, but its relation to the ideological system. The visual form is merely apparent – a lesser reality, not worth imitating. Thus in Christian art the important eye is not the observer's but God's, to which all objects are equally close: a notion of space which corresponds to the traditional Christian concept of time, which with God is a single eternal present moment.

With the development of Gothic style all this begins to change in the direction of secular realism and naturalism. In sculpture we find individualised facial expressions, realistic proportions, gracefully suggestive body postures, and an intensely humanised Jesus, Mary and army of saints. In paintings, the world is now represented as a worthwhile place to be; it is God's creation, the scene of good deeds and of effective preparation for the afterlife. Physical objects, the human body and the old cult-images are now recognisably real. But it is primarily during the fourteenth century, with the decadence of Gothic, that the most important innovations appear in the treatment of space, with the work of Duccio and Giotto. The observer's eye becomes the criterion for spatial dimensions; proportion and perspective as we know them are discovered; space itself becomes three-dimensional. These changes, as Bunim notes, 'mark the transition from the medieval to the Renaissance concept of space' (p. 134).

Like the other tendencies summarised above, late-medieval developments in the visual arts participate in a general cultural movement from abstract to concrete, from ecclesiastical to secular, from universal to particular. Yet while such terms provide a closer definition, they explain nothing but require themselves to be explained. To what new social needs does that general cultural movement respond?

For the period under discussion, the dominant fact of economic history is the transition from feudalism to capitalism. It is the major contradiction of the later Middle Ages, and I am proposing that the phenomenon I have isolated for study here is a cultural manifestation of that contradiction. As an important ideological weapon in the arsenal of the feudal class, analogical patterns of thought and modes of representation could not express the perceptions and values of groups competing with that ruling class. The attack on analogy, with the substitution of other modes of argument and representation, does express the values and perceptions of such other groups at a particular moment in their evolution; that is, it articulates ideological needs which are partially constitutive of their social reality. We may begin with a brief general sketch of the conflicting social realities of the late Middle Ages.

My presentation is schematic – necessarily so, for in constructing a model of feudalism I have taken salient features and minimised uneven development (difference from country to country and from century to century). In the interest of brevity I have also had to omit many subtleties of medieval class structure, as, for example, degrees of stratification among tenants. Nonetheless my aim is not to offer an exhaustive study of feudalism, but rather to focus on those of its aspects that are most pertinent to my subject. In responding to criticisms of the medieval section of his work *Der moderne Kapitalismus* Werner Sombart is reported to have replied, 'I have made a construct which is called the Middle Ages. What may have been the actual conditions of that era is a matter of complete indifference to me, and it is ridiculous to claim to refute my theories with objections drawn from historical essays.'[5] Though I neither claim such indifference, nor take the statement literally, the tone of the response is tempting in face of some recent historical writing on feudalism. I have in mind particularly an article by Elizabeth A.R. Brown – a sophistical and implicitly quite reactionary piece which denounces 'feudalism' as a deceptive term and concept, calling for its abolition in favour of a narrow history of individual subjectivities.[6] I shall take for granted here the usefulness and general validity of the term, as well as its major features, without discussing such matters as the weight of demographic factors in 'the crisis of feudalism' or the use of 'feudalism' to describe a mode of production.[7] By the thirteenth century, Perry Anderson notes, 'European feudalism had produced a unified and developed civilisation that registered a tremendous advance on the rudimentary, patchwork communities of the Dark Ages' (p. 182). That such a coherency presumes the interrelatedness of art and economics I hope the present essay will show.

Feudalism is that set of economic and political arrangements, originating in the Merovingian age, which dominated Europe for nearly a millenium. Its economic base was rural and agricultural, with the large country estate (villa, seigneurie, manor) as its basic social and economic unit. The estate was more or less self-sufficient economically; it produced nearly all the agricultural products and small hand-manufactures it required, and its surplus was almost entirely consumed by the inhabitants of the estate.[8] Production on the feudal estate was planned to meet the known needs of a stable community; its surplus was for the most part use-value.

Class structure on the estate was multi-layered and it varied with time and place. In general, though, its inhabitants can be divided into two groups: those who worked the land and produced its surplus but did not appropriate that surplus; those who did not work the land but who controlled it and appropriated its surplus. The first group included tenants, free and servile, some poor and others prosperous. The tenant (villein) owed his lord a fixed portion of his labour in working and maintaining the lord's land; he also owed certain tributes in money and in kind, and money taxes for necessary services held in monopoly by the lord: compulsory use of the lord's ovens, brewhouse, mill, stud animals, permission to marry, etc. An elaborate system of manorial policing ensured that there were no individualistic departures from this scheme, such as grinding corn at home in a hand mill. Infringements were tried and fined in manor court. The villein could not dispose freely of land or produce; he had to buy a licence to sell beasts; only grain (within certain limits) could be sold without permission, in order to raise money for rents and taxes. In exchange for this and innumerable other oppressions the tenant population received the privilege of retaining a certain portion of their produce and labour for their own needs, and some limited military protection from the lord. The political features of this system are recognisable in the North American company town, or in the great plantations of Brazil and other Latin American countries (though of course neither of these can be called 'feudal' in the economic sense since they produce for the world capitalist market).

As for those who consumed the manorial surplus, they too occupied various ranks and degrees. They constituted a chain of command, linked by the institution of vassalage. This was a mutually binding contract in which the landowner ceded to his vassal the income from a portion of land (the fief) and some degree of legal jurisdiction over it. In exchange the owner received military service and supplies, and financial aid. The vassal might in turn subdivide his fief among lesser vassals and so distribute the burden more widely in a process of subinfeudation. In this structure, the ecclesiastical ruling class participated as well as the secular, for the villein was indeed servant to two masters. As the largest landlord in Europe, the Church had the power to levy taxes, raise armies and wage war, make laws and enforce them in its own courts. The ecclesiastical estate functioned no differently than its secular counterpart; and in the *Chanson de Roland* it is the valiant Archbishop Turpin of Reims who confirms the vassal's military duties, crying, 'Ne sui mie vencut. / Ja bon vassal nen ert vif recreut' (*laisse* 155, 2087–8.)

Hierarchal order is key to the feudal social system. It can survive only when each individual correctly fulfills obligations to those above and below; and as we will shortly see, it was in part the failure or inability of the ruling class to meet its traditional obligations that led to the dissolution of the feudal structure. To such a system the importance of analogical cosmology, ontology and logic is clear. It permits the powerful to justify the present social structure as eternal, inevitable and immutable by analogy to cosmic structure. It mystifies human life and human suffering by relegating them to a secondary, derivative, and merely analogical order of reality. It encourages the 'virtues' of humility and obedience by placing earth and mankind at the bottom of the universe. As a literary manifestation of these principles we may look to Chaucer's allegory, adapted from a folktale, *The Clerk's Tale*. Griselda is at once the ideal wife, serf and human being. Domestic, social and theological virtues are united in her. In order to transfer meaning from literal to figurative levels, as the Clerk insists we do, we must accept the isomorphic structure of those three areas, together with the naturalness and permanence of that structure.

The notions of limit and stasis are also important to the feudal world view, with its regular and predictable cosmic movement and its carefully circumscribed universe. It is a world-view whose stasis and limits duplicate those of social structure. A social system which is economically static offers no basis for social mobility, for social mobility is made possible by increased wealth and productivity. In early feudal economy, increased productivity was pointless, so that social mobility was anomalous. Given a more or less stable population, a substantially increased surplus on the manor would only be wasted because there was no large national or international market to absorb it. Sold in small local markets it would only drive prices down and threaten the tenant's ability to pay money rents. Moreover, increased productivity would require too hard a hand on the already exploited tenant population, thus threatening the productive base itself (indeed this was a factor in the crisis of feudalism when, later on, increased productivity became economically necessary). And, given the static economy there was little need for technical innovation or for the intellectual ambition and inventive genius whose social effect is to increase productivity. Even when a technical innovation appears in this kind of economy it is not widely used: ample human labour is available, and that labour has no other place to go.[9]

The concept of human nature as we know it today can scarcely exist in such a system. Instead, human nature and virtue tend to be defined as class nature and virtue. Plato defines them as such in the *Republic*; so does Andreas Capellanus, speaking of peasants, in a passage from *De Arte Honesti Amandi* which makes no secret of the social function of its concept of human nature:

But lest you should consider that what we have already said about the love of the middle class applies to farmers, we will add a little about their love . . . for a farmer

hard labour and the uninterrupted solaces of plough and mattock are sufficient.
And even if it should happen at times, though rarely, that contrary to their nature
they are stirred up by Cupid's arrows, it is not expedient that they should be
instructed in the theory of love, lest while they are devoting themselves to
conduct which is not natural to them the kindly farms which are usually made
fruitful by their efforts may through lack of cultivation prove useless to us. (pp.
149–50)

It is not the nature of peasants to love, because it is not socially expedient
for them to do so; for a peasant to love would be 'unnatural'. Virtue too
becomes the correct fulfillment of class duties: how else can one understand the 'virtue' of Roland, the chivalric prowess for which he is taken
directly to heaven, despite his rejection of Oliver's sage advice?
Custom is the rule of life, and we recall that in its earliest meaning,
'custom' is the feudal labour obligation: the manorial *consuetudines*.

   Though this static notion of society and human nature did correspond
at first to economic reality, it survived among the ruling class even after
the development of trade and towns began to change that reality. Here is
what Andreas considers the correct line for a noblewoman towards a
bourgeois suitor. 'I am very much surprised', she says—

it is enough to surprise anyone – that in such a great upsetting of things the
elements do not come to an end and the world itself fall into ruin. . . . It is not
without cause or reason that this distinction of rank has been found among men
from the very beginning; it is so that every man will stay within the bounds of his
own class and be content with all things therein and never presume to arrogate to
himself the things that were naturally set aside as belonging to a higher class. . . . As
for [your good character] this makes you very worthy of the love of a woman of
your class. But even if a falcon should sometimes be put to flight by a buzzard, still
the falcon is classed with falcons and the buzzard with buzzards – the one being
called a worthless falcon, the other a very good buzzard. (p. 52)

The concept of individual character or merit has little meaning in a feudal
society. In the sense that the particular person is comprehended mainly
by reference to the general category or class, the feudal concept of
human nature is itself, loosely speaking, allegorical: the concrete is
meaningful only when translated into the abstract. The ideology is perfectly expressed in pre-Gothic conceptual art, with its refusal to render
the physical world meaningful in its own terms.

   Arnold Hauser remarked that feudal society lacked 'the intellectual
dynamism induced by the competitive idea' (vol. 1, p. 181). That competitive idea entered European life when the feudal system began its cen-
turies-long process of disintegration: toward the mid-eleventh century,

when the economic base of feudalism, already weakening, was further challenged by rival forms of economic activity. So pronounced was the change in direction at this time that Marc Bloch was prompted to speak of 'two successive "feudal" ages, very different from one another in their essential character' (*Feudal Society*, p. 60).

Among the internal weaknesses of feudalism was intense competition among lords for land and vassals. This resulted in increased expenditure, partly for sumptuary display (which in any case was an important use of surplus production). In the Middle English poem, *The Parlement of the Three Ages*, Medill-elde reproaches Youthe:

For alle thy ryalle araye, . renttis hase thou none.
Ne for thi pompe and thi pride, . penyes bot fewe.
For alle thi golde and thi gude . glowes on this clothes,
And thou hafe caughte thi kaple, . thou cares for no fothire. (Stanza 1, 186–9)

But the condition treated here in moral terms was in fact a wide-spread economic situation. Competition among lords also generated prolonged warfare, such as the twenty-year battle which opens the story of Aucassin and Nicolette. The Crusades were a special drain, for they required an enormous initial outlay, and ruined many a noble family. The impoverished vavasor in Chrétien's *Erec et Enide* spoke for many when he told his story:

tant ai esté toz jorz an guerre	I've been in such a continual war
tote en ai perdue ma terre,	that I've lost all my land
et angagiee, et vandue. (515–17)	and mortgaged and sold it.

These factors combined to create a need for increased manorial production and, consequently, overexploitation of the manorial labour force in taxation, labour dues, and other ways. The worsening condition of the manorial worker, so eloquently described in the opening lines of the *Second Shepherds' Play*, drove many to leave the manor.

Simultaneously with these events, the feudal system felt the external impact of a complex of closely related developments: the growth of trade and manufacture, the development of national and international markets, and the revival of towns as centres of commerce, industry and culture.[10] A new social class was called into being: the bourgeoisie, which began as rival to the feudal aristocracy and ended, a few centuries later, as the new European ruling class.

In contrast to the relatively self-sufficient rural estate, the development of trade generated the urban centre connected by mutual need to a network of other towns across the nation and abroad: raw materials, processing, manufacture, markets, division of labour were the ties that bound. In contrast to manorial use-value, trade created exchange-value. Surplus product could now be sold at a profit, in an infinitely expandable market. With exchange-value, therefore, increased productivity became both a goal and a need, along with the mental and social qualities required. The thrift, saving and reinvestment of early capitalists could only appear avaricious to the feudal landlord; while the feudal lord's conspicuous consumption of surplus product must appear wasteful to the bourgeois. That conflict of values is reflected, in rather crude terms, in the alliterative poem *Winner and Waster* (1352).

Perceptually, experientially, the world changes when exchange-value replaces use-value. The Coast Salish Indian may see in a cedar the form of a canoe, a roofbeam or a totempole; but Mr. MacMillan or Mr. Bloedel must see in it so many board feet worth so many dollars in Japan. In part the new naturalistic perception of the late medieval artist had to do with his social background: art had moved out of the monastery into the hands of laymen. These craftsmen were professionals, people of good family, often with fortunes of their own gained by investment and in any case dependent on wealthy bourgeois patrons. Their interest was very much in the real world. Moreover, how could the late medieval artist continue to reproduce two-dimensional space when its inaccuracy was demonstrated all around him? He need not know that fourteenth-century philosophers had recently demonstrated the probability of an infinite universe; but he could scarcely help noticing the apparently limitless expansion of markets, of geographical horizons, of commodity production, and of personal fortunes. I am suggesting, then, that the so-called 'inaccuracies' of conceptual art express quite accurately not only a religious ideology, but the values of the economic and social structure supported by religious ideology. By the same token, natural space, distance and measurement begin to exist psychologically and aesthetically when they come to exist socially.

From the start the medieval bourgeoisie were in competition with feudal lords. They competed first for labour-power, for they required a pool of free workers and artisans to produce what they would sell. Free, that is, from feudal ties, free to move where they were needed, free to work when they were needed, and free from property.[11] To this end most town charters guaranteed freedom to any serf who lived peacefully in the town for a year and a day, who worked and paid taxes. But the bourgeois himself, whether merchant, employer or financier, also required freedom from domination by lay and ecclesiastical lords. He wanted freedom to trade unimpeded and travel safely, freedom to hire and release employees, to raise or lower prices, wages or interest, to accumulate a fortune, marry a noblewoman or purchase an estate. The political privileges granted to the urban bourgeoisie were known as 'liberties'. Indeed the notion of 'liberty' was the distinctive contribution to European thought of the bourgeoisie breaking free of feudal bonds; it culminated in the slogans of French and American bourgeois revolutionaries of the eighteenth century.[12]

If it is true that humanity creates God in its own image, then it is interesting that the notion of an absolutely free God emerged during the fourteenth century. At the same time we find William of Ockham demonstrating the perfect freedom of human will: 'There is no demonstrating', he remarks, 'that what God intends is done by God or by anyone else'. Humanity is bound neither by instinct nor by any analogical relation, as Aquinas taught, to seek the good. But the pervasive notion of freedom carries uncertainty with it. The perfect freedom of God's will makes contingency the only reliable law of nature, and the perfect freedom of human will means the practically unlimited multiplication of possibilities – possibilities of motives, desire, will, action, and so on.

When that sense of possibility, or contingency, becomes part of the writer's perceptual set – and it can only do so when it is a fact of social life – then s/he will not, I suggest, find allegory a satisfactory mode of expression. That is because the allegorical character can display no free will, no irrational or inexplicable ambivalence. Even the composite character, like the love-object in Guillaume's *Roman de la Rose*, is no greater than or different from the sum of her named parts. The allegorical character may make mistakes, but even mistakes are easily rationalised by reference to the dominating abstract ideology. In the long run the allegorical persona is perfectly predictable, functioning within a narrative frame which is also perfectly predictable. But the vagaries of free human will in a fluctuating society and in a contingent universe are not so easily circumscribed or predicted. In a period of turmoil, the writer's concern with experiential truth must lead him or her to develop a narrative mode which can accurately reflect the environment. That Chaucer did not reject allegory out of hand, testifies to his own divided will: the dual commitment to experiential truth and to doctrinal truth which is so movingly expressed in his retraction to *The Canterbury Tales*.

The bourgeoisie also rivaled feudal lords for social status and political influence. Their wealth, and the gradual decline of aristocratic fortunes, enabled them to buy an aristocratic life-style, an estate, a title, or a noble marriage. Political influence the bourgeoisie began to acquire in several ways. One was that they were able to turn to their own advantage a contradiction within the ruling class, making convenient alliance with the king against lay and ecclesiastical lords. City charters granted by the king, privileges bought from impecunious local lords, parliamentary manoeuvring in England especially, in France the protected status of bourgeois du roi – by all these means the bourgeoisie won influence in local and national government. Their payment for these privileges – the taxes, tolls, firma burghi, and ad hoc grants – in turn guaranteed the king a steady cash income with which to finance foreign wars and strengthen his hand against ever-troublesome barons and ecclesiastics.

This alignment of class forces was a new factor in the old struggle between papal and royal or imperial powers. The conflict had always been chronic, at least since 390, when Ambrose, Bishop of Milan, had excommunicated the Emperor Theodosius over the question of ecclesiastical versus imperial authority. From the late eleventh century conflict had entered an acute stage, focused on the issue of royal versus papal investiture of civil servants who were also ecclesiastics. But despite the continuous existence of the conflict from the earliest Middle Ages, the royalist camp never produced a copious, detailed and convincing polemic until the late thirteenth and fourteenth centuries. Walter Ullmann hints at the reason when he observes that in the earlier period 'those whose "natural vocation" it would have been to propound a royal blueprint, an educated laity, did not exist' (p. 131). In one sense they did not exist because modern European intellectual life did not exist: the great universities that produced the educated laity were founded mainly in the twelfth and thirteenth centuries, and the Aristotelian tracts they would study were translated then as well.

In another sense, the educated laity – that is, the bourgeois civil servants and propagandists – did not exist as a class because the bourgeoisie was not yet a decisive political force. With the centralised monarchy, with the idea of the state, with the national bourgeoisie and its mutually productive alliance with monarchy – all of which developed from the thirteenth century on – it became, not the 'natural vocation' but the class interest of the educated laity to support, with all its intellectual resources, the claims of royal power in opposition to those of king and state: to establish strong jurisdiction over the state bureaucracy, over law, education, taxation and trade. Though the political theorists mentioned earlier occupy various points on the antipapal spectrum, their concerted attack on analogical argument is as much the product of late medieval class structure as is their very existence as a group.

Given the new importance of the bourgeoisie, social mobility became not only possible but necessary, accompanied by redefinitions of virtue and human nature. Though the concepts were as old as the Gospels, they were revived now in context of a social situation which gave them new relevance. The thirteenth-century Middle English romance *Havelok the Dane* shows the meteoric rise of Grim from serfdom to commercial prosperity, the reward for his loyalty to the king. No longer are noble sentiments and social mobility 'unnatural' to men of Grim's class (see Chapter 4). Human nature begins to be severed from considerations of class, and Andreas's *bourgeois gentilhomme* hopes to be judged on merit alone, saying to the noblewoman he courts,

> Love is a thing that copies Nature herself, and so lovers ought to make no more distinctions between classes of men than Love himself does. . . . If I have cultivated a character excellent through and through, I think that puts me inside the walls of nobility and gives me the true virtue of rank, and so my character puts me among the nobles. . . . I cannot see any reason why if a man of the middle class excels a nobleman in the excellence of his character he ought not to receive a greater reward, since we are both descended from a common ancestor, Adam.

Chaucer's praise of natural 'gentilesse' in *The Wife of Bath's Tale*, the insistence of the *stilnuovisti* on the nobility conferred by love – these eloquent testimonials to the aspirations of a new class would echo widely in European literature over the next several centuries. In human relations, as well as in logic, painting, poetry, science and political theory, the particular demanded accurate representation in its own right, refusing to be subsumed in abstraction.

I hope that the present chapter, sketchy as it must be, has at least shown the futility of looking for single causes of cultural change. The economic base remains clearly a dominant cause and should therefore be incorporated into history, history of ideas, and art criticism; yet it is not isolated from other kinds of cause: military, natural, cultural, and so on. Ockham's view of causality may be relevant here:

> the whole multitude of both essentially and accidentally ordered causes is caused, but not by some one thing which is part of this multitude, or which is outside this multitude, but one part is caused by one thing which is part of this multitude, and another by another thing, and so on ad infinitum.[13]

It is a concept of causality not far removed from that of Engels, who, deploring mechanistic materialism, wrote,

> What these gentlemen all lack is dialectic. They never see anything but here cause

and there effect. That this is a hollow abstraction, that such metaphysical polar opposites only exist in the real world during crises, while the whole vast process proceeds in the form of interaction (though of very unequal forces, the economic movement being by far the strongest, most elemental and most decisive) and that here everything is relative and nothing is absolute – this they never begin to see. (Letter to C. Schmidt, October 27, 1890)

If we can incorporate that sense of dialectics into medieval scholarship, we will have taken a step toward overcoming the isolation we have often felt.

The romance of kingship:
Havelok the Dane

In claiming romance for the 'mythos of summer', Northrop Frye
associates the genre with 'wish-fulfillment dream'. At the same time, Frye
introduces an important qualification to the utopian or fantastic dimension of romance: the quest-romance 'is the search of the libido or
desiring self for a fulfillment that will deliver it from the anxieties of
reality but will still contain that reality' (p. 193). The Middle English verse
romance Havelok the Dane exemplifies this double perspective in the two
dimensions in which it explores the nature of kingship – a topic of the
first importance in English public life of the thirteenth century, when
Havelok was composed. The poem operates simultaneously on mythic
and political levels, defining kingship in the same terms as were used in
contemporary discussions of kingship: a compromise between the royal
prerogative conferred by divine ordination, and the practical limitations
imposed on royal power by social structure. That compromise is
incarnated in the person of Havelok, who rules in two registers: as
theologically ordained monarch and figural hero, saviour of the kingdom; and as socially responsible leader of a multi-class nation united
under law.

A brief resumé of the historical background must precede my reading
of the poem.

By the late thirteenth century, the Norman and Angevin effort to centra-
lise government had produced in England a strong sense of national
unity. It had also engendered significant baronial resistance to royal
power. And, especially with the thirteenth-century boom in the wool
trade, a powerful bourgeoisie was clamouring – or, more accurately,
manoeuvring – for extended influence in local governments and in
Parliament.[1] The net result of these social forces was neither an outright
rejection of absolute monarchy, nor thorough repression of dissidence
and ambition. Instead, a balance was eventually achieved between royal
power and the rights of subjects of various classes, which some scholars

have called a 'partnership' of the interested parties: king, barons, wealthy merchants and burgesses (Tout, p. 135; Wilkinson). From a modern point of view this balance remains a conservative one, in which theocratic notions were not fully replaced but were rather tempered by the exigencies of English class structure.

Such an adjustment appears, for example, in the Great Charter of 1215. John, 'by the grace of God king of England', acting 'by the will of God, . . . to the honour of God and for the exalting of the holy church and the bettering of our realm', is forced nonetheless to limit the power of the Crown, to specify the rights of barons and other classes, and, in article 61, to reassert the legal right of resistance.[2]

But Magna Carta is a programmatic and not a theoretical document. A more fully developed statement of limited monarchy appears in the work of the jurist Henry Bracton (d. 1268), De Legibus et Consuetudinibus Angliae. So finely balanced is Bracton's treatise that it was quoted during the seventeenth century by royalists and parliamentarians alike. Bracton conceives the king both above and below the law, divinely appointed but, just because of this, obliged to govern properly:

The king himself must be, not under Man, but under God and the Law, because the Law makes the king. . . . For there is no king where arbitrary will dominates, and not the Law. And that he should be under the law because he is God's vicar, becomes evident through the similitude with Jesus Christ in whose stead he governs on earth. For He, God's true Mercy, though having at His disposal many means to recuperate ineffably the human race, chose before all other expedients the one which applied for the destruction of the devil's work; that is, not the strength of power, but the maxim of Justice, and therefore he wished to be under the Law in order to redeem those under the Law. For he did not wish to apply force, but reason and judgment.[3]

The success of Bracton's book (it became the basis of legal literature in the reign of Edward I) reflected the attempts being made in historical practice to redefine the nature, rights and obligations of kingship. Those attempts were evident throughout the century in several ways: the constant claims of barons and burgesses to participate in government, the baronial crisis of 1298 and the subsequent Confirmation of Charters, the development of Parliament as a legislative organ.

The concern with the nature of kingship that dominated English public life in the thirteenth century was given literary expression in Havelok the Dane. In its Middle English version, Havelok was probably composed during the reign of Edward I (1272-1307), though the precise date is uncertain.[4] The stylistic simplicity of Havelok, its humor and energy, and its attention to physical detail have caused many critics to call it 'bourgeois romance'. Yet since the medieval bourgeoisie included a very wide range of wealth and social status, from great banking families and mercantile magnates down to the local brewer and baker, the adjective 'bourgeois' does little to pinpoint the actual politics of a given work. My view of Havelok is that the main purpose of the poem is to define the nature of kingship in the person of its eponymous hero. What emerges is the characteristically English resolution, familiar from thirteenth-century theory and practice: Havelok reigns by divine right and also by consensus; he is born to rule, but, unaware of this, he earns the right to rule. In this chapter, therefore, I want first to show that Havelok is established as theocratic king, and then to indicate how that status is qualified and limited by contractual notions.

The single extant copy of Havelok is found in a collection of saints' lives (MS. Laud Misc. 108, Bodleian), and its imposing title seems more appropriate to a religious story than to romance: *Incipit Vita Havelok Quondam Rex Angliae et Danemarchie*. This placement need not be coincidental, for the romance presents Havelok as a worker of miracles. As rightful king, moreover – king by heredity and divine right – he is not only protected by God but becomes the instrument of divine justice. In this sense, Havelok is a figural hero: not a Christ-figure, but one whose literal or historical role in the narrative duplicates the archetypal victory of good over evil.

After an invocation to Christ (15-22), the story opens with a description of the idyllic reign of Athelwold, the English king whose daughter Havelok will marry and whose ideal government he will duplicate. The description is a conventional one, with many antecedents and analogues in medieval literature and historiography.[5] Yet the convention serves a special literary purpose here, and is tailored to show particular virtues. Athelwold's piety takes the form of justice, as it ought to do when the king is God's representative on earth; in Bracton's phrase, 'Dum facit justiciam, vicarius est Regis Eterni, minister autem diaboli dum declinat ad iniuriam' (f. 107b). As we will see, the story includes both types. Athelwold, however, administers the strait retributive justice expected of 'vicarius Regis Eterni':

He lovede God with all his might,
And holy kirke and soth and right.
Right-wise men he lovede alle,
And overall made hem forto calle.
Wreyeres and wrobberes made he falle
And hated hem so man doth galle; . . . (35-40)

Friend to fatherless, protector of widows and maidens (71-97), Athelwold practises the primary Christian virtue of *caritas*, feeding the poor and winning Christ's reward in duplicating Christ's goodness (98-105). Loved by all, Athelwold is mourned by all in his fatal illness. He entrusts his small daughter Goldeboru to the wardship of Earl Godrich of Cornwall. It is a sacred trust, and the ceremony is a religious one which includes

> the messebook,
> The caliz, and the pateyn ok,
> The corporaus, the messe-gere . . . (186-8)

Thereupon the king takes to his deathbed; his preparation is that of a saint and includes prayer, confession and self-flagellation. Then Athelwold distributes all his goods and money (218-25), an act which reminds us that 'it is easier for a camel to go through the eye of the needle than for a rich man to enter the kingdom of God' (Mark 10:25). Athelwold dies calling on Christ and repeating Christ's dying words (from Luke 23:46; lines 228-31).

After the sorrow of the populace is somewhat abated, bells are rung and masses sung,

> That God self shulde his soule leden
> Into hevene biforn his Sone
> And ther withuten ende wone. (245–7)

The extended portrait of Athelwold and his reign has thus set a standard for godly rule which will not be easily met.

The idyllic condition of England ends abruptly, less by Athelwold's death than by the treachery of the evil Earl Godrich. Despite his holy vow to guard both Goldeboru and England, Godrich establishes a strict and oppressive bureaucracy (248-79), and when Goldeboru comes of age withholds the kingdom from her. As Athelwold was linked with Christ and the saints, Godrich is compared with Judas and Satan (319, 1100-1, 1133-4). Like Judas, Godrich betrays God and his leader for material gain: he has broken a religious vow and usurped the throne from its divinely ordained occupant. The author calls for miraculous intervention to restore Goldeboru (and, by implication, England), like Lazarus, to her former condition (331-3).

Godrich's usurpation figurally re-enacts the archetypal Christian conflict of good and evil; plainly the hero who can perform the prayed-for feat of liberation must be Christ's agent.

The narrative turns now to Denmark, where the preceding story of betrayal is repeated (though it is told less amply). Birkabein, the good and holy king, entrusts his heirs to Earl Godard. Godard kills the two girls in a particularly bloody way (465-75), and arranges to have Havelok killed by his serf, Grim. Godard's momentary pity on the boy is called 'miracle fair and good' (500), and Godard, like his English counterpart, is compared to Judas and to Satan (422-5, 482, 496, 506, 1409, 1411, 2229, 2512). Christ's curses are heaped on him (426-46), and another miracle is prayed for so that Havelok may avenge himself (542-4). In fact a sequence of 'miracles' has already begun, as noted above. The first of them (not explicitly labelled as such) was that which caused 'the dumb to speak': the seven-year-old Havelok's extraordinary access of rhetoric which had prompted Godard's pity. Another providential miracle occurs immediately after the prayer: in the dimness of their cottage, Grim and his wife see a light shining from Havelok's mouth 'als it were a sunnebem'; they also notice the 'kine-merk' on his shoulder (later we discover that it is a golden cross: 1262-3, 2139-40). These signs of divine appointment cause Grim to commit himself to Havelok rather than to the diabolical Godard. He does so in a prayer-like passage which deliberately exploits the ambiguity of the words 'lord' and 'freedom':

'Loverd, have mercy
Of me and Leve, that is me by!
Loverd, we aren bothe thine,
Thine cherles, thine hine . . .
Thoru other man, loverd, than thoru thee
Shal I nevere freeman be.
Thou shalt me, loverd, free maken.
For I shall yemen thee and waken;
Thoru thee wile I freedom have.' (617-31)

The theological dimension of this speech is intensified by the resemblance of Grim's repentance to that of Peter after he denies Christ; as Peter 'broke down and wept' (Mark 14:72) so Grim 'sore gret' (615). We may add that Grim, like Peter, is a fisherman; that he is Havelok's first subject, as Peter was the first apostle; and that his role as founder of the town of Grimsby parallels Peter's as founder of the Church (Matthew 16:18). Again the symbolism is a deft and unobtrusive reminder of Havelok's theocratic role.

With his family and Havelok, Grim sails to England, settles at Grimsby, and becomes a prosperous fisherman and merchant. Havelok finds work in nearby Lincoln, where his good qualities endear him to all

(945-88). So well-known is Havelok that Godrich, attending Parliament in Lincoln, decides to use him in order to rid himself of Goldeboru. Having promised to wed Goldeboru to the 'hexte' (highest) man in the land, Godrich thinks he will observe only the literal meaning of that promise (the tallest man), unaware that in so doing he providentially fulfills its moral and social meanings as well (the best man, the most exalted) and prepares his own downfall. The forced marriage is performed by the Archbishop of York, who 'cam to the parlement / Als God him havede thider sent' (1179-80). Thus the marriage is consecrated by the highest ecclesiastical authority.

Havelok now returns with his royal bride to Grimsby, where the holy marks of kingship are revealed for the second time. Goldeboru does not understand their full significance until an angel's voice interprets them and reveals Havelok's destiny. With this heavenly communication Goldeboru is able to interpret Havelok's prophetic dream and to help him plan a strategy for winning the throne of Denmark. Havelok consecrates his project at church, and sets sail for Denmark.

In Denmark Havelok does battle with a group of thieves who, as 'Caimes kin and Eves' (2045) participate in the nature of archetypal Biblical sinners. After this victory the holy king-marks are again revealed, this time to the royal justice Ubbe. Recognised at last as rightful heir in his own land, Havelok is able to bring Godard to the hideous death he deserves. Returning to England, Havelok engages in climactic single combat with Godrich. He shows his mercy by offering to forgive if Godrich will renounce all claim to the throne. When mercy is rejected, justice must be done, and Godrich meets as painful a death as Godard had done. Havelok is made king, rewards are distributed, fealty is taken 'on the bok'. A new golden age begins for England under a divinely appointed king who equals Athelwold in strength, virtue and piety

To read *Havelok* from a religious point of view reveals a king who is virtually a saviour-figure: he defeats diabolical opponents, avenges those who have been wronged, and brings a new reign of harmony, love and peace. But the poem also develops another aspect of Havelok's rule, simultaneously with the theocratic. That is the political or contractual side of his rule, to which I now turn.

Reviewing the beginning of *Havelok*, we find that England's golden age under Athelwold is defined in political as well as in religious terms. The king is distinguished by his ability to make and enforce good laws (27-9), and his reign by a remarkable consensus among all social classes:

Him lovede yung, him lovede olde,
Erl and barun, dreng and thain,
Knight, bondeman, and swain,
Widwes, maidnes, prestes and clerkes,
And alle for hise gode werkes. (30-4)

The theme of consensus is constant in the story, and it is as important a
key to judgment as the religious symbols discussed above. Again and
again the author emphasises that the good ruler governs on behalf of and
with the approval of his population, at least the middle and upper classes.
Thus when Athelwold falls ill,

He sende writes sone anon
After his erles evereich on:
And after hise baruns, riche and povre,
Fro Rokesburw all into Dovere . . . (136-9)

This council of earls and barons chooses Godrich as ward of Athelwold's
daughter, just as Godard is chosen ward of Birkabein's children by a
similar council of Danish barons and knights (364-82).

Havelok's influence when he works as a cook's helper in Lincoln
transcends class lines (955-8), a trait which anticipates the contractual
character of his rule. When Goldeboru interprets Havelok's prophetic
dream, she is careful to include among his future loyal subjects 'Erl and
baroun, dreng and thain, / Knightes and burgeys and swain' (1327-8).
When Ubbe discovers Havelok's holy light, he summons his entire
retinue of 'knightes and sergaunz'. The formulaic list is repeated when
Ubbe promises that Havelok shall take fealty of the entire population
(2138-85), when he summons them (2194-5) and when the oath is sworn
(2258-65). When the ceremony is done, Ubbe sends out an even more
general writ throughout the entire country to castles, boroughs and
towns, knights, constables and sheriffs (2274-89). When Godard is
caught, his sentence is decided by a popular assembly which includes
knights and burgesses (2465-73). Godrich is judged by a more limited but
still representative jury of his peers (761-5).

In contrast to Athelwold and Havelok, the usurpers Godrich and
Godard govern autocratically. Godard makes decisions solely on the
basis of personal will (249-59). He demands a loyalty oath from all
subjects without admitting any to partnership in government (260-2),
and Godard does the same in Denmark (437-42). Godrich rules by fear
alone, creating an oppressive bureaucracy in order to enforce his ambitious schemes (266-79). When Godrich rallies his barons for battle with

Havelok, not only does he fail to seek their advice, but he coerces by threatening to reduce them to thralls (2564-5) – a flagrant and unheard-of violation of custom and law.[6]

Although consensus is an important feature of kingship in Havelok, the poem puts forth nothing like what we would now call a 'democratic' social ideal – nor did political and legal theory of the time. The 'partnership' mentioned earlier included barons, smaller landholders (knights) and the upper bourgeoisie. Peasants and labourers were not considered to have legitimate class interests other than what was defined for them by their lords or employers: this was to remain generally true in England well into the seventeenth century, and even through the Civil War (MacPherson, Part 3). The interests represented in Havelok are those of the newly powerful propertied classes: they hoped to share the privilege of government, but had no intention of extending that privilege beyond themselves.

Among Athelwold's virtues is his prompt attention to crimes against property. Thieves are the particular object of his hatred (39-43), and his zeal against them makes England a safe place for wealthy people and travelling merchants (45-58).[7] Indeed the prosperity accruing from commercial activity seems to constitute a large part of England's 'ease' in praise of which the author concludes this passage (59-61).

Acquisition of wealth and property appears in the poem as an honourable pursuit and one requiring virtuous character. Grim's loyalty to Havelok, as well as his industry, is rewarded by prosperity, which, by the time he dies, amounts to a large family fortune in money, goods and livestock (1221-8). Even as Godard's thrall, Grim had not been badly off; he owned substantial livestock (699-702) and a well-equipped ship sturdy enough to sail to England (706-13). Still, Grim is not free, and he acknowledges that only Havelok can make him free (618-31). This would seem at first to infringe contemporary feudal law, for a serf could be directly manumitted only by his overlord (in this case Godard), not by the king. The only way in which the king could be said to confer freedom was through the law of year and day. This privilege, included in many borough charters, provided that any person who lived peacefully in the borough in his own house for the stipulated period, would automatically become free.[8] What Grim seems to anticipate, then, is that his path to freedom lies through the borough privileges which were the essence of the alliance between king and upper bourgeoisie.

As a youth, Havelok heartily adopts the middle-class work ethic; he helps Grim to sell fish, for

It is no shame forto swinken;
The man that may well eten and drinken
That nought he have but on swink long;
To liggen at hom it is full strong. (799-802)

But a shortage ('dere') of grain forces Havelok to seek full-time work in
Lincoln instead. The situation there is grim. Havelok remains unemployed and hungry for two days, until

The thridde day herde he calle;
'Bermen, bermen, hider forth alle!'
Povre that on fote yede
Sprongen forth so sparke of glede,
Havelok shof dune nine or ten
Right amidewarde the fen,
And stirte forth to the cook,
Ther the erles mete he took
That he boughte at the bridge;
The bermen let he alle lidge,
And bar the mete to the castel,
And gat him there a ferthing wastel. (867-78)

Noteworthy in this passage are, first, the large number of unemployed
who, at the cook's call, 'spring forth like sparks from a coal'; and, second,
Havelok's brutal fervour in shoving his hungry competitors into the
mud. The incident is repeated the next day. So impressed is the earl's
cook with this eagerness that he offers Havelok a steady job. Havelok
accepts, stipulating no other wages than enough to eat (901-20). Havelok
is as conscientious a worker as we might expect from his behaviour so
far: he does everything (931-42) and afterward does more:

Wolde he nevere haven rest
More than he were a best.
Of alle men was he mest meke,
Lauhwinde ay and blithe of speke;
Ever he was glad and blithe;
His sorwe he couthe full well mithe. (943-8)

In short, Havelok is presented as an ideal worker. Yet we must acknowledge that he is an ideal worker only from the point of view of an
employer. He is extremely competitive with other workers, works for
nothing, gladly works to the point of exhaustion, and never complains
but always smiles. None of this behaviour could be considered either
realistic or admirable by an audience of ordinary workers, though it
would suit the taste of their urban employers or manorial supervisors.

With Havelok's experience in Lincoln we see that his movement through the story, after Godard's usurpation, is to be a progression from lowest to highest social class. He begins as the foster-child of a serf, at Grimsby becomes a free fisherman's assistant, and at Lincoln an employee in the earl's household. That progression continues when, after marrying Goldeboru, Havelok returns to Denmark as a merchant, is knighted by Ubbe in token of his victory over the thieves, and finally achieves the throne. Presumably Havelok's experience of all classes will enlarge his political sympathies when he is king, and teach him the needs of his entire population. At the same time Havelok's social ascent permits him to display, in each condition, the noblest side of his nature and the one most appropriate to the particular class, whether cheerful acquiescence or valiant self-defense.

Nearly two hundred lines are lost from that portion of the poem which narrates the crossing to Denmark, a project supported and financed by Grim's (now wealthy) sons. When the text resumes we find Havelok conversing with Ubbe. It is Ubbe's function, as justice, to grant foreign merchants permission to sell their goods, and to receive for that privilege a toll or hanse: in this case a very valuable gold ring (1632-4). Ubbe invites Havelok and Goldeboru to dine with him, guaranteeing, with an elegant play on her name the safety of Havelok's most valuable property':

'And have thou of hire no drede;
Shall hire no man shame bede.
By the fey I owe to thee,
Thereof shall I myself boru be.' (1664-7)

Despite this assurance, Havelok worries lest someone abduct his wife (1668-73), and Ubbe himself, acknowledging the possibility, sends a special guard to Havelok's lodging. When the attack occurs, its motive is unclear. Huwe Raven is sure that *raptus* is the aim of the sixty armed invaders (868-70), but Havelok's wealthy host Bernard Brun thinks it is robbery (1955-9). Though the local burgesses agree with Bernard, rejoicing that he has lost no property ('tinte no catel', 2023), Ubbe continues to emphasise the protection of Goldeboru.

Beside letting the poet display some of his most vigorous verse, and Havelok his formidable courage and strength, the battle episode underscores the need for a strong just king and a centralised administration. Again this point of view coincides with the interests of the upper bourgeoisie, whose property and fortunes could be protected, whose liberties and privileges could be granted and maintained, only by a strong centralised government. When we recall that under Athelwold no merchant travelling in England would have encountered the least trouble (45-8), the entire episode shows Godard's abysmal failure to sustain the moral tone of Denmark and to make it safe for the middle classes. Since Godrich has been unable to establish a judicial system or a public police force, Ubbe, fearing retaliation from friends of the slaughtered thieves, removes Havelok to his own well-protected house – where of course the recognition scene occurs.

A curious feature of Havelok's accession to kingship is its complete secularity. In Denmark, Ubbe summons the population, who confer the kingdom upon Havelok (2316-19). Of the English accession we hear only that the feast lasted more than forty days (2948-50). The Danish accession emphasises the ancient electoral principle, and conspicuously absent from both accounts is any mention of a traditional coronation ceremony. There is no reference to a crown; no bishops or other ecclesiastical figures are present; Havelok is neither consecrated nor anointed with holy oil; he wears no coronation robes, so closely resembling sacerdotal vestments; nor does he take anything resembling the traditional English coronation oath with its promise to safeguard the Church.

My argument is admittedly *ex silentio*: nonetheless the omission of a coronation ceremony, with its heavy ecclesiastical overtones, is significant. First, such a ceremony could have provided the author with an ideal opportunity for ceremonial description, an opportunity most medieval authors welcomed in such events as weddings, dubbings, battles, and so on. Indeed we have already seen that our author enjoys and excels at physical description and detail: the death of Athelwold, the battle at Bernard's, and other *loci* prove that. Second, even more surprising than the poet's bypassing a splendid literary opportunity is his ignoring an event which in his own time was an extremely important one in English public life, and which had been important for generations.[9] Both literary and social tradition, then, suggest that a coronation scene would be an obvious climax in the poem. Its omission, however, is neither accidental nor inconsistent.

In part the secularity of Havelok's accession may reflect the nationalistic sentiment that infused thirteenth-century English public life, for that sentiment was largely a product of England's assertion of sovereignty against papal intervention to emphasise the rights of *regnum* over those of *sacerdotium*. It stresses the inviolable unity of the nation.

But beyond this, the secular coronation rounds out the new definition of kingship offered in *Havelok*, and here a historical analogue cannot be ignored. Like Havelok, Edward I became king in an unusual manner. Since he was abroad when his father died in 1272, Edward's succession was proclaimed immediately by hereditary right and will of the magnates. This was confirmed by oath of fealty from knights and burgesses, and Edward began to reign from the date of his election. It was the first time that full legal recognition had been extended to an heir before coronation, for Edward was formally crowned – that is, he received ecclesiastical approval – only two years later, on his return to England. Thus Edward's accession itself showed that the English notion of kingship had already moved well away from the theocratic extreme, and that the will of those governed had become as significant a factor as the will of God. 'The double note, of conservatism and experiment, which was to sound throughout his reign, seemed already struck before he began it' (Johnstone, p. 393). It is the same double note that *Havelok* strikes.

At the end of the romance, the theme of social mobility emerges again. The rise of Grim and Havelok has already validated social mobility, while the villainy of Earls Godard and Godrich indicates that rank cannot guarantee character. Havelok himself underlines the importance of moral, rather than social, superiority when he refers to Godard as a 'thrall' (1408); later the author calls Godrich a 'mixed [filthy] cherl' (2533), rhyming 'cherl' with 'erl' to intensify the paradox.[10] Now, social mobility is extended to Havelok's supporters. Grim's three sons are elevated to knights and barons (2346-53), and Grim's daughters are raised even higher. One of them is given in marriage to the Earl of Chester, the other to Havelok's former employer, the cook, who is now by Havelok's grant Earl of Cornwall. These rewards, especially the last, may seem extravagant, and Halvorsen has called this scene 'a peasant fantasy'.[11] But the scene is neither fantastic, nor expressive of peasant aspirations; it represents the social reality and realistic ambitions of the upper bourgeoisie and knighthood.

I would point out, first, that a post in a noble household was often a prestigious sinecure. The Earl's 'cook' may have been himself a wealthy tenant-knight with merely supervisory duties. Though the exact duty of a nobleman's 'cook' is not known, it is known that William the Conqueror gave his 'cook' half a hide of land, and that the Count of Boulogne conferred on his 'cook' the estate of Wilmiton (Pollock and Maitland, pp. 262-71). Moreover, the period was one of rapid and often dramatic social change. Serfs left the manor to become free labourers or artisans; artisans might amass sufficient capital and property to become burgesses;

recently wealthy merchants and financiers bought estates and titles, intermarried with nobility, adopted an aristocratic life-style, and aspired to participate in government. In 1307, perhaps only a few years after *Havelok* was composed, the young Edward II created Piers Gavaston, a knight's son, Earl of Cornwall – a title whose two previous holders had been king's sons. Joan, daughter of Edward I and widow of the Earl of Gloucester, in 1295 married a knight, to whom Edward eventually entrusted the Gloucester inheritance. However it was not only in Edward's private life that he confirmed social mobility, but also in his deliberate expansion of 'the community of the realm' to include the upper middle classes, as in the 'Model Parliament' of 1295. For Edward recognised that the upper bourgeoisie was both a valuable financial resource, and a reliable ally against the barons. Thus the reward scene in *Havelok* represents little that had not been, or would not soon be, accomplished in reality.

The idea of theocratic monarchy in England would long outlive the thirteenth century, though the history of Richard II shows that Tudor and Stuart monarchs could assert with impunity what their predecessors could not. Still, the origins of its demise in the Civil War of 1642 lay precisely, and paradoxically, in the 'partnership' – the gradual institutional adjustments – by which monarchy survived in the thirteenth century. To the beginning of that fruitful change *Havelok the Dane* bears witness.

Rewriting woman good: gender and the anxiety of influence in two late-medieval texts

In 'The Laugh of the Medusa', Hélène Cixous proposes 'marked writing' as a term for gender-influenced work. She goes on to maintain that writing is 'a locus where the repression of women has been perpetuated . . . and in a manner that's frightening since it's often hidden or adorned with the mystifying charms of fiction'.[1]

I want in this paper to offer two examples of such 'marked writing', one by a male and one by a female author, in order to explore what it might mean, in a given historical period, to write not like a man but *as* a man, not *like* a woman, but *as* a woman. As my title indicates, I am extending Harold Bloom's theory of 'anxiety of influence' beyond Bloom's *terminus a quo* in the seventeenth century. I am also using it in a social rather than a psychoanalytical context. This is appropriate usage for a theory itself so heavily committed to revision, and my 'misprision' (to use Bloom's phrase) – a 'strong' one, I hope – has its origins in the social reality of the present.

My exemplars or test cases will be Geoffrey Chaucer's *Legend of Good Women* and Christine de Pizan's *Livre de la Cité des Dames*, written within 25 years of one another (about 1385 and 1405 respectively) by late-medieval courtly poets of similar social status, intellectual background and ideological assumptions.[2] The stimulus for each work was the author-narrator's anxious confrontation with the western misogynistic tradition in literature. The result in each case was a compilation of short biographies of famous women, each preceded by prologue containing a fictionalised but intensely self-conscious account of how the writer resolved his or her relations to the authoritative (though not uncontested) misogynistic tradition. Both works purport to rewrite that tradition in order to present a new image of woman, that of the good woman: courageous and loyal, prudent and kind. That Christine actually does this, while Chaucer (sheltering in irony) does not, strikes me as an interesting opportunity for speculation in the murky problematic of gender-linked aesthetics.

Doubtless such juxtapositions are possible for any historical period whose literature survives and includes women writers, though each period must confer intellectual and ideological specificity of form on the issues at stake.[3] I do not see gender-'linked' as synonymous with gender-'determined', because the mediation of social factors is clearly decisive in transforming gender into anything beyond biology, and this social mediation between gender and culture renders hollow the predictive certainty of 'determined'. To my mind both the specificity and the decisiveness of social forms argue against a distinctively feminist critical theory, for if the latter does not make gender itself the decisive factor, it becomes something else; and if it does, it commits a falsification.

Nowhere is social mediation more strikingly and more painfully evident than in the contrast between these two late-medieval encounters with misogyny, and in the aesthetic strategies arising from them. Chaucer's position is that of speaking subject, Christine's that of spoken object. Chaucer meets the misogynist tradition as a male poet accused, by the God of Love, of belonging to it; that is, of having written ill of women and of love (LGW, F text, 320-40). Christine meets the tradition, represented by the work of one Matheolus, as a woman reader whom it defines as inherently inferior to men; that is, without the high moral or intellectual capacity required of scholars and writers (sec. 1). For Chaucer the issue is what kind of writer to be, with the representation of women the test case. For Christine the issue is the possibility of her writing at all, with the representation of women offering role models. For her, then, the stakes are much higher, and the issue is gender-specific.

If programme generates theory (as is the case in politics), then Chaucer's backhanded vindication of misogynistic literature will require an epistemology and an aesthetic, as will Christine's propagandistic revision of that tradition. How, then, does each of them justify his or her project? I will start with LGW as the earlier and culturally 'normative' text.

First, a brief plot summary is in order. The Chaucerian poet-narrator begins with a discussion of the value of old books (tradition), then reveals his intense love for the daisy. He falls asleep and in a dream is visited by the God of Love whose companion, Alceste, personifies the daisy. Love wrathfully accuses the narrator of having slandered women and love in previous writings (Chaucer's actual earlier works). Alceste intercedes, imposing as penance that the narrator shall now compose a 'legend of good women' who were true in love. The extant collection has nine stories, the last unfinished.

Geffrey's self-defence begins with the first words of the Prologue, whose discussion of old books is the vehicle for a statement of a sceptical and fideistic epistemology.[4] Where we cannot know by direct experience, there we must believe,

> For, God wot, thing is never the lasse sooth,
> Thogh every wight ne may it nat ysee. (F, 14-15)[5]

This is as true for history as it is for religious doctrine; therefore we must give 'feyth and ful credence' to authoritative traditional texts (17-28). The opening section of the prologue, then, constitutes a depreciation of personal experience, for to rely on mere personal experience is to risk vulgar empiricism and solipsism. The stage has begun to be set for the legends. What are women really like? What was Cleopatra or Hypsipyle really like? Since we cannot know empirically we are compelled to trust tradition.

Nothing distracts the narrator from his books, he says, except devotion to the daisy, an emotion whose intensity triggers a crisis of confidence. Doubting his ability to do poetic justice to his emotion or its object, the narrator abases himself before the memory of his predecessors the great love-poets. (They are not named, but a list would include Ovid, Dante and Petrarch, perhaps Chrétien de Troyes and one or two of Chaucer's contemporaries at the French court.) Will the poet-narrator survive in the English tradition as an important and original author, or merely as minor and derivative, someone who can only follow those who have 'of makyng ropen' ('reaped [the grain] of writing poetry'), someone limited to 'glenyng here and there' (F, 66-83)? Implicit in this agony of influence is the question whether such vulnerability to one's predecessors supplants one's own passion: does one follow nature and reality or merely manipulate the formulae of other, more innovative writers?

Help is at hand in the fideistic resolution, which now allows the narrator to transcend the dilemma of originality versus imitation by shifting responsibility to the daisy which, as his muse, controls the narrator's creativity and is now invoked:

> ye ben verrayly
> The maistresse of my wit, and nothing I.
> My word, my werk ys knyt so in youre bond
> That, as an harpe obeieth to the hond

And maketh it soune after his fyngerynge,
Ryght so mowe ye oute of myn herte bringe
Swich vois, ryght as yow lyst, to laughe or pleyne.
Be ye my gide and lady sovereyne!
As to myn erthly god to yow I calle . . . (F, 87-95)

The passivity inherent in fideism is striking here: we see the poet as instrument played by a superior hand. The song it plays on his heart may be a joyous or a plaintive one, for in sharp contrast to the God of Love's demands later on, tone and content are not prescribed. The narrator asserts the validity of virtually any material. That the object of passion is not a woman is no impediment to creative intensity, for 'Ther loved no wight hotter in his lyve' (F, 59). But whatever his material, the narrator's intellectual posture can scarcely generate a frontal assault on tradition, for it is a posture of receptivity rather than of reconstruction.

We return now, with the narrator, to Mayday celebration. In the description of spring we get a curious and beautifully-wrought little drama: two of them, actually. The first, short and traditional, paints a miniature of the conflict of seasons, the cyclical persecution and relief of earth:

Forgeten hadde the erthe his pore estat
Of wynter, that hym naked made and mat,
And with his swerd of cold so sore greved;
Now hath th'atempre sonne all that releved,
That naked was, and clad him new agayn. (F, 125–9)

What is the nature of nature? It is contradictory: poor and rich, cold and warm, naked and clothed, violent and temperate, suffering and rejoicing. The next scenario makes the same point, though this time with brilliant originality:

The smale foules, of the sesoun fayn,
That from the panter and the net ben scaped,
Upon the foweler, that hem made awhaped
In wynter, and distroyed hadde hire brood,
In his dispit hem thoghte yt did hem good
To synge of hym, and in hir song despise
The foule cherl that, for his coveytise,
Had hem betrayed with his sophistrye.
This was hire song, 'The foweler we deffye,
And al his craft.' And somme songen clere
Layes of love. . . . (F, 130-40)

Nature itself has two faces; so, therefore, must our, or any creature's, experience of it. Hence the natural singer, the bird, has two kinds of song. One is of hatred, contempt and defiance against the 'foule cherl' who traps birds in winter; the other of devotion, tenderness and praise in honour of St. Valentine and a sweetheart: each at its appropriate moment, each 'true'.

If such is reality, how can the truthtelling realist poet do other than show us what is contradictory in nature – including woman? If he is faithful to nature and reality, to that extent his portrayal of women must be contradictory, ambivalent or ironic. To show woman all good – as the God of Love demands – would be indeed to manipulate hollow formulae, and to rewrite nature itself. Such an effort would be unrealistic, presumptuous, virtually heretical in its utopian thrust.

Just for good measure this point is made again some lines further on, in the narrator's comment about flower versus leaf. The narrator refuses to take sides in this courtly fad:

> But natheles, ne wene nat that I make
> In preysing of the flour agayn the leef,
> No more than of the corn agayn the sheef;
> For, as to me, nys lever noon ne lother.
> I nam withhoolden yit with never nother;
> Ne I not who serveth leef, ne who the flour. (F, 188-93)

Flower and leaf, corn and sheaf: frivolous courtiers may set them in competition, but in nature they are part of a single organism. To insist on one or the other is at best an innocuous pastime. At worst it might indicate a taste for verbal or intellectual structures that are unnaturally rigid, unnecessarily divisive. Good women or bad women: should the one be 'lever or lother' than the other? Is any woman all bad or all good, or do the two aspects of personality coexist as closely as corn and sheaf?

What the Prologue constructs, then, is an aesthetic and a definition of nature against which the God of Love can only appear absurd in demanding a poetry that effaces contradiction. His aesthetic is a kind of Proletkult of love, a prescriptive bureaucratic utopianism where women are always true and good. It is an 'eroticist unrealism' based on the maintenance of his own power:

> And thow [art] my foo, and al my folk werreyest,
> And of myn olde servauntes thow mysseyest,
> And hynderest hem with thy translacioun,
> And lettest folk from hire devocioun

To serve me, and holdest it folye
To serve Love. Thou maist yt nat denye,
For in pleyn text, withouten nede of glose,
Thou has translated the Romaunce of the Rose,
That is an heresye ayeins my lawe,
And makest wise folk fro me withdrawe;
And of Creseyde thou hast seyd as the lyste,
That maketh men to wommen lasse triste. . . . (F, 322-33)

The God of Love asks for tales of clean maidens and steadfast widows and true wives (G, 282-306), for women 'trewe in lovyng al hire lyves' (F, 485). He asks, in short, for propaganda. It is from the standpoint of a self-interested courtly bureaucrat and propagandist that the well-intentioned Narrator is accused of participating in a tradition not realist but misogynist.

Now there speaks the only plausibly good woman in the poem: Alceste, personification of the daisy and companion to the God of Love. Her intervention is a strong one, though rhetorically as tactful as can be. She remonstrates gently with her lord, calmly bringing out extenuating circumstances for the accused poet. She balances the narrator's dossier by listing his works that do praise love. She lectures on the duties of kings and administrators. Alceste is the complete lawyer and courtly adviser – and no less a virtuous, attractive woman. We observe, therefore, a rather interesting role reversal which conveniently exonerates the poet from charges of misogyny, for he gives us a male deity who is narrowminded, selfish and temperamental, with a female adviser who is balanced, objective and controlled. It is as if Chaucer shows us that he can indeed portray good women – but not to order.

Like the good fairy in 'The Sleeping Beauty', Alceste cannot avert a penalty but she can mitigate it. Her compromise requires the narrator to compose a penitential piece honoring the God of Love 'as muche as he mysseyede / Or in the Rose or elles in Creseyde' (F, 440-1). The relativistic ambiguity of that directive, together with the ironic subversion of its intention in the tales that follow, can be read as the poet-narrator's vindication of the Roman de la Rose (which Chaucer had translated) and of the Troilus.

Alceste's significance here resembles that of Penelope invoked in Hades (Odyssey XI): living evidence that the poet is not a misogynist, proof that there are good women. Penelope is the poet's trump card against the genuinely misogynistic claim that all women are tainted by the misdeeds of one – a claim made by the understandably embittered Agamemnon, and contradicted by Odysseus using his wife as example. But after all, the world is not made up exclusively of Penelopes and Clytemnestras. These are the extremes on a spectrum of female nature. I believe that 'Homer' intends to say two things about women: one, that women are capable of moral choice and action; two, that from a cosmic viewpoint a woman's 'natural' role is that of subordination to men. I suggest that Chaucer would support both statements. Neither poet considers the second notion misogynistic, but rather a fact of life, a more or less self-evident verity, a socially necessary and valuable arrangement which is for Chaucer, moreover, a consequence of the Fall. Indeed, each poet takes the trouble to defend himself against the charge of misogyny: Homer by having Agamemnon utter the 'really' misogynistic sentiments that are refuted with the example of Penelope; Chaucer by having the accusation of misogyny tactfully fended off by Alceste.[6]

The movement of Chaucer's poem, then, is that of a double subversion. The God of Love's directive to rewrite woman good is supposed to subvert the traditional anti-feminist representation of woman. But the Chaucerian response is to subvert that directive in accordance with a world-view and an aesthetic which see all created nature as inherently contradictory, and the poet's task as fidelity to that reality. The legends assert contradiction after all. They do so indirectly to be sure, but just as inevitably and 'naturally' as birds in spring defy the fowler's 'sophistry'.

When we turn to Christine de Pizan we meet the first woman in European letters to earn her living as a writer and to describe herself as a writer. In a work composed the year Chaucer died, Christine attributes her career to the necessity imposed by her husband's premature death: Fortune transformed her into a man, she says, so that she might steer the ship of her life (La Mutacion de Fortune, c. 1400). Now plenty of bourgeois and artisan women – married, single or widowed – worked, ran businesses, and prospered financially in the late Middle Ages. Christine was not of the bourgeoisie but of the courtly Parisian intelligentsia; nonetheless the example of urban middle-class and artisan women was not far to seek. What Christine had to do when her husband died was, first, to straighten out complicated legal and financial affairs by arguing her case before various officials and courts, and then to earn a living: in short, she had to speak in her own behalf and to write in her own support. It seems, then, that the process Christine represents as gender-mutation was not her movement toward financial independence per se but rather her assumption of a far less common role, that of speaking subject.[7]

Some five years later Christine was able to use her power as speaking subject to do something about woman as written object: she compiled the *Cité des Dames* as an antidote to the tradition of scholarly misogyny. Let me sketch the scene and structure of Christine's text.[8] Like *LGW* it is a first-person narrative, a dream-vision whose narrator is presented as author of the text. The story opens in Christine's library, where the scholarly narrator is pursuing her studies. She takes up a borrowed book, the *Lamentations* of Matheolus.[9] It provokes a crisis of doubt and despair, for Matheolus had written a deeply misogynistic social satire against women and marriage. Why do so many poets, clerics and philosophers have a bad opinion of women? Could God really have created such an abomination as woman? Am I such an inferior creature? Tormented by these questions and thrown into deep depression, Christine suddenly perceives three crowned ladies in her room. They are Reason, Righteousness and Justice; their task, they declare, is to restore Christine to good spirits and to combat the misogynist heresy. This they do by providing a scathing critique of misogyny, then by vindicating the goodness of woman as God's creation, finally by calling on Christine to help create a new tradition ('ce nouvel heritaige'): a fortress and refuge for women, a City of Ladies. The construction of this City is the writing of the text, each of whose stories – about 130 in all – is a unit in the foundation, walls or roof of the City. Each of the crowned ladies presides over a section of the text and a corresponding portion of the edifice: Reason tells of warriors, queens and inventors; Righteousness of chaste, loving and prudent women; Justice of holy women. The conclusion exhorts women to humility, patience and submission toward husbands, advising them to avoid the flattery of flirtatious men 'whose laughter conceals deadly venom'.

The directive to rewrite woman good comes to Christine, as to Geffrey, in a dream-vision and from a female personification. Yet the personification is treated very differently in each text. Chaucer's Alceste externalises part of the poet's inner debate about his own work, but this function is suppressed in the text: we have to read it in. Thus the figuration of Alceste shows a distancing that is a function of the writer's gender, for it consecrates the notion of woman-as-object. The poet as man is writing subject; the female figure is not portrayed as an aspect of himself but rather as critic of his work and as object of his devotion. Christine's Lady Reason, on the other hand, is explicitly portrayed as an aspect of the author's self: her own capacity for reason, as well as the personification of human reason at large.

Moreover, Chaucer's Alceste is a deeply ambiguous figure, whose kindness is limited by her loyalty to the angry God of Love. She becomes the instrument for a double-bind. Does Geffrey deserve the punishment he gets? If yes, then it is because he was a misogynist and therefore includes Alceste in his warped judgment of women. If no, then she is wrong to assist in the punishment and proves a misogynistic point: women can't think for themselves but act as agents of men's judgment; women lack courage, independence, farsightedness. Finally, Alceste is obeyed in form but not in spirit, for her directive is to produce a propagandist work, not an ironic one. There is no such ambiguity in Lady Reason.

Christine's Lady Reason gives no orders. She suggests and supervises and works along with Christine as a constant presence throughout the text, engaging in frequent dialogue with her. The author-narrator is not working against herself but rather, with Reason's help, for herself, for full integration of personality. It is after all herself she must rewrite, not, as in Geffrey's case, an Other.

Hence Christine confronts the misogynist tradition in a way wholly different from Chaucer's. The Chaucerian narrator is already a famous poet, already able to compare himself with great predecessors. His concern is to assure his reputation and to fend off the restrictions of a misogynistic tradition that (he fears) may already have assimilated him as one of its own. Christine's position is nowhere near so secure and her defensive posture is far more urgent, for the tradition she confronts does not encourage her to be a writer. It excludes her from any authoritative or exemplary role, excludes her from tradition itself. It is problematic for her in that way, and for Chaucer in his, precisely because of gender and the social mediation of gender.

As a woman writer Christine can afford no such passive tolerance toward tradition as is evidenced in Chaucer's fideistic stance. Indeed, to 'give faith and full credence' to 'old books' would amount in her case to abandoning the role of writer altogether. Her first task as a writer must be to enable herself to work: to confirm woman's intellectual and moral capacity. She begins, as Chaucer did, with an epistemology, but an epistemology opposite to his. She asserts personal experience as a source of genuine knowledge – a position neither unique nor original in the high Middle Ages, but important to Christine's strategy.[10] We have come, Reason says in her first speech,

pour . . . te gitter hors de l'ingnorence qui tant aveugle ta meismes congnoissance que tu deboute de toy ce que tu scez de certaine science et adjoustes foy ad ce que tu ne scez, ne vois, ne congnois autrement fors par pluralité d'oppinions estranges. Tu ressembles le fol dont la truffe parle, qui en dormant au moulin, fu revestu de la robe d'une femme, et au resveiller, pour ce que ceulx qui le mouquoyent luy tesmoingnoyent que femme estoit, crut myeulx leurs faulx diz que la certaineté de son estre. (sec. 4)

to get you out of the ignorance which so blinds your consciousness that you debate with yourself what you know as certain knowledge, and lend faith to what you neither know nor see nor understand except through the multiplicity of different opinions. You resemble the fool that the joke tells about, who while sleeping at the mill, was dressed up in a woman's clothes, and on waking, because those who were mocking him assured him he was a woman, believed their false assertions rather than the certainty of his being.

It isn't simply her own experience that Christine brings forward as a basis for knowledge. Constantly Reason urges her – and implicitly the reader, whether male or female – to use personal experience against misogyny. Women are said to show off at church? It would be strange if young, pretty and wealthy women were not seen there, but for every such you will see 20 or 30 older women soberly dressed. Women are supposedly self-indulgent? Just recall the drunk you saw the other day whose wife's utter sobriety compensates for his sins.

What then of textual authority? Reason points out that philosophers differ among themselves: their words are not articles of faith and they can err. Poets often speak figuratively or ironically; some lie. 'Chiere amie', Reason concludes,

Or te reviens a toy meismes, reprens ton scens et plus ne te troubles pour telz fanffelues. Car saiches que tout mal dit si generaument des femmes empire les diseurs et non pas elles meismes. (sec. 4a)

So return to yourself, take hold again of your good sense and don't trouble yourself any longer on account of such nonsense. Know that all evil spoken so generally about women vitiates the speakers and not women themselves.

Now Chaucer also understands the contradictory nature of written authority; it is what The House of Fame is about. Scepticism he shares with Christine, yet her scepticism does not take the fideistic resolution. Rather Christine pushes through to faith in herself. 'Experience, though noon auctoritee / Were in this world, were ryght enough for me. . . .': it is the Wife of Bath's stance and her revisionist methodology, but seeing it in the flesh, as it were, lets us appreciate (as I believe Chaucer was ultimately unable to do) not its solipsism but its survival value, not its distortive but its corrective function. It is an epistemology – 'the certainty of one's being' – that, for all its modest presentation in context of an old French jest, heralds Renaissance individualism and the Cartesian *cogito*.

The God of Love asks Geffrey for propaganda. Though Geffrey will not oblige, Christine not only will but must. She has to rewrite woman good in order to provide herself with role models, with a line of mothers to think back through (to paraphrase Virginia Woolf). Christine also writes on behalf of other women: to keep them from despondency such as she had experienced, to offer positive role models, to give sage counsel and to influence men in favor of educating well-born women – a point Christine amplifies at every opportunity. Does Christine flatten out contradictions in her version of womanhood? She does. Does she skew the tradition, omit what is unsuitable to her purpose, rationalise aberrant behaviour? Certainly. Are her figures realistic, balanced or contradictory characters? By no means. Xantippe empties no pisspot over Socrates's head, but is a loving and reverent wife. Medea kill her children? No children are mentioned in either of Christine's versions of Medea. Semiramis did marry her son Ninus, but only for reasons of state. Women invented virtually all the technology of civilisation: the Roman alphabet and the science of grammar (Carmentis), agriculture (Ceres), metalwork, music, arithmetic, the Greek alphabet and the wheel (Minerva), law and horticulture (Isis), textiles and nets (Ariadne).

It is a tedious performance in its relentless recital of female excellence, and Christine's legal-bureaucratic style scarcely lightens the tedium (though as Curnow points out, such a style suits Christine's presentation of the work as a legalistic defense of women). Yet Christine's revision is not without its world-view, for her valorisation of personal experience has implications for her sense of history and human nature. Christine acknowledges the existence of individual bad women, but she has no reason to portray them, and she denies any generalisation of their behaviour to the sex at large. Indeed an evil woman is unnatural,

monstre en nature, qui est chose contrefaitte et hors de sa propre condicion naturalle qui doit etre simple, coy et honeste . . . (sec. 16a)

A monster in nature, thing wrongly made and outside its own natural condition which must be simple, quiet and honest.

Someone of the Chaucerian persuasion might consider this a Pollyannaish view of nature: certainly it is optimistic. Its optimism extends to history, for since women produced civilisation, Christine must reject any anti-technological nostalgia or golden-age primitivism. She is firmly for progress, asserting that the more we receive from God the better we can serve him. If we use those gifts badly it is we who err, not the things themselves that are bad (sec. 174).

Two revisionary texts, then, and revising traditions – Chaucer the courtly, Christine the misogynistic – that are but two sides of the same coin: Woman as sign, as myth, as Other. For Chaucer, to write in unambiguous praise of women is to reduce the natural complexity of reality. To write such poetry is punishment; it must be set right again, rendered complex again, by irony. For Christine it is the clerical-misogynist tradition that distorts reality, reducing the natural complexity of women by effacing their goodness. To read such poetry is punishment, and the proper balance is restored by a necessarily one-sided completion of the picture.

Now I want to muddy the waters a bit by looking at Christine's sources, for her propagandistic revision of the image of woman was not entirely original. She had precursors who were neither female nor misogynistic, and whose methods and results she was able to borrow for her own project. Her main and nearest source was the De Claris Mulieribus (c. 1360) of her countryman Giovanni Boccaccio,[11] from whom she took not only a great deal of material but also the euhemeristic interpretation of pagan divinities, a relatively rationalistic approach to Scripture, and a healthy scepticism about tradition that resulted in the certification of nature and experience as moral guides. Boccaccio too undertook to rewrite woman better, if not entirely good, and to redress the imbalance produced by misogynistic literature. As a Christian humanist, Boccaccio is for the education of women and against involuntary nunhood, condemning the latter as an especially vicious form of oppression (Chap. 43). He denounces the low self-esteem of women who consider themselves fit for nothing but motherhood. Although he does include evil or ambiguous characters in his collection, Boccaccio is as positive as possible toward Eve and Medusa, cleans up the image of Dido and exposes the presumptuous Pope Joan as a purely legendary figure.

Another of Christine's sources was Jean le Fèvre, who, after translating the Lamentation of Matheolus into French, was overcome with guilt. He expiated by producing a 4000-line apology to women, Le Livre de Leesce, describing the joys of marriage and the virtues of women. Jean denies the truth of certain myths unflattering to women (e.g., Pasiphae's lust for the bull of Minos) and revises figures such as Medea, Circe and Dido into examples of largesse.

In still another late-medieval tradition that is neither humanistic nor satirical, numerous figures from classical myth had already been rewritten good through the good offices of allegorical interpretation. I refer particularly to the *Ovide Moralisé*, that massive versification and reinterpretation of Ovid's *Metamorphoses* composed in the early fourteenth century by an anonymous Franciscan cleric. The purpose of this text has nothing to do with the literary representation of women. It claims rather to demonstrate the capacity of Christian doctrine to absorb, by reinterpretation, its classical antecedents. This method, in accordance with the advice of St. Paul – 'Whatever was written in former days was written for our instruction' (Romans 15:4) – became a standard medieval hermeneutic. Christine was thoroughly familiar with the *Ovide Moralisé*, even if not with the many other allegorical commentaries on Ovid that proliferated from the twelfth century on. As a sample of its method, I cite the story of Medea (deBoer, Book 7). In the (much expanded) narrative itself, Medea is not whitewashed. She is a sorceress. She is lustful, unable to take her eyes off Jason, whom she thinks at first is a god from heaven. Long internal monologues show her selfishness and pride. Her murders of brother and children are not omitted. Despite these vices, multiple interpretations of the literal narrative force a reversal of evaluation on several levels. Historically Medea represents the Golden Fleece. Allegorically, the Fleece signifies the virginity of Mary, to which deity joined itself 'par mariage / Charnelment' (745-6). Medea's herbs and roots are the medicine of salvation. The murder of her brother parallels Jesus's delivering his body to pain in order to save humanity. Jason's second wife, Creusa, burnt by Medea with a poisoned shirt, is the 'fel' full of deception who saddens God and provokes revenge. Medea's final escape in a dragon-drawn chariot represents God's ascent to the skies where he reigns in permanent glory. This multiple allegorical transfiguration, as wonderful as any achieved by ancient sorcery, represents an important strand in the medieval revision of classical tradition as it came down to Christine.

Clearly, then, one did not have to be a woman to see what was wrong with misogyny or to try to correct it. One did not have to be a woman, an antimisogynist, or a humanist to revise the classical representation of mythic female figures. Nor did being a woman – even an exceptional woman – certify one's social radicalism. The only social reform Christine mentions is education for women – in 1400 by no means a daring demand. She has Dame Raison rationalise women's exclusion from public office on the grounds that each sex performs duties appropriate to it; and, as I argue in Chapter 6, Christine was in general very conservative by the standards of her time.

Yet though the relation of gender to aesthetics cannot be rigidly predicted, nonetheless we can discern gender-distinctive features in the two works at hand. Christine does root her text in a reading experience which is explicitly gender-linked. She does offer her crisis and its cure as representative and therapeutic: she does produce the text explicitly on behalf of women, and her revisions are dictated by her purpose. The very image she chooses for her text, that of the city-fortress, says everything about the vulnerable and beleaguered condition of even the exceptional woman of her day.

If Christine writes as a woman in Cité des Dames, does Chaucer write as a man in LGW? Of course one doesn't have to be a man to endorse sceptical fideism, or to see nature as inherently contradictory, or to dislike formulaic and simplistic courtly verse. Nonetheless, the Chaucerian narrator's role as daisy-lover and as alleged misogynistic poet are clearly gender-defined features of his text. Equally important is the subject matter he chooses in order to define and test his aesthetic: the representation of women.

At issue, though, is not one or another specific intellectual position, but rather the tendencies and interests of those whose gender, translated into privilege or exclusion and indeed partially created by privilege or exclusion, produces a different relation to love, to nature, to oneself, to tradition, to the other sex: a different consciousness, in short.[12] Not completely different, of course, and there remains between Chaucer and Christine de Pizan a good deal of ideological solidarity. They share an orthodox, old-fashioned Augustinian Catholicism, dependency on the aristocratic ruling class, and a general acceptance of the status quo – including the subordinate condition of women. Yet it is possible to find such solidarity a cause for optimism, for in the service of different values than theirs, solidarity can help to rupture the bonds that still link gender, social condition and aesthetic production or response.

'Mothers to think back through': Who are they? The ambiguous example of Christine de Pizan

My title comes from Virginia Woolf, who claimed in *A Room of One's Own* that 'a woman writing thinks back through her mothers' (Chapter 6). The book attempted to revive the tradition of the writing woman and to explore some of the special problems of that tradition. Woolf's notion of 'mothers to think back through' poses a problematic of its own, and it is this I shall address here, using as my test case the late-medieval French courtly writer Christine de Pizan.

The problem of antecedents has begun to be explored by contemporary gender-oriented scholars stimulated as much by the work of Harold Bloom as by that of Virginia Woolf. In *The Anxiety of Influence* Bloom offers a more or less Freudian and Oedipal theory of poetic history as a history of influence in which the strong poet 'corrects' or completes the work of his precursor poet. The poet does so through 'strong misprision': a misreading or misinterpretation which is actually a complex defence mechanism permitting him to absorb and transcend the influence of his powerful precursor. Gender-oriented scholars have both appropriated and criticised Bloom's theory. Sandra Gilbert and Susan Gubar write that their well-known study of nineteenth-century female writers, *The Madwoman in the Attic*, 'is based in the Bloomian premise that literary history consists of strong action and inevitable reaction' (p. xiii). Simultaneously they point out that the female poet does not experience anxiety of influence as her male counterpart would do, for she experiences something much more fundamental: 'anxiety of authorship', the fear that she cannot become a precursor: 'The creative I AM cannot be uttered if the "I" knows not what it is' (p. 17).

For those who have used Bloom's thesis, whether pro or con, the consensus appears to be that Bloom's theory itself requires a strong 'creative misprision', a rewriting that will free it from the male-oriented Oedipal perspective and allow the notion of influence or models to operate in context of female experience. Such a rewriting must restore the social dimension that seems marginal in Bloom's project but which, as Virginia Woolf stressed, has profoundly moulded the woman artist's relation to her work. It must recognise as a primary component of female experience the fact of exclusion. This is exclusion, often, from production and consumption of the means of culture: more generally, exclusion from that range of experience that writers write about, including the experience of personal and institutional power.

One of the aims of contemporary gender-oriented scholarship has been to acquaint us with our antecedents and to provide role-models – 'mothers to think back through' – by rehabilitating earlier women writers whose work has been neglected. Thus we have learned – to mention only a few examples from my own period of specialisation – about Hrotswitha, the tenth-century German nun and playwright; about some two dozen trobairitz (women poets of courtly love) in twelfth and thirteenth century France; about the women humanist scholars of quattrocento Italy; about women poets of the Renaissance; and about the early fifteenth-century courtly writer Christine de Pizan.[1] It is a valuable effort, and not only for women. Everyone needs to know what women have done and what they have not done, and the reasons why; for as the utopian socialist Charles Fourier long ago declared, the condition of women in any society is an index to the advancement and limitations of that society as a whole.

Paradoxically, the very effort to reconstitute a full understanding of women's participation in cultural history can result in a skewed perception of individual contributions and of history at large. This need not happen, but it can happen, when we do not firmly anchor the figure in question in her own historical milieu. If we desire the full equality and genuine liberation of women, then we desire the transformation of social life and we cannot afford an inaccurate view of past or present, for that would condemn us to ineffectuality. If we do not wish to maintain a falsified history, then we have to assess every rehabilitated woman writer in relation to her social context as well as in other ways. Without a rounded and balanced analysis of this kind, the search for 'mothers to think back through' becomes simply a scholarly version of 'sisterhood', which the revived women's movement in our era has confronted as one of its basic theoretical and political questions. I want in this paper to challenge the idea that the act of writing by itself suffices to qualify an early woman writer as a feminist, a radical, a revolutionary or a model for us. We have, in short, to select the mothers we wish to think back through.

Interestingly, Christine de Pizan has a place-setting in that powerful and controversial monument to 'sisterhood', Judy Chicago's installation *The Dinner Party*. One criterion for including a given figure in *The Dinner Party* was her ability to 'represent a role model for the future', and it is this criterion that gave the artist a moment of doubt. 'As I worked on research for *The Dinner Party*', she writes, 'and then on the piece itself, a nagging voice kept reminding me that the women whose plates I was painting, whose runners we were embroidering, whose names we were firing onto the porcelain floor, were primarily women of the ruling classes' (p. 56). But Judy Chicago shies away from the difficult implications of this nagging voice, with the truism that 'History has been written from the point of view of those who have been in power. It is not an objective record of the human race.' Does this mean, then, that we are to reject the notion of ruling class, or to reject all historical data recorded by men? Judy Chicago's evasion implies a deep scepticism that would render any historical understanding impossible, including that of *The Dinner Party*, which reveals a strongly biased (and in my view inaccurate) conception of history. The nagging voice that Judy Chicago heard and dismissed is the one I want to pay attention to here, in arguing that we need not clasp every woman writer to our collective bosom merely because – as Virginia Woolf remarked of the eighteenth-century novelist Eliza Haywood – 'she is dead, she is old, she wrote books, and nobody has yet written a book about her' ('A Scribbling Dame').

It has become especially important to take a hard historical look at Christine de Pizan because of the large claims that have been made for her. Jeffrey Richards, for example, translator of Christine's *Livre de la Cité des Dames*, adopts a tone nearly hagiographical, with the vocabulary of 'mothers to think back through' very pronounced. We are told of 'the experimental and innovative nature of her prose' (xxi), 'her enormous range' (xxii), 'her participation in the intellectual currents of her age' (xxvi). Christine is 'revolutionary . . . profoundly feminist', completely dedicated 'to the betterment of women's lives and to the alleviation of their suffering' (xxviii). This appreciation, which seems to me wrong on every count, is surely one of the most extreme in Christine-scholarship, and particularly odd since the view of Christine as proto-feminist is not a new one.[2] It emerged and was debated a century ago in the heyday of the international feminist movement; it was laid to rest as early as 1912 by Matilde Laigle in her study of Christine's *Le Livre des Trois Vertus*. Later I will suggest some reasons for the latter-day revival of this 'querelle de Christine'.

My purpose in presenting a cautionary dossier on Christine is to show that she was not, even by the standards of her own day, a reformer or proto-feminist. She is at best a contradictory figure, admirable in some respects, deplorable in others. I approach Christine as a reader and a writer who has been moved by Christine's account of her own 'anxiety of influence' at the beginning of Cité des Dames, where she confronts head-on the literary tradition of medieval clerical misogyny. I have, I think, understood her subversive propagandistic effort to 'rewrite woman good' in that text (see Chapter 5). I have been charmed by some of her lyrics, impressed by her determination to educate herself and above all by her will to write. Yet I have also been terminally bored by the tedious, mind-numbing bureaucratic prose of Cité des Dames, imitated from the style of royal notaries and civil servants.[3] I have been angered by Christine's self-righteousness, her prudery, and the intensely self-serving narrowness of her views. I have been repulsed by the backwardness of her social attitudes, attitudes already obsolescent in the early fifteenth century when Christine lived and wrote. If in this paper I emphasise the negative axis of my response to Christine de Pizan, it is in order to foreground the kind of historical interrogation that is necessary in selecting the literary mothers we wish to think back through.

We know a good deal about Christine's life, much of it from her own pen.[4] She was Italian by birth, the daughter of a prominent physician-astrologer who took up residence at the French court under Charles V. Christine was born about 1365, educated at home by her father, happily married to one Etienne de Castel (a notary in the royal service), widowed at twenty-five with three children and a mother to support. With small inheritance and only a little land, Christine eventually turned to writing as her profession, manoeuvring skillfully among the murderous rivalries that plagued the French ruling houses. She was a prolific author with a substantial reputation among the French and English aristocrats whose patronage was her livelihood. The oeuvre on which her reputation rests was mainly produced over a period of about fifteen years. Later there followed an interval of more than a decade (1418-29) during which Christine withdrew to a convent at Poissy, outside of Paris, and evidently produced nothing. She was one of many courtiers who followed the Dauphin into 'exile' upon the Burgundian invasion of Paris in 1418. Her last work, a patriotic poem honouring Charles VI and Joan of Arc, was produced in 1429. We do not know Christine's response to Charles's betrayal of La Pucelle the following year, nor exactly when Christine died, except that she was dead by 1432. Until 1600 or so her reputation flourished, with translation of her works into several languages (Mombello).

Those who are not familiar with the period of transition from feudalism to capitalism – Christine's period – are often surprised by its radical aspects, for it was an age self-consciously modern which in theory and in practice had begun to attack traditional ideas and institutions. What was the social context in which Christine lived and wrote? What would 'radicalism' actually mean in early fifteenth-century Europe?[5]

To begin with, the Catholic Church was in crisis. Clerical abuses and high living had generated a tradition of anti-clerical sentiment on both scholastic and popular levels. (The latter would include, for instance, German polemical poetry, French fabliaux and the Roman de Renart, and several of Chaucer's Canterbury Tales.) Simultaneously there flourished, from the eleventh century on, a network of popular heresies which, despite varying origins and programmes, challenged the Church by practising pacifism or apostolic poverty, denying the sacramental nature of marriage, advocating the right of laymen to administer the sacraments, the right of women to preach, or salvation through women. The Church was sufficiently worried about the appeal of such heresies that it founded not only the Inquisition to combat them, but the orders of preaching friars. Moreover, a low-level but widespread scepticism about the efficacy of prayer and priestly ministration was probably inevitable when the Crusade movement failed, the Black Plague invaded Europe in 1348, and the Great Schism in the church from 1378 to 1417 offered the unedifying spectacle of rival popes excommunicating one another. Reinforcing these centrifugal tendencies was the consolidation of national monarchies and, in Italy, of city-states, or communes, governed by elected councils of the high bourgeoisie. Monarchs and republicans had their theoreticians – the corpus of lawyers, scholars and theologians such as Marsilius of Padua, Pierre DuBois, John Quidort and William of Ockham – whose task was to rationalise the dismantling, or at least the limiting, of ecclesiastical power in the temporal sphere. The English Protestant Reformation was still more than a century in the future when Christine de Pizan died, but already in the thirteenth century, the nobles of France had formed a society for the disendowment of the Church.

On the intellectual scene, philosophers of the via moderna – the revolutionary new 'nominalistic' logic – were well established at the universities of Eastern and Western Europe, and nowhere more firmly or more notoriously than at the University of Paris. They challenged the certainty of orthodox doctrine on such basic questions as creation *ex nihilo* and transsubstantiation. The goodness of God and even his existence were interrogated as logical propositions, and found wanting. In science, the diurnal rotation of the earth was already proposed by Nicolas Oresme, economic adviser to Charles V and colleague to the father of Christine de Pizan. While Tommaso da Pizzano continued in astrology, the work of Oresme in physics and astronomy anticipated that of Copernicus and Galileo.

Socially, feudalism was dying, stifled by the efflorescence of international commerce and the political and economic demands of the urban bourgeoisie. Social mobility both vertical and horizontal was the order of the day: that is, changes in social rank, and travel. Symptomatic of these changes were major revolts in every European country and involving every social class: peasants, artisans, bourgeois, university intellectuals, even aristocrats. I list a few of the best-known of these insurrections to give the flavour of the period, but each of them is only the tip of an iceberg, preceded and followed by decades of struggle that often erupted into strikes and lockouts, sit-ins and occupations, armed confrontation and guerrilla warfare. There was the great anti-feudal revolt of English peasants and artisans in 1381, which nearly took London. There was the people's militia in Flanders led by the wealthy merchants Jacob van Artevelde and his son Philip who twice during the fourteenth century ousted the Count of Flanders. There was the guildsmen's overthrow of the city government of Freiburg in Germany in 1388.

In France – mother of revolutions – the normal tensions of the transition period were exacerbated by war with England and by a ruling elite whose self-indulgence literally turned every holiday into a national financial disaster. The country was in constant turmoil which during the lifetime of Christine de Pizan coalesced into several nationwide insurrections. The Jacquerie – the great national peasant revolt of 1358 – linked up with dissatisfied bourgeois in many cities who were already organising general strikes against royal fiscal policy. The Maillotin insurrection of 1382 culminated months of tax-riots by bourgeois and artisans in major cities, taking its name from the police mallets seized by the rebels. During 1383 and 84, guerrilla warfare was carried on throughout the south by bands of dispossessed peasants and urban poor, the so-called Tuchins.

Christine herself witnessed and wrote about one of the most important of these insurrections, the 1413 Cabochian revolution, centred in Paris (see Coville). Here, a multi-class coalition (today we would call it a popular front) developed around a programme of fiscal reform. The bloc was led by Jean Sans Peur, Duke of Burgundy and Christine's long-time patron, who saw the reform movement as a convenient anti-Orleanist weapon. His main bloc partner was the pro-Burgundian University of Paris, official think-tank of the day. The real muscle of the coalition was the working population of Paris – artisans, apprentices, servants, shopkeepers, guildsmen – spearheaded by the wealthy guild-corporations of skinners and butchers, whose leader, Simon Caboche, gave his name to the rising. The rebels placed princely advisors and courtly hangers-on under house arrest, including fifteen of the queen's ladies-in-waiting. They forced the king to 'dis-appoint' (*desappointer*) officials and replace them with the rebels' university allies; they made the king establish a committee of inquiry into abuses and proclaim a series of reform ordinances. The rebels achieved, in other words, a short-lived period of dual power. But it is typical of cross-class blocs that the threat of force, while effective, alienates the ruling-class partners. So the nobles and the University dumped their embarrassing allies along with the reforms already won. A new coalition was formed on a slogan of 'peace at all costs', a slogan appealing to the high or 'respectable' bourgeoisie who had no particular desire for fiscal reform. (It was this new party that won the sympathy of Christine de Pizan.) The reform ordinances were revoked, the corporations of butchers and skinners were destroyed, and the country returned to the *status quo ante*, just as the rebels had warned: civil war and economic disaster.

Such was the tenor of Parisian life as Christine was able to observe it. Even at court, though, there was a long tradition of criticising government and royalty, continued by – among others – Christine's fellow poets and courtiers Eustache Deschamps and Alain Chartier. Deschamps sympathised with the poor whose labour produced the country's wealth:

. . . This grain, this corn, what is it but the blood and bones of the poor folk who have plowed the land? Wherefore their spirit crieth on God for vengeance. Woe to the lords, the councillors and all who steer us thus, and woe to all who are of their party, for no man careth now but to fill his bags. (Tuchman, pp. 396-7)

Chartier went so far as to give voice to the peasant directly.[6] To be a courtier, clearly, one did not have to suspend all critical faculties.

The last aspect of medieval society I wish to refer to is the role of the urban middle-class woman, which, like others I have mentioned, reflects the radical social changes of the epoch.[7] From the eleventh century, expanding mercantile and manufacturing capital had called more and more women into the labour force and given them numerous legal and social rights (though these would be lost during the Renaissance). In Christine's day the bourgeois woman owned, inherited and bequeathed property independent of her husband; she sued and was sued in court; she lobbied Parliament; in some cities she held minor office, in others voted in municipal elections. She apprenticed, worked in, owned and operated virtually any trade or profession, from apothecary to shoemaker, brothel-keeper to weaver. The huge food and textile industries were often staffed and controlled by women, who also joined the guilds of their craft. Though women were not admitted to university, they could receive education at home or at church or public schools. Some Italian women scholars gave public orations or lectures at university. The ideal of the educated woman penetrated even the literary romances of the day, for some of them present a heroine skilled in languages, literature and science.

We begin to appreciate, I hope, that in the Middle Ages, dissent from received norms was neither impossible nor unusual. Radical ideas and practices were current in this pluralistic and seethingly modern society – but not in the work of Christine de Pizan.

She was, of course, a courtier and a foreigner. In this age of international marriages, alliances and cultural exchange, many Italians lived and worked in France. Few can have been so intensely loyal to their employers as Christine, who – the Rosemary Woods or Fawn Hall of her day – praises her corrupt and fratricidal patrons as the most benign and humane nobility in the world (Policie 3:7). When Christine, 'plus royalist que le roi', asserts it is literally a sin to criticise king or nobles – 'Je dy que c'est pechié a qui le fait' (Varty, no. 118 or Roy, vol. 1, no. 49) – we must surely see her very much in the rearguard of social thought of the period. Christine seems to think little of Parliaments, councils, cabinets, or any of the institutional means whereby a ruler might consult the ruled. Republican government with rotating administration, such as already existed in Bologna and elsewhere, she rejects. The principle of electoralism frightens her deeply: why, if a ruler can be elected, he can also be deposed (Policie, 3:2)! For the Parisian reformers and their project Christine shows nothing but hatred and contempt. The Livre de la Paix is filled with her execrations against 'le vile et chetive gent, le fol gouvernement de menu et bestial peuple' (Pais, 2:1) who flout the will of God in their dissatisfaction against the nobility (Paix, 3:9,10). Even an Italian despot is better than such people, who should keep silent 'de ce de quoy

ne leur apertient a parler' (Policie, 1:3). Her sketch of a political meeting –
'celle diabolique assemblee' (Paix, 3:11) – is nothing short of vicious. For
Christine, social justice and harmony consist in each rank fulfilling its
divinely-appointed duties according to its divinely-determined nature
(Paix, 3:10,11). By the fifteenth century this was a sadly outmoded model,
completely out of touch with late-medieval social life and political
theory. The image that comes to mind is of King Canute trying to beat
back the tide with a broom. So Christine tries to beat back the tide of
social change, of protest and nascent democracy, with her little broom of
pious anecdotes and exhortations gathered from the Bible and other
ancient authorities. In a time when even courtiers and clerics wanted
change, Christine continued in her quiet neo-Platonic hierarchies and
her feudal nostalgia.

It is not inconsistent with a static neo-Platonic world-view that
Christine should consider rural labour the most necessary social group
of all, and advise us to be grateful for their services. In this Christine only
repeats the truisms of classical and Christian rhetoric: Adam and Noah
tilled the soil, so did some famous Romans, therefore we ought not to
have contempt for those who till the soil. Besides, a life of poverty is the
most morally perfect of all (Policie, 3:10). Christine herself did not, of
course, aspire to this particular form of perfection but strove mightily to
avoid it. In fact her brief edifying reflections on rural life consist of a set of
literary topoi echoing the pastoralism then in vogue among the French
nobility.[8] Perhaps Christine was among the retinue of Queen Isabel
when the latter retreated, as she often did, to her farm-estate, 'Hostel des
Bergeries', the gift of her fond husband Charles VI, 'pour esbatmente et
plaisance'.

What about Christine as champion of women? Surely this is the
arena in which, for feminists, her credentials as proto-feminist must
stand or fall. The Cité des Dames is usually cited as the strongest evidence of
Christine's dedication to the cause of women. Here Christine offers
models of female courage, intelligence and prudence, to show that
women are indeed capable of these virtues and to bolster women's
self-image insofar as this might be undermined by clerical misogyny.
Though this is a laudable aim it is surely a very minimal one given the
already prominent role of women in medieval social life. Moreover in
several ways the text subverts its own 'subversion'. We are told of ancient
warriors, queens, goddesses and scholars, and of a few present-day
noblewomen said to be of surpassing virtue. But for all its valorisation of
female strength and ingenuity we hear of no modern working woman

whether rich or poor. The sole exception is a painter, Anastasia, who illuminated some of Christine's manuscripts (sec. 113). France was full of strong, clever, industrious and ambitious women, but one would never guess it from *Cité des Dames*. The reason, I suspect, is that these women were of a class that Christine had little affection for – they were, after all, trouble-makers in the realm, so that the considerable virtues of the bourgeois or artisan woman were lost on our arch-courtier. In the same text Christine's *porte-parole* Dame Raison justifies the exclusion of women from public office on the grounds that it is not their God-given place (sec. 40). Though many women were their husband's partners both domestically and commercially, Christine fears the implicit egalitarianism of such an arrangement, advising the married woman to submit humbly to what comes her way (3:19; Laigle, 237-59).

In *Le Livre des Trois Vertus*, Christine ignores the independent woman of her day, presenting her only in relation to a husband's 'professional conscience'. It is the wife's duty to ensure her husband's honesty, especially if the husband should be a rural labourer:

If your husbands work land for others, they should do it well and loyally, as if for themselves, and at harvest they should pay their master in wheat . . . and not mix rye with the grain. . . . They shouldn't hide the best sheep with the neighbours to pay the master the worst ones . . . or make him believe the sheep have died by showing him the hides of other animals, or pay the worst fleeces or give short count of his goods or fowl. (Laigle, p. 300; my translation.)

Thus Christine sees woman domestically as 'the angel in the house', socially as an agent of control on behalf of the ruling elite.

Christine is sometimes mentioned as an early crusader for the education of women. This is far from the truth. In reality Christine merely argues the standard Catholic truism that women are *capable* of learning. Despite her own thirst for knowledge, though, she does not in fact recommend education for women generally. The point is that most women do not require an education in order to fulfil their social obligations. They do not need Latin, nor scholarly texts such as Christine herself knew: vernacular romances and saints' lives will do for most girls, and only as much arithmetic as will enable them to keep household accounts (Laigle, pp. 173-86). One need not wonder what Christine's countrywoman, the learned Laura Cereta, would have thought of such a limited programme. We know what her countryman Giovanni Boccaccio thought, for he denounced the narrow domestic aspirations of women – who 'have in common the ability to do those things which

make men famous' (DCM, chap. 84). We know, too, how highly the
fourteenth-century French theologian Pierre DuBois valued the
capacities of women, for he proposed to the Pope a scheme for sending a
large corps of educated women into the Muslim East, to regain by
propaganda and fraternisation what the Crusades had lost (Shahar, p.
155). By contrast with the ideas of these contemporaries, Christine's
proposals seem timid at best.[9]

The last aspect of Christine's career that I will consider here is her part
in the well-known debate on the Roman de la Rose, one of the most
popular, influential and durable works of the entire Middle Ages. It is not
difficult to see why the Roman has often been interpreted as a subversive
text. The poem denounces numerous social ills such as clerical hypocrisy
and the perversion of justice by wealth. It propounds a rationalistic –
though by no means unorthodox – Christianity threatening to more
conservative churchmen such as Jean Gerson, chancellor of the
University of Paris and Christine's ally in the debate. It offers a fictional
representation of fornication – that is, sex without benefit of the marriage
sacrament – which implicitly removes sexuality from the ecclesiastical
control to which it had been subjected in the ecclesiastical reforms of the
eleventh and twelfth centuries: a campaign which also established clerical celibacy, persecuted homosexuality, and intensified clerical
misogyny.[10]

If we can speak of a Phyllis Schlafly of the Middle Ages, surely that title
belongs to Christine. Her main complaint against the Roman is that its
author talks dirty. In context of a discussion of the nature of justice, Jean
de Meun has Dame Raison recount the story of Saturn's fall. Raison's
narration includes a reference to 'les secrez membres' – specifically the
'coilles' (testicles) – of Saturn, whose castration by his son Jupiter ended
the Golden Age. Raison argues (as did many defenders of the Roman) that
because all creation is good, such naming is permissible. Christine
refutes this justification of obscene language: since the beauty of creation
is a paradisal condition, to name the genitals is to deny the polluting
effects of original sin; hence it is not only a socially offensive act but
virtually a heretical one. Nor may we excuse an author because it was
only a fictional character who spoke: Christine insists that an author take
full responsibility for every word written. Luckily Christine did not
explicitly apply this criterion to her contemporaries: Geoffrey Chaucer
for one would scarcely have passed muster with his apologias for plain
speaking (Canterbury Tales, GP 725–46 and A 3167–86). French popular literature must have been agony for Christine inasmuch as words like 'con',

'foutre', 'merde', 'vit' and 'pet' were quite common in *fabliaux*, riddles, jokes and popular songs, even finding their way occasionally into the *chansons de geste* and other courtly literature.[11] It was not, by and large, a prudish age.

After its use of obscenity, Christine objects to the *Roman*'s potential influence. Since human nature is already inclined to evil, the *Roman* will encourage abominable behavior and dissolute living through its portrayal of unmarried love. It is a dangerous book, all the more so for being well written. Finally, the author or his characters (for Christine, the same thing) slander women by portraying in certain episodes their love of gossip and their ability to deceive a jealous husband. (Curiously, Christine ignores numerous examples of virtuous women in the text.)

Christine's solution to the 'problème de la Rose' is simple: burn the book. She proposes it not only in her letters but in a balade where she self-righteously compares herself to Aristotle and Socrates, who had also been attacked for telling the truth. 'Le Roman', she writes, 'plaisant aux curieux, / de la Rose – que l'en devroit ardoir!' Interestingly, Jean Gerson, the most influential of several parties to the debate, seems virtually obsessed with fire: the imagery of fire recurs constantly in his letters, in proverbs and metaphors as well as in actual recommendations. Gerson demands the flames not only for the *Roman* and for the letters of those who defend it, but also for the works of Ovid, for popular songs, poems or paintings that incite to lubricity, for homosexuals or those who practise any other 'vice against nature' (which for Gerson would include sodomy, oral copulation, or abortion). 'Justice les arde!' 'Au feu! bonnes gens, au feu!' he writes in the exalted hysteria of crusade rhetoric. If applied, Gerson's recommendations would have decimated the ranks of the Church, not to mention society at large, as well as a good deal of medieval literature and art.[12] Fortunately neither the ecclesiastical nor the civil power-structure was as committed as Gerson to the salubrious ministrations of the flames.

Now censorship was a genuine issue in Christine's day, and burning – of books and of people – was its most extreme expression: not a common one, but a possible one. Need we recall that many of the heretics burnt before and during Christine's lifetime were women, that most of the witches who would later go to the stake were women, and that Christine's heroine Joan of Arc met her death by fire? Political censorship was not unknown at the French court. In 1389 Christine's colleague Philippe de Mézières proposed a ban at court on all poets except those using moral or religious themes, and in 1395 Charles VI forbade all poets and balladeers to mention the Pope or the schism. Burning had been rare in France since the extermination of the Cathars in 1330. Nonetheless at the time of the *Roman* debate, Jean Gerson was engaged in polemical struggle against a sect of which a group had been burned in Paris in 1372 for heresy. As Pierre-Yves Badel has shown, there was for Gerson a close association between the errors of the *Roman* and those of the heretics, particularly on the subject of sex (447-61). Christine does not go so far as to demand the burning of individuals, not even Jews: them she merely denounces, endorsing Fortune's continual punishment of them, though such uncompromising hostility was neither the 'official' position nor was it held by all educated laymen and clerics.[13] Yet Christine's advocacy of book-burning has a logic of its own that should give us pause. We should be clear that Gerson's intervention in this seemingly innocuous literary debate was motivated by no chivalrous gallantry but by the most conservative of political interests. And while I do not doubt Christine's sincerity, any more than I do Gerson's, we should not forget that it was she who first publicised the documents of what began as a private literary discussion, and that this publication, though not her first, effectively enhanced her career at court.

It seems to me, then, that Christine's role in the *Roman* debate shows her again less the friend of woman than of the powers that be at their most oppressive: a position no more inevitable in her time than in ours. If Christine stood in advance of her day it was in anticipating the prudish moralism of nineteenth and twentieth-century literary censorship. If Christine was correct on the *Roman de la Rose*, then so were the censors of James Joyce, Henry Miller and D.H. Lawrence. If Christine was correct, then we should not be able to read Djuna Barnes or Anais Nin either. In fact it was Christine's opponents, the defenders of the *Roman* – male, clerical, arrogant and patronising as they were – who nonetheless made the same arguments that today permit us to read some of the most interesting writers, male and female, of our own time.

This completes my short dossier on Christine de Pizan, and I should like to return now to the late twentieth century and to gender-oriented criticism. The kind of overestimation that I have tried in this chapter to correct is not limited to Christine. I have noticed it, for instance, in some scholarship on the American feminist Charlotte Perkins Gilman, who shows a number of interesting parallels with Christine and whom I have elsewhere characterised as 'representative of a day that was drawing to a close rather than as harbinger of a day that was dawning' (*Writing Woman*,

p. 169). Phyllis Rose, a biographer of Virginia Woolf, has warned against imbalanced appreciation of women writers. 'Recent feminist biography', she notes, 'has been challenging in exciting ways our accepted notions of major and minor. But just because an artist has been underappreciated does not mean her work is major. . . This partisanship, this absence of perspective produces some outrageous statements . . .' (New York Times Book Review, June 26, 1983). Nor is the phenomenon limited to literary studies. In reviewing two books about activist women, the sociologist Bernice Fisher writes, 'It is especially important that we do not incorporate role models uncritically. We need to examine carefully our portrayal of women as models, to ask ourselves what message these images convey . . .' Fisher goes on to call for 'the radical social analysis that shows the objective constraints under which industrial women have achieved.'

I believe that the data assembled above are conclusive with respect to Christine's conservatism. What doubtless remains open for some, though, is interpretation. Was Christine's view of things inevitable or predictable precisely because of 'objective restraints?' Bluntly: was she forced to ultraconservatism by complete dependence on royal patrons, a dependence created by lack of opportunities for women? If so, ought we not to sympathise rather than to judge? The first is primarily a historical question, the second moral. To treaty them fully would require another long chapter, but I shall address what seem to me the major problems with this approach.

Historically, the position is less tenable for Christine's epoch than for those preceding and following it. The tenth century, or the sixteenth, might offer more convincing evidence, but the high and late Middle Ages did in fact open significant opportunities to women. Moreover, ultraconservatism is only one possible response to constraint, and many medieval women found other ways. Women participated in the rebellions of the time, joined heretical sects, banded together in collectives to do good works (the Beguines), ran businesses, petitioned Parliament for legislative change in their industry, and regularly disobeyed the Church's teachings on contraception, abortion and sexuality.

Nor was Christine herself without resources. She might perhaps have remarried. She might have lived at a convent (as in fact she would do later in life), there to continue her scholaarship and social life as was the norm for well-placed covent boarders. She might have retired to the Château de Mémorant, a property given her father by King Charles V and which Christine eventually sold to Philippe de Mézières. She might have gone into business as a bookseller, a notary, or a copyist, or in some other branch of the burgeoning book industry. She might have accepted invitations from Henry IV to take up residence at the English court, where her son was companion to the young prince, or from the Duke of Milan to grace his court. These invitations and refusals were made in 1400 and 1401 – 'even before she had begun to produce her major works', as Charity Willard points out (*Life and Works*, p. 165). In France she was supported by many members of the royal family, male and female. All this suggests that the search for patronage was considerably less urgent a matter for Christine than it must have been for many another courtly writer.

Despite opportunities available to urban women generally, and to Christine individually, even the exceptional woman had neither complete freedom nor complete equality with men. Nor do we today, and there can be no doubt that the special oppression of women deforms consciousness. Nonetheless, to adduce special oppression, then or now, in mitigation of reactionary social attitudes strikes me as condescending, naive aand ultimately irresponsible.

Condescending because it implies that women ought to be exempt from moral or political polemic because of their gender. About Christine it implies that her stated opinions were insincere. Indeed, in its effort to exculpate Christine from the unfashionable charge of conservatism, the defence from sheer economic necessity (besides being inaccurate) paradoxically reduces her to an unprincipled and hypocritical opportunist. I prefer to think that she understood the choices available to her, and chose as she believed. This preserves at least her dignity.

Naive because the position implies that an individual can hypothetically be removed from her social environment and inserted in an ideal, ahistorical existence, one in which special oppression no longer deforms her consciousness and in which therefore her 'true', 'authentic' opinions can be known or guessed. In literary terms this is a version of the old 'sincerity fallacy'. For better or worse, though, all we have is the text, and all we have is individuals in their social context.

Irresponsible because while any opinion surely has both personal and social determinants, these don't, in my view, justify the denial or abdication of choice. Here I mean both Christine's choice and ours. To take an extreme instance: in our day the woman fascist or the woman racist can be understood; the special oppression of women is doubtless relevant to her position; but then what? or even so what? If we don't accept a passive-deterministic attitude toward life, then we ought not to gloss over reactionary views, though they be voiced by a woman and in the name of womanhood.

What I find interesting about the revival of Christine's reputation as proto-feminist is that it seems to reflect a much more conservative feminism than was typical of the women's movement two decades ago: a backlash, if you will, observable in academic life, among the organised left, in the labour movement, in national electoral politics. It is a telling sign of the times that Jeffrey Richards can adduce, as Christine's fellow so-called 'revolutionary', the humble pacifist Martin Luther King (p. xxix), the same whose slogan 'If there is blood in the streets, let it be ours' was once rightly denounced by activists of both races and varying political persuasions. But if King is your idea of a revolutionary, then it isn't hard to make the leap to Christine de Pizan. If the censorship of pornography strikes you as progressive social action – as it does some feminists today – then it will not be hard to see Christine as progressive. If you cannot imagine any alternative to the institution of the family than what now exists, then you may well endorse Christine's admonitions to women. And if you believe that the special oppression of women – even the exceptional woman – foredooms women to conservatism, then Christine's conservatism will appear perfectly 'natural'.

But I would like to suggest another model in keeping with the metaphor of 'mothers to think back through' with which I began. We learn from our mothers in various ways, not exclusively by imitation.[14] We also learn by struggling against them, by coming to terms with our ambivalence about them, by making the effort to understand historically their success and their failure. It is the least we can expect from a genealogical inquiry.

Clerks and quiting in *The Reeve's Tale*: social structure as a source of irony

In the pair of *fabliaux* narrated by Chaucer's Miller and Reeve, two sets of young clerks have a special function: they are agents of the kind of retributive justice called 'quiting'. The theme of quiting controls this section (Fragment I) of *The Canterbury Tales* from the Miller's prologue through the conclusion of *The Reeve's Tale*,[1] and the various shades of meaning given the word by Host, Miller, and Reeve offer a clue to the moral nature of each. Moreover, while both the Miller's and Reeve's tales illustrate the principle of even-handed justice, our appreciation of the latter work depends especially on the fact that the victors are clerks, and on the unique suitability of clerks to that role. The source of the literary role of the medieval clerk is his oddly ambiguous social position, which, since it carries the final irony of *The Reeve's Tale*, allows us to judge the narrator of the tale as well as its characters.

Harry Bailey first uses the word 'quite' in his request that the Monk tell the second story of the day:

> 'So moot I gon,
> This gooth aright; unbokeled is the male.
> Lat se now who shal telle another tale;
> For trewely the game is wel bigonne.
> Now telleth ye, sir Monk, if that ye konne
> Somwhat to quite with the Knyghtes tale.' (I, 3114-19)

Harry Bailey's notion of quiting reveals that instinctive, sometimes undis-criminating, approval of harmony and propriety which governs his res-ponse to many of the tales. His request serves an aesthetic and a social end at once for he hopes that in matching the standard of excellence established by the Knight, the second teller will again draw the pilgrims together in unanimous approbation. These good intentions are subver-ted when the Miller announces that he will follow the Knight:

> 'By armes, and by blood and bones,
> I kan a noble tale for the nones,
> With which I wol now quite the Knyghtes tale.' (3125-7)

The Miller wishes to quit by contrast, not by similarity. In this he succeeds, providing a vulgar counterpoint to the amenities of rhetoric, philosophy, and courtly love in The Knight's Tale. Further, the tale told by the Miller is constructed according to the requirements of retributive morality. Every fault (except Alison's adultery) is punished at its source: the old carpenter's folly, Absolon's foppishness, the lechery of handy Nicholas. In spite of its scurrility, The Miller's Tale is well received by the general company – except for Oswald the Reeve. For whatever reasons, Oswald interprets the tale as an offense to himself. In his prologue, quiting degeneerates into a narrow vengefulness which is not related to any larger scheme of order or justice, and a note of personal spite is introduced:

> 'So theek', quod he, 'ful wel koude I thee quite
> With bleryng of a proud milleres ye,
> If that me liste speke of ribaudye . . .
>   This dronke Milere hath ytoold us heer
> How that bigyled was a carpenteer,
> Peraventure in scorn, for I am oon.
> And, by youre leve, I shal hym quite anoon;
> Right in his cherles termes wol I speke.
> I pray to God his nekke mote to-breke; . . .' (3864-6; 3913-18)

As used by the Reeve, quiting is equivalent to simple vindictiveness, but the operation of quiting in the tale itself indicates some limitations of this definition of morality. To the Reeve it is appropriate that Simkin, the miller in his own fabliau, be cuckolded as was John the carpenter in The Miller's Tale. It is appropriate too that Simkin be deceived by clerks as John was. But this very insistence on symmetrical justice defeats the Reeve's attempt to vindicate himself and those of his profession. His tale demonstrates only the ingenuity of clerks at the expense of a proud miller, just as the preceding tale had shown their ingenuity at the expense of a foolish carpenter. The Miller's and Reeve's tales do not assert the superiority of millers and carpenters respectively; they only confirm the superiority of clerks to both.

Why did Chaucer consider the clerk to be a particularly suitable agent of quiting? One reason is found in the tradition of the French fabliau, where the clerk is conventionally a conquering hero. In his study of the fabliaux, Per Nykrog shows that the clerk-lover is uniformly successful, and that his success, unlike that of other types of lover, does not depend on the social rank of the challenged husband.[2] Moreover, since the clerk does not appear in the fabliaux as a husband, he himself cannot be cuckolded. Clerks are opposed to a miller in the extant French analogues to The Reeve's Tale, and while this may partly account for their presence in Chaucer's version, it does not explain their function. For that we must turn to the actual social position of the medieval clerk.

Town-gown hostility has always been a feature of academic life, but during the Middle Ages it approached the dimensions of continual warfare. The so-called 'slaughters' at Oxford (1228 and 1354), Toulouse (1332) and Orleans (1387) are only a few of the best-known in a long series of raids, assaults, and brawls. Some of these conflicts were provoked by specific trivial incidents, but the results are so disproportionately violent that most of them are understandable only as manifestations of a relation that was strained at best, one created largely by the special privileges enjoyed by all University students and personnel.[3] The establishment of scholarly privileges was usually initiated when a representative of the University petitioned the king for redress of grievances suffered at the hands of townspeople or the mendicant orders. The privilege was confirmed by papal approval, and interference with it might incur excommunication as well as fines and imprisonment, so that the Universities enjoyed protection of the highest civil and ecclesiastical authorities. Most significant among these privileges was ecclesiastical immunity, or exemption from normal civil judicial process. This meant, among other things, that an accused clerk could not be tried in civil court but was bound over to the Chancellor for trial. The converse of clerical immunity was lay liability, for in a case to which a clerk and a layman were parties, the layman was also subject to Chancellor's jurisdiction. Punishment was often administered to the satisfaction of the offended clerk: in the event of murder or of serious injury to a clerk the entire community might be fined.

Clerical privileges intruded on other areas of civil life than the judicial, especially on those affecting the petty bourgeoisie. Rent and repairs in all houses letting to students were controlled by a University commission, and in many towns the University was also responsible for the inspection and control of weights, measures and prices. Scholars were usually exempt from such civic obligations as military service, local purchase and property taxes, tolls and duties while travelling to and from the University. At Bologna, all noisy occupations (smiths, wheelwrights, coopers) were prohibited from the University area; the butchers of Paris were required, at University pressure, to clean streets at their own expense and to slaughter animals only outside city limits; the citizens of Oxford were similarly made to clean and pave their streets. Besides the supervision of professional conduct, it was at Oxford the University's right to investigate and correct the morals of the laity. For this purpose the town was divided into districts, and offenders were summoned to the Chancellor's court. With typical vividness, Rashdall writes that by the middle of the fifteenth century, the town of Oxford 'had been crushed, and was almost entirely subjugated to the authority of the University. The burghers lived henceforth in their own town almost as the helots or subjects of a conquering people' (vol. 3, p. 79).

The nascent aristocracy of intellect found its natural ally in the courtly aristocracy. The two were united partly by a common opponent, the bourgeoisie, and partly by shared special influence with king and Pope. More than this, the University often owed its physical existence to aristocratic patrons (including ecclesiastical aristocrats) who donated libraries, endowed lectureships, and founded residential colleges. Remarkable, but hardly surprising, is the absence of the *haute bourgeoisie* among the founders of colleges: in England the single exception is the founding of Corpus Christi College (Cambridge) by the united guilds of Corpus Christi and the Blessed Virgin Mary. The political and economic connections between University and aristocracy, together with the University's estrangement from the bourgeoisie, placed the medieval clerk in an unusually flexible social position which had little to do with his own actual origin. This position helps qualify the clerk for his unique role in the *fabliaux*, and intensifies the irony of John's and Aleyn's vengeance in *The Reeve's Tale*.

In placing his Cambridge students in 'a greet collegge / Men clepen the Soler Halle' (3989-90), Chaucer shows his acute awareness of these social alignments. The clerks' college was called 'Solar Hall'[4] because of its upper rooms or sun-chambers, but its proper name was King's Hall, and it epitomized the intimate relation of University and state. Maintained by direct royal patronage, its fellows and wardens appointed by the crown, King's Hall specialized in civil law. The college

had as one of its chief functions the provision of a reservoir of educated personnel for ecclesiastical and governmental service. . . . The King's Hall was intended to play a central role in the perpetuation and renaissance of civil law studies at the English universities prompted perhaps partly by the need to meet an increased demand for civil law graduates arising from movements such as the Hundred Years War and European conciliarism, and partly to engender a climate of legal thought generally favourable to the more theocratic aspects of kingship. (Cobban, pp. 114-15)

Hence the trans-class alliance is firmly built into Chaucer's tale, and however impoverished or provincial his two clerks may be at the moment, their future is assured as that of the Miller or his daughter can never be.

The first encounter between Simkin and the two clerks reveals the miller's resentment of scholars as a group. He responds as follows (albeit silently) to John's simple-minded scheme for supervising the grinding of grain:

> 'Al this nys doon but for a wyle.
> They wene that no man may hem bigyle.
> But by my thrift, yet shal I blere hir ye,
> For al the sleighte in hir philosophye.
> The moore queynte crekes that they make,
> The moore wol I stele whan I take.
> In stide of flour yet wol I yeve hem bren.
> "The gretteste clerkes been noght wisest men,"
> As whilom to the wolf thus spak the mare.
> Of al hir art ne counte I noght a tare.' (4047-56)

Later, when the theft is accomplished, Simkin gloats:

> 'I trow the clerkes were aferd.
> Yet kan a millere make a clerkes berd,
> For al his art; . . .'   (4095-7)

The contempt that Simkin displays in these two passages is directed partly at the clerks' practical naiveté, partly at the intellectual preoccupation of clerks in general. Traditional bourgeois hostility is evident in the proverb which Simkin wrenches round to his own malicious use, and in the phrases 'for al the sleighte in hir philosophye', 'for al his art'. The motif reappears when Simkin agrees to let the exhausted clerks stay with him for the night:

> 'If ther be eny,
> Swich as it is, yet shal ye have youre part.
> Myn hous is streit, but ye han lerned art;
> Ye konne by argumentes make a place
> A myle brood of twenty foot of space.
> Lat se now if this place may suffise,
> Or make it rowm with speche, as is your gise.' (4120-6)

Here the miller, secure in having deceived John and Aleyn, dares to taunt them openly about the dubious achievement of their training, for Simkin's own values are above all materialistic. He goes so far as to flaunt his own verbal cleverness in the pun on 'rowm' (echo/spacious).

Chaucer has taken pains, in his version of the *fabliau*, to provide the proper social background for Simkin's values. In 'Le Meunier et les .II. Clers', the miller is clearly of the villein class and is referred to as 'li vilains' in text A of the *fabliau* (line 157). His poverty is also apparent in the limited hospitality he is able to offer:

> Li muniers lor fait aporter
> Pain et lait, et eues, et fromage,
> C'est la viande del bochage;
> Aus .II. clers assez en dona. (A. 170-173 in *Sources and Analogues*)

By contrast, Chaucer's miller feasts his guests on roast goose, bread, and strong ale. Simkin is something more than a villein, for red stockings, a sword, and hopes of a daughter's high marriage are outside the villein's world: they do not appear in the analogues. Nor does a wife who, as illegitimate daughter of the local priest,[5] considers herself 'ycomen of noble kin' (3942). On this shaky status her husband relies 'To saven his estaat of yomanrye' (3949); that is, to maintain his present legal position as a freeman which otherwise might revert to that of a churl or serf, a position evidently occupied in the uncomfortably near past. Moreover, Simkin is an oppressor, in his own modest way, for his thefts would be practiced not only on students but equally on the peasants who were forced by manorial law to grind at his mill. Had Simkin been unequivocally a villein, he would have had neither incentive for advancement nor the means to achieve it. As an established bourgeois, on the other hand, he would have had small reason for insecurity about his social position or that of his daughter. Chaucer has deliberately given Simkin an ambiguous social rank: the miller is a parvenu, anxious to keep and augment his share in what he conceives to be the good life. He grasps anything that may advance his status, particularly the hope of a profitable marriage for his daughter – which hope is so effectively blasted by Aleyn.

It is easy to overlook the miller's daughter here, twenty-year old Malyne with her snub nose and broad buttocks, for the Reeve's narrative presents her as a standard joke-figure, the vulnerable and forgettable pawn of the men who use her for advancement or revenge. Yet she is, by that very function, in a sense the center of the story, 'the observed of all observers', and it is she who will not escape this comic adventure without serious consequences. She has been, essentially, raped, for Aleyn had surprised her in her sleep so that 'it had been to late for to crie' (4196). Her evident feeling for Aleyn, her 'deere lemman' and 'goode lemman' (4240, 4247) will go unreciprocated, though it prompts her to betray her father by revealing the latter's subterfuge. When she does so, 'almoost she gan to wepe' (4248) – whether from knowledge 'about the ways of college men', or ambivalence about the betrayal, or fear of its consequences at her father's hands, we are not told. Very possibly she will bear a child from this casual union, so that whether she marries or not, Malyne's life is likely to be very different and her choices far fewer than if she had maintained her virginity. By giving away something for nothing, Malyne has shattered the carefully constructed matrimonial economy projected for her, and indeed challenged (albeit ineffectively) the quid pro quo of the genre itself.

Are the rustic clerks really Simkin's social inferiors? He thinks they are, and according to his strictly materialistic standards, Simkin is right. But other criteria are present in the tale, which would have been apparent to Chaucer's audience: the literary reputation of the clerk as love-hero, and the long-standing sympathy between clerks and aristocracy. This double tradition allows the clerks to transcend Simkin's measure, and offers another means of judging the miller's morality and his short-sighted social aspirations. Chaucer might after all have used another villein as the agent for frustrating the miller's ambition; there is some precedent in the French fabliaux for that situation. That treatment would obliterate one dimension of irony, for the villein could in fact be classified as inferior by Simkin's standards. The audience would have to concede the quiter's genuine social inferiority, and, by sharing that opinion with Simkin, would implicitly have to accept his values. Hence to maintain perspective on the near-bourgeois Simkin, The Reeve's Tale requires a 'hero' whose social position is fluid enough to be considered inferior by the miller, and simultaneously to be recognized as inherently, because potentially, superior by an aristocratic or bourgeois audience. The clerk's ambivalent social status accounts for his presence in the tale, and doubtless for his role in the French fabliaux as a tool of satire against all classes of deceivable husband.

The Reeve ends his tale with the remark, 'Thus have I quyt the Millere in my tale' (4324), and his last lines maliciously parody the Miller's own conclusion. In the narrowest sense the Reeve has quit the Miller. But Oswald's values, like Simkin's, are crude, and through them he exposes himself to the kind of justice he is so eager to apply to others. While blaming the Miller's ribaldry, the Reeve produces a confession of lascivious old age far more offensive than anything in the preceding tale. His instruments of vengeance, two clerks, would as gladly and successfully deceive a carpenter as a miller. His 'justice' includes the rape of an innocent young woman and the sacrifice of her future. Finally, the Reeve's character, as revealed in the General Prologue and in his own confession, makes him an unusually suitable target for retaliation: he is lecherous, spiteful, and doubtless as practised a thief as Simkin.

Nonetheless the Reeve thrives, and there is no sure sign that he has been or will be punished. In refraining from quiting the Reeve, Chaucer dissociates himself from a too-narrow definition of morality as mathematical retribution. In any case, life itself is not necessarily so finely tuned. Yet if narrative does not provide explicit judgment, this will not be lacking in the audience response, nor, eventually, at the seat of merciful justice.

The orthodox religious conclusion just specified – a charitable silence if you will – is paired with a social stance that many critics are reluctant to accept as equally characteristic. In directing his satire against the miller's 'illusions', the poet tilts at an overwhelming fact of the day: the social mobility and social aspirations that made the late medieval period so fertile. No one 'likes' Simkin, though everyone 'likes' the Wife of Bath; but they are the same kind of obnoxious upstart – the kind who would renovate English society. When Napoleon was able to describe England as 'a nation of shopkeepers', the Simkins would have the last laugh.

Strategies of silence in the Wife of Bath's recital

The second half of my title is misleading. It is a concession to habit and convenience, for the essay does not focus on the fictional character who supposedly 'speaks' the Chaucerian text. Instead, I invite the reader to regard the verbal strategies composing the text not as the monologue of a garrulous female weaver but rather as the production of an accomplished male courtier-poet voicing certain values of the culture inscribed in him. Ideally my title would read 'Strategies of silence in *The Canterbury Tales*, Fragment III, 1-1264.'

This essay can be seen as organised, on three levels, around three pairs of questions. In the most general strategic way the questions I have posed are these: 1) How is medieval social life, including ideology, articulated in the piece of literature at hand? 2) How is our social life, including ideology, articulated in the ways we speak of that piece of literature or of literature more generally? Here the thematic of silence is central: on one hand the silences or gaps in the text; on the other, the ways we interpret those textual silences or gaps.

In a closer and more tactical way, I think of this essay as oscillating between the two questions posed by Michel Foucault in 'What Is An Author?' The two questions are 'Who speaks?' and 'What difference does it make who is speaking?' By oscillating I do not mean that the paper wavers or is indecisive: I don't mean vacillating. I mean that each of these questions has been useful in its turn, to assist me in producing the meaning I wish to produce. At one moment I have needed to ask 'Who speaks?', taking an author-oriented biographical or psychoanalytic angle in order to bring forward a certain view of the poet in his time and in relation to his work: a view, it happens, which has often been suppressed as unacceptable. At other moments I have needed to ask 'What difference does it make who is speaking?' in order to foreground the ideological dimension of the text as opposed to the usual biographical or psychological realism it is so often said to represent. I should say also that although Foucault counterposes these two questions, I do not believe that they are necessarily mutually exclusive if one has a sufficiently broad definition of 'who': that is, to accept the second question is already to alter the first, but not necessarily to reject it.

Finally, the text itself can be said to be organised around two questions that themselves, with absolute acuity, pose the entire politics of gender. The first is 'Who painted that picture?', the Wife of Bath's question in her prologue; or, as she puts it, specifying the content of the picture, 'Who painted the lion?' At issue here is the appropriation and control of the means of cultural production. As we will see, this becomes paradigmatic of power relations in general. The second question, from the tale, is the riddle around which the plot turns: 'What do women want?' This is the power issue from another angle: the desire of the excluded other and the meaning of that desire for the dominant power.

Because these three pairs of questions are not strictly isomorphic, cannot be lined up in two lists A and B, I have not organised this essay in a schematic progression from one to another. I have instead integrated the registers in which they occur, so that one or another question will be recognised at various moments in what follows.

Once more to the lion

What is curious about the verbal patterns with which Chaucer has characterised the Wife of Bath is the several kinds of silence they include. Among these is the odd blend of flaunting and suppression that constitutes her mode of quotation from authoritative texts. Her scriptural hermeneutic often distorts by omission: a tactical silence about the context of a cited locus, or about its traditional and authoritative significance, or even the omission of subsequent words that might contradict the meaning she wishes to produce. The Wife's treatment of classical myth is similarly suppressive, as in her version of the tale of Midas: she simply ignores the usual version of the tale – or, more accurately, Chaucer has her ignore it and substitute another, so as to make her inadvertently affirm the old clerical-misogynist stereotype of woman as incontinent of speech, woman as disrespectful of authority.[1]

Besides scriptural and classical texts, the Wife refers to a relatively modern source, Marie de France's version of the Aesopian fable of the lion.[2] Her reading of it, I want to argue, is of a piece with her other interpretive efforts, offering a neat example of the would-be subversive subverted. The Wife alludes to this story in justifying her destruction of

her fifth husband's book of misogynistic writings, a source of annoying
nightly lectures:

Who peynted the leon, tel me who?
By God! if wommen hadde writen stories,
As clerkes han withinne hire oratories,
They wolde han writen of men moore wikkednesse
Than al the mark of Adam may redresse (III, 692-6).

The fable 'Del leun e del vilein', like many others in the collection, is
about power: physical, moral and social power. The two main characters
are a lion and a villein (a peasant, not necessarily poor). As the two walk
along, their topic of conversation is their *parage* (rank or status) and their
lignage (ancestry, race, perhaps species). Noticing on a wall a picture in
which a man kills a lion with his hatchet, the lion asks, 'Who made this
image, man or lion?' 'A man', the villein replies, 'with his intelligence
[*engin*] and his hands'. 'Everyone knows', agrees the lion, 'that man can
sculpt and paint, but the lion doesn't know how'. Next occurs an odd
episode in which the pair arrive at the emperor's castle, where a treasonous baron has just been stripped and thrown to – the emperor's lion!
Indeed the story is full of lions, for as the pair set out on the road again
they meet yet a third lion, who reproaches the first with his poor choice
of companion, one who knows how to set traps for lions. This third lion
offers to kill the man. The first lion refuses; hearing which the man is
deeply grateful: 'I see differently now!' he exclaims. 'Before, you showed
me a picture', the lion admonishes; 'but [since] I have shown you more
truth, you look at it more clearly.' The explicit morality is that we ought
not to trust stories or paintings which are like dreams or lies, but only that
'dunt hum veit l'ovre' (of which one sees the practical result), and which
therefore reveals the truth. Such too is the *moralitas* that survives in
Caxton's much shorter and much less interesting version: 'Men ought
not to byleve the paynture but the trouthe and the dede . . . And therfore
at the werke is knowen the best and most subtyle werker' (Liber Quartus,
XV). The point seems to be that individual character ought not to be
judged by species prejudice only: lions and men may behave with
generosity toward one another, they can coexist in the right circumstances. If we translate this as an allegory of gender relations, as the Wife
of Bath does, it may appear to make a liberal statement: don't judge on
gender alone. But let us look more closely, for this morality is completely
undercut by the story itself, in both narrative and symbolic structure.
   A number of curious things occur in Marie's fable. This first lion rejects

the advice of its own kind in order to remain loyal to the man. It remains complicit, therefore, in its own subjugation. The homicidally-inclined third lion, on the other hand, displays mere bestiality in its instinctive distrust of mankind. It ignores this particular man's proven good nature toward lions and concentrates only on the species potential for hostility. In other words we have a 'good' lion and a 'bad' lion. The good lion remains explicitly conscious of its own species-inferiority to the man, and is therefore able to display loyalty to the man. That is the condition of their coexistence. The bad lion is capable only of knee-jerk hostility because of its stereotyped thinking about men. Its projected violence is therefore inappropriate to reality.

What of the second lion, the one whom we never see but who accomplishes the execution of the treasonous baron? This lion too is exemplary, representing sheer natural strength channelled into (what would then have been considered) socially useful and humanly controlled institutions: the punishment of criminals, specifically, the capital punishment of offenders against the state. So that this criminal baron must also enter our interpretation as a reminder of what happens, or should happen, when in social life one or another element steps out of its place in the prescribed scheme. The second lion is therefore also a good lion, helping to enforce that hierarchal structure. It shows that physical strength alone cannot make for civilisation; strength must be linked with judgement. On its own, a lion (or a baron, or a woman) will not necessarily use its powers for good; but controlled by, or loyal to, a superior intelligence it can do so. We discern here a favourite medieval theme, expressed in numerous texts from the *Chanson de Roland* (the preu/sage pair) to *The Knight's Tale* (the competing lover-knights regulated by Theseus).

One thing lions will never do is produce art; that is acknowledged from the start. Of course a human being made the painting – it could not be otherwise, both lion and man agree. This appropriation of discourse and of representation is a privilege of the intelligence that can also invent a hatchet with which to kill a much stronger creature – or can invent a trap to do so, as the third lion correctly asserts, or incorporate a lion into a system of justice, as the emperor does with the second beast. So that the lion's question 'Ki fist ceste semblance?' can have only one answer, because lions *cannot* paint. It is simply not within their nature to do so, and however strong a lion may be it will always remain inferior to the human being. It may roar, it may attack, it may even kill, but it will never paint. Thus the 'bad' lion can only speak against itself in speaking against mankind, and only so can the 'good' lion do in speaking for mankind. It is a Catch-22.

It will be clear, then, how my reading of this fable relates to the Wife of Bath's recital. She reads the fable as an allegory of men and women – a quite legitimate application, as also would be an application to social class, since the fable is about relations of power. But in solidarising with the lion, Alice makes the same mistake made by the treasonous baron or the third, bad, lion. Like them, Alice speaks as if lions could or some day might paint: that is her basic misreading. For as written by Marie and as used by Chaucer, the fable conveys that sense of essential alterity carried in Ludwig Wittgenstein's remark, 'If lions could speak, we could not understand them.'

If the fable is read as an allegory of men and women, then its meaning is shockingly misogynistic. It tells us that women have not appropriated the means of cultural production because it is not their nature or capacity to do so, rage as they may. A woman may be a very clever woman, even a well-read woman, but she will never be equal to 'clerkes . . . withinne hire oratories' (694). It is not merely digressive to note that the word-play in this line richly and subtly supports my reading. A 'clerk' may be either a university intellectual, or a person ordained into holy orders; yet a woman may be neither one, banned by law both from university and from the ecclesiastical hierarchy. 'Oratory' (Fr. oratoire) is a private chapel in a monastery or a house; but the Latin oratio contained in the word points to the public exercise of rhetorical skills, whether the preaching of clerks or the legal, parliamentary or diplomatic presentations of university graduates and lawyers. 'Oratory' as public discourse is as inaccessible to women as the professions that employ it: on this matter Church and state agree. If the exceptional individual should imitate it in the private realm, she exposes herself to the charge of being a nag and a shrew, or to such malice as the Pardoner's snide address to the Wife as 'noble prechour' (165). More serious was infringement on the clerkly monopoly of public preaching. This exposed the lay individual, whether male or female, to the charge of heresy, often a capital offence. Given the dissemination of Wycliffism during the period when Chaucer was composing the Tales, given the civil and ecclesiastical authorities' growing alarm about lay and especially female preaching, the Pardoner's comment has a particularly nasty edge. His point, though, is that women are not meant to preach, just as Marie's point in her fable is to disclose the limits of cultural appropriation.

To return to the painting of lions: If we interpret the fable consistently, we find that its narrative line forces the conclusion that woman's best hope is to work within the controlling sphere of a superior (presumably male) intelligence. In this way the Wife of Bath, like the lion she quotes, also speaks against herself, and can only do so in citing this story whose givens – animal versus human – already constrain interpretation, already load the dice. Chaucer must have savoured the multiple irony in his female character's appropriation of a female author's antifeminist poem. Marie did appropriate the means of discourse, she did paint the lion, and what she produced was a reaffirmation of the traditional order. Marie's *moralitas* is a pragmatic little piece of anti-utopianism advising the reader not to waste time on abstract imaginations, but to go with what works and what has always worked. Chaucer's strategy in this section of The *Canterbury Tales* is equally complex and equally retrograde.

Two women critics have recently produced interpretations of the Chaucerian reference which duplicate the interpretation given by the fictional character. I want to say immediately that the Wife of Bath does perform as what Judith Fetterley calls a 'resisting reader', and that this is for us a laudable thing. But I also want to say that if we think that Chaucer thought it a laudable thing, then we are suppressing a number of important critical issues. We are rewriting history and authoritative texts according to our utopian desire – much as the Wife of Bath does – and we are adding to the Wife of Bath's silences our own in effacing the really unpleasant dimensions in our cultural past, including its best-known literature. The question, I suppose, comes down to what constitutes effective resistance for the critic who sees the 'author-function' known as 'Chaucer' as something to be resisted, and who wishes therefore to be a resisting reader of Chaucer. We are, as critics, in the position of the Wife of Bath; but we are not written by a medieval writer and we do not need to adopt the tactics of a medieval fictional persona.

Mary Carruthers and Marjorie Malvern offer a much 'nicer' Chaucer than I do, a far more liberal one, in their interpretation of the Aesopian reference. As they see it, the fictional character uses the fable of the lion to teach the true relativity of perception and of moral judgement. The fable ultimately vindicates the Wife's recital by proving her position to be as valid as any other.

I am reminded of a similar interpretive controversy that appears in Laurie Finke's discussion of an essay by Josephine Donovan. The text in question is a *New Yorker* cartoon of a couple watching television. The woman remarks to the man: 'You missed the end, but it came out happily. She shot him.' Donovan argues that this caption represents an authentic, woman-identified interpretation of the TV show based in the woman viewer's empathic identification with the murderess which in turn is rooted in women's cultural experience. This is right as far as it goes, but it has to go further. Laurie Finke asks, on the other hand, 'Who is the butt of the cartoonist's joke, and why?' She suggests that the humour of the cartoon derives from our seeing this empathic identification as wrong or at least as stereotypically female, subjective even to the point of approving immorality: 'How like a woman to miss the point altogether, to substitute her experience for the author's intention.' This is right too, as far as it goes, and to take it further would be to see another, grimmer, humour in the dark impulses lurking beneath the quiet domestic scene. A temptation to violence can be approved while safely distanced on the TV screen, but it expresses dissatisfactions not admissible into the daily life of a comfortably married couple. To deconstruct all of these layers of meaning is important, but we would evade most of them by simply seeing the cartoon as unwittingly (or even purposely) pro-woman.

That some women critics have interpreted Marie's fable and Chaucer's allusion to yield a proto-feminist point is an ironically mistaken strategy in rewriting medieval culture. It is equally ironic that a Marxist critic, Terry Eagleton, should use a similar exemplum to conclude his discussion of political criticism: 'I shall end with an allegory. We know that the lion is stronger than the lion-tamer, and so does the lion-tamer. The problem is that the lion does not know it. It is not out of the question that the death of literature may help the lion to awaken' (*Literary Theory*, p. 217). The hope implied here is one that I endorse, and elsewhere in his book Eagleton puts it more openly: 'If literary theory presses its own implications too far, then it has argued itself out of existence. This . . . is the best possible thing for it to do' (p. 204); or, 'There is no way of settling the question of which politics is preferable in literary critical terms. You simply have to argue about politics' (p. 209). Nonetheless the lion-allegory is a particularly unfortunate and self-defeating piece of rhetoric. The vehicle does not yield the desired tenor, for many reasons. Oppressed and exploited people are not like animals; social revolution is not an instinctive, animalistic attack; a circus lion may wake or sleep without this affecting its subordination to the tamer; we can scarcely applaud a lion's attack on a human being; a lion-tamer remains intellectually superior to even a wakened lion, etc. To replace Orwell's pigs with Eagleton's lions is not much of an improvement. The task of extracting from this mini-allegory its significance for the author's overall political and moral vision isn't one that can be undertaken here. Still, it remains as true for critics as for novelists that their imagery stands like a herm at the edge of their assertions, indicating limits or extensions.

'Natural' and 'real'

I should like now to turn to another kind of silence that constitutes the Chaucerian representation of his female character. This is the omission of information about herself, which may seem a paradoxical assertion in view of the character's evident volubility.

Incontinent speech was presented, in the clerical tradition of social satire, as a female characteristic and vice. Certainly incontinent speech typifies the fictional speaker of III, 1–1264, a feature largely responsible for the ages-old critical consensus that 'she' is an especially 'real', 'natural', and convincing character. The autobiographical recital placed in the character's mouth is usually received as excruciatingly honest in its 'self'-revelation, while the character itself is analysed as an uninhibited extrovert, a libertine, a mysterious, complex and fascinating human being. Such psychologism is a stubborn residue of the now generally discredited 'roadside realism' approach to Chaucer.[3] That it persists indicates how hard the old habits die; but old habits die hard because attitudes do, and in the course of this chapter I should like to investigate some of the issues at stake in a reading of the Wife of Bath as a realistic character.

Whatever Chaucer has Dame Alice tell us, he keeps her silent about her work and her travel, those two arenas of experience that define her most distinctively as proto-modern woman. One approach to this absence might be to fill the gap with information about the realities of work and travel in the fourteenth century. This was Mary Carruthers's aim in her meticulously researched article on the WBT, the same one discussed from another angle in the first section of this chapter. If there the interpretation of a fable posed the problematic of feminist reading, here the supplying of factual background data requires us to consider how history is present in, or to, art. It is not necessarily the case that this presence will be most important at the empirical level. Nor is it necessarily true that the omission of empirical facts is an authorial oversight to be supplemented by the critic. I want to consider both a historical and a rhetorical approach to the silences in a text.

From a historical viewpoint, it is sometimes the case that long-term or large-scale factors of social stability and change are more relevant to artistic representation, or to conditions of production and consumption of art, than any specific immediate or local fact. It is also sometimes the case that long-term factors at least partially determine the specific immediate or local fact. This is why the cultural phenomena so lavishly and interestingly arrayed by new historicists often leave one, like the proverbial consumer of a Chinese dinner, hungry half an hour later. Not to beat about the bush, I am talking about substructure and superstructure here, and it is a shortcoming of the new historicism in various disciplines – not only literary criticism – that it often confines itself to the empirical or superstructural register without penetrating to longer-range developments. The price of wool does little, I think, to explain the Wife of Bath; the nature of early capitalism does a great deal more.

For instance: Despite her apparent volubility, Alice of Bath fails to discuss work and travel as aspects of her experience, though we know she is well able to do so. Nonetheless these activities are not completely absent from the text. They have been, as it were, internalised into the character's consciousness. By this I mean that Chaucer has given the character an idiom which is itself expressive of work and travel, even though these topics do not appear as explicit content. Chaucer has the Wife describe her sexual behaviour in the imagery of commerce: buying and selling, cheap and dear, market psychology.[4] He makes us believe thereby that the character has commodified her own sexuality. Moreover, we meet the character on a journey, during which she reveals that her entire being is predicated in mobility. She is constantly in motion, always ready for change. Stability is not her mode. This change or mobility may be literally horizontal: the gregariousness or lust that impels her to walk or ride about and that leads her eventually to take up a horizontal position in the sexual act. Or the movement may be figuratively vertical: social ambition and pride, embodying the aspiration and the social reality of the artisanal bourgeoisie.

In short, social reality or experience may make itself felt in a text in subtle and implicit ways, and it may appear only to be co-opted for the purposes of authority. The confrontation of misogynistic authority with female experience and desire is a case in point. The authoritative misogynist tradition is part of the Wife's experience. By way of the Church – sermons, liturgy, confession, dramas – it would have been part of her experience even without nightly readings by her scholarly fifth husband, Jankyn. Alice has absorbed this authority to refute it in light of her desire and her experience. Buut this intended subversion of orthodoxy is itself subverted by what the surrounding culture acknowledged as inadequacy. The character's exempla and allusions backfire; her 'self-revelation' confirms the worst stereotype as she reveals herself to be an ambitious, indiscreet, disloyal, lustful woman: 'a scourge and a blight', according to William Blake, 'a scarecrow' (Erdmanp. 528). Blake was right insofar as the representation does in its multiple ironies operate as a negative exemplum, affirming the values of the hegemonic culture.

Let me now move my argument to rhetorical or semiotic grounds. In 'Menelaiad', one of the pieces collected in Lost in the Funhouse, John Barth experiments with the problem of multiple voicing and direct discourse several times removed. At one point his narrator remarks, 'No matter; this isn't the voice of Menelaus; this voice is Menelaus, all there is of him.' Robert Jordan borrowed this line in his response to the Carruthers article, reminding readers of PMLA that the Wife of Bath's Prologue and Tale are 'not the voice of Alison; this voice is Alison, all there is of her.' The comment concerns the status of the letter, or in this case the status of the letter's absence. It is not that the character has neglected anything, it is not that the poet has neglected anything, it is that we are in the presence of a deliberate rhetorical strategy – a strategy of silence as I have chosen to call it.

Another response to the Carruthers article came from James Wimsatt. This stressed conventionality, suggesting that the medieval materials most relevant to our text are not experiential but authoritative; that is, not the economic conditions of cloth-makers but the literary tradition of marital satire. Jill Mann has shown how much the portraits of Chaucer's pilgrims owe to the literary tradition of medieval estates satire. The Chaucerian representation of women tends to support this sense of conventionality, for in several tales Chaucer strips a female character of individuality in order to highlight her exemplary function or to polarise moral conflict. Constance in The Man of Law's Tale is deprived of the blue-stocking education she had in Trivet's romance. Virginia in The Physician's Tale is not affianced to a champion of the people as in Livy, but becomes a passive twelve-year-old child. Ovid's eloquent Coronis shrinks to the anonymous victim-wife of The Manciple's Tale. Pertelote is no longer right, but wrong.

Moreover, very few of the Canterbury pilgrims of either sex reveal much about the ordinary details of their work. The Pardoner does, that Chaucer may the more clearly pose the paradox of the vicious cleric. And from the latecomer Canon's Yeoman we hear a description of his employer's fraudulent alchemical practices, that these may be rejected for old-fashioned faith. Characters within the tales are sometimes shown practising their trade as objects of social satire: one thinks of Oswald's Miller, or the Friar's Summoner. But for the pilgrims themselves, most are as silent about their work as is the Wife of Bath.

As for travel, John P. McCall remarks that although Chaucer himself had travelled in Italy, his description of that country in *The Clerk's Tale* is not derived from observation but from the literary source for the tale. 'Chaucer had seen a great deal of his world and has told us practically nothing about it', comments McCall. This is because setting 'was for Chaucer largely a matter of metaphor and symbol . . . a literary topos, a motif . . . to emphasise a moral condition of to amplify an idea' (p. 87).

The same principle may well apply, in Alice's case at least, to work; for her cloth-making is very likely a parody derived from no less authoritative a text than Holy Scripture: the Vulgate *Encomium mulieris fortis* (Proverbs 21: 10-31) with its portrait of the virtuous wife who spins and weaves and clothes herself in 'fortitudo et decor' (Boren). Indeed the Wife's clothmaking is overdetermined. Mann points out that 'the assumption that cloth-making is the duty of the feminine estate' is a commonplace in late-medieval satire, adding, 'The fact that we never hear again of the Wife's "clooth-makyng" strongly suggests that the only reason for introducing it . . . is to emphasise her estate function' (p. 122). That these literary sources coincide with a major English industry of the period, an industry in which women were strongly present, does not necessarily certify the priority of the real (that is, the social or experiential) in the Chaucerian hierarchy of value or in the poet's method of composition.

Analogous arguments can be made with respect to character, certainly in the case of the Wife of Bath. To have included genuinely realistic material about the experiences of work and travel would have meant producing a very different character, a very different text. It would have individuated the fictional character too much for Chaucer's moral (or moralistic) purpose. It would have rendered her too much a person, too little a type or exemplum of fallible human desire. In omitting from the explicit level the experiential dimensions of work and travel, Chaucer deliberately reduces the complexity of Dame Alice. There is certainly a logic to her as a literary figure or a sign, there may well be a psychology discernible through her recital – but it is not the logic or the psychology of a 'real' 'woman'.

To make my point from another angle I shall recall a modern work that shows interesting similarities to the Wife of Bath material. I have in mind D.H. Lawrence's story 'The Woman Who Rode Away'. Lawrence gives us another woman on horseback who travels on pilgrimage to a holy place (in this case an Indian ceremonial site in the mountains of Mexico). Lawrence's protagonist, like Chaucer's, is a middle-class woman with a history of marital dissatisfaction, and she is looking for something better. Like *The Canterbury Tales*, Lawrence's story is full of naturalistic, circumstantial detail: the appearances and clothing of characters, the physicality of horses, the exotic Mexican landscape. But who can believe in Lawrence's character as a 'real' woman? This empty, emblematic figure leaves her home, husband and children without a regret. She can imagine no other destination than the grim mountains. She never thinks about divorce or return to an American city. She never protests her abduction by Indians, or a tedious weeks-long imprisonment in an Indian mountain village, or the forced ingestion of hallucinogenic drugs. She never tries or wants to escape; she is never bored or lonely. In the end she accepts her death at the Indians' hands with utter passivity. In short, this character is defined not simply by silences, but by a virtually total silence. She is Lawrence's Griselda, only worse, since Chaucer's Griselda at least is shown to experience and express both love and sorrow. So grotesquely silent is the Lawrence figure that we can only read her as an iconic projection of the author's desire. There is nothing 'real' about her. Leo Steinberg furnishes me with a brilliant example of a related discussion in the visual arts. The genital display so often featured in Renaissance portraits of the infant Jesus has often been accounted for as simple naturalism, the product of close observation of ordinary life. Steinberg offers another explanation:

What is involved here is a misunderstanding of a critical truth: that naturalistic motifs in religious Renaissance art are never adequately accounted for by their prevalence in life situations. There are many things babies do – crawling on all fours, for instance, before they start walking – which no artist, however deeply committed to realism, ever thought of imputing to the Christ Child . . . In short, the depicted Christ, even in babyhood, is at all times the Incarnation – very man, very God. Therefore when a Renaissance artist quickens an infancy scene with naturalistic detail, he is not recording this or that observation, but revealing in the thing observed a newfound compatibility with his subject. (p. 8)

That compatibility, Steinberg proposes, lies in the doctrine of the humanation of Christ, which the genital display visually represents. It is not primarily a question of baby-portraits, any more than in the Chaucerian text it is a question of what real weavers' lives were like. It would be foolish to deny the importance of distinctively renaissance styles, commitment to the physical and to what Svetlana Alpers has called 'the art of describing'. What I think Steinberg intends is a broad view of other cultural developments that accompanied and enabled these styles. These comments return us to the problematic of 'roadside realism' with its assumption that a textual silence manifests either authorial oversight or individual psychology of the fictional character. The Wife of Bath's silences, Chaucer's silences, are the kind that Pierre Macherey has written of incisively:

It remains obvious that although the work is self-sufficient it does not contain or engender its own theory; it does not know itself . . . Critical discourse does not attempt to complete the book, for theory begins from that incompleteness which is so radical that it cannot be located.

Thus, the silence of the book is not a lack to be remedied, an inadequacy to be made up for. It is not a temporary silence that could be finally abolished. We must distinguish the necessity of this silence. For example, it can be shown that it is the juxtaposition and conflict of several meanings which produces the radical otherness which shapes the work: this conflict is not resolved or absorbed, but simply *displayed*.

Thus the work cannot speak of the more or less complex opposition which structures it, though it is its expression and embodiment. In its every particle, the work *manifests*, uncovers, what it cannot say. This silence gives it life. (pp. 83–4; italics in original)

To try to make this silence speak, as I am doing here, is not to ignore Macherey's own silence, which speaks volumes of history. I refer to his suppression of any reference to the writings of Leon Trotsky on literature, art and culture, though Trotsky's ideas suffuse Macherey's book. 'Like a planet revolving round an absent sun, an ideology is made of what it does not mention; it exists because there are things which must not be spoken of' (p. 132). To be sure, the Stalinists know this better than almost anyone else. The preceding words of Macherey, his gloss to Lenin's comment that 'Tolstoi's slences are eloquent', permits a glimpse of the unresolved conflict his own book displays, a glimpse of what is not said: the history of French intellectuals, of the PCF, of Stalinism itself.

To return now to the Wife of Bath: A real person with the Wife's experience would qualify as an authority in much more than 'wo that is in mariage'. If we take it on Chaucer's authority that such is the sum of the Wife's 'real' 'experience', do we not acquiesce in some version of 'biology is destiny' or 'woman's nature'? The portrait is partial and conventional. Based in estates satire, the *Roman de la Rose*, Scripture and other sources, it lacks work, travel and other dimensions of subjectivity.[5] In accepting such a portrait as 'realistic', do we not implicitly assent to a version of humanity produced by authorities we no longer take for granted?

We need not identify emotionally with the Wife of Bath to understand that we already are the Wife of Bath. We do work, we do travel, we do remarry, we do love more than one man in a lifetime, we do, many of us, revise or reject Scriptural authority. It would satisfy few of us of either sex to be criticised as the Wife of Bath is criticised by Chaucer and by many contemporary scholars: natural but wrong. As a summary of Chaucer's viewpoint, and that of the hegemonic culture that speaks through him (albeit not without its and therefore his contradictions), this is not incorrect. But as a statement about life – which is implied in the terms 'realistic' or 'natural' – it is indequate at best, at worst homicidal: an implication realised in the Lawrence story discussed above. We would want, I think, to claim what Arlyn Diamond has called 'the authority of experience': our own experience.

What do women want?

In a limited way the claim of experience was made in writing during Chaucer's time by a few women. One of them – Margery Kempe, fifteenth-century author of the first English autobiography – did write about work, travel and the subjective dimensions of marriage. Moreover, she did assert her unique religious experience against the authority of husband and Church, though at serious cost to her health, sanity and reputation. Another – the Franco-Italian courtier and scholar Christine de Pizan – asserted the validity of individual experience and perception. In doing so, Christine put the Aristotelian-Thomistic discussion of 'certaine science' (certain knowledge as opposed to mere opinion) to a new use: the validation of women's experience against the clerical miso-gynist tradition (Cité 1:2). That Chaucer was unable or unwilling to voice a similar social or psychological realism is surely the consequence of his own experience and desires, mediated as these are by gender, social position, religious tendency and choice of textual authorities.

'What does Woman want?' asked Freud ('Was will das Weib?'), and so Chaucer has his knight ask in The Wife of Bath's Tale. It is what logicians term a non-question, a pseudo-problem, for there is no way to verify, or even to find, a single and 'correct' answer. That is doubtless why Chaucer locates and resolves the question in the realm of magic. It is as unanswerable as the question posed at the end of The Franklin's Tale as to which man was most generous. It is a conundrum which we answer only by demonstrating our gullibility; that is, our acceptance of its deceptive terms. If at the end of The Franklin's Tale we want to decide whether the husband was most generous in giving his wife, the lover in renouncing his paramour, or the magician in cancelling his fee, then we have already accepted the premise that a woman is a possession on a par with money, an object without will or moral responsibility. And that would be as misleading an illusion as any the magician can produce. If we have taken the ideological point of The Franklin's Tale, we will have understood that some questions are better left unanswered – or, like Dorigen's questions about marriage and nature, answered by faith and authority. One might add that Dorigen does provide an example of what Mary Carruthers calls 'painting the lion': she tries to create a new social form (the egalitarian marriage) only to abandon the effort in crisis and return, humbly, to the protective authority of an old-fashioned man, her husband.

'What do women want?' has always seemed to me a silly question. Its silliness can be appreciated if we substitute any other group for 'women', such as 'Jews', 'men', or 'blacks'. When we do this, we see that it isn't really a question about women but a question about excluded groups. 'What does anybody want?' is the import of the question, and the answer is so simple and obvious as to be a non-answer: everything, of course, whatever there is; and why should women be any different? To have to ask this question requires the suppression of one's own experience and desires, for to consult them is to know what is generally wanted. It requires also the distancing of the given group from a concept of normative humanity, the idea being that even if one knew what oneself wanted this surely could not be what They want too. Much of this is already implied in the collective singular Freud used in his formulation rather than the plural: woman rather than women. He chose the abstract universal which in denying specificity also denies similarity to oneself, thus maintaining radical otherness.

What has always intrigued readers about the Wife of Bath is that she has managed in spite of everything to get so much and to maintain her desire for more. She would welcome a sixth husband 'whenever he shal', and would even like to be young, rich and gorgeous again. Who wouldn't? Perhaps even Chaucer would. If we read the tale as the Wife's projection of her own desires, we may see it as a kind of regressive utopianism, a revision of the national and personal past in magical accordance with impossible ideals.

But utopianism is no virtue in the Middle Ages, and we have been taught to dissociate author from character. Whose is the pre-feudal nostalgia of the tale, though; and whose wishes are being fictionally fulfilled? Who asks the question 'What do women want?' One thing we can be sure women do not want is rape.[6] The criminal knight does not know this at the start of the tale, or does not care. Presumably the protest of his victim's outraged family, and the subsequent death-sentence, provide enlightenment. This sentence, however, is averted by the intervention of noble women in a gesture of class solidarity over sex solidarity and even, evidently, over the law of the land. Other questions arise. Should rape be a capital offence? Should King Arthur accept his wife's proposal of a lesser punishment? Should the rapist be rewarded, after a year, with a wife at once beautiful, rich and true? Is the knight's crime expiated by his year of anxious searching for an answer to the 'riddle' of what women want? Such questions are often approached through character: the tale is the fantasy of a woman who has so thoroughly internalised male chauvinism, even against her conscious will, that her own proto-feminist desires are subverted in the end. So enthusiastic is she about the idea of a husband who is young, rich, noble and malleable that she is willing to forgive his crime. Or – a variant – we are given a character who, try as she may to revise traditional antifeminist values, can only affirm them in spite of herself, thus proving the inescapable, necessary or 'natural' force of those values. Or – another variant – rebellious character successfully challenges hegemonic values which are shown to be alterable.

But the story is equally convincing as the fantasy of a courtier-poet whose experience with rape and betrayal may have been uncomfortably close to hand. Of the many extant versions and analogues of the tale, only Chaucer's has the questing knight a rapist. It is a bold revision; it ups the ante about as far as it can go. The social motive it provides for the life-and-death plot was legally realistic: penalties for rape in Chaucer's day included 'loss of life and of member'. The rape is a node that concentrates legal, moral, sexual, psychological and class issues in a single act. If pastorale commemorates and romanticises the chance meetings of knights with country girls, the Wife's tale represents the magicalised aftermath of pastorale.

It is easy enough – too easy – to deny the rapist knight any role in the figuration of the poet's experience or desire. We are reluctant to hear in this text a male and culturally dominant voice because the text presents itself so stridently as 'female'. Does it protest too much? Is the presentation convincing? It certainly has been, by and large, though that must depend on one's critical orientation. In interrogating the question the knight asks, we might detect beneath it another one: 'What do men think that women want?' Which translates in turn as 'What do men want women to want?' and 'What do men want?' or, more directly, 'What do I want?' It doesn't matter that in the tale the original question is both set and answered by a woman, because only a man could ask this question, and it can only be asked on behalf of men.[7]

This would remain a narrowly feminist line of inquiry if I did not go on to ask 'On behalf of which men?' Medieval misogyny is blatantly the product of political struggles within and by the Catholic Church over a period of several centuries. In order to give itself an image of moral rigour with which to compete with the popular heresies; in order to assure to itself the inalienable property of its bureaucracy; in order to secure its privileges by controlling the lives, down to the most intimate details, of its mass membership – for all of these reasons at various times the Church developed and maintained a long-lasting campaign of ascetic reform. Clerical celibacy, the exclusion of women from orders, the monogamous nuclear family, supervaluation of virginity, and the accompanying propaganda depreciating women and sexuality were the tactics in this campaign. To know how well it succeeded we need only observe ourselves. Yet this tendency was not absolutely hegemonic in medieval culture, it was contested. Heresies contested it, often quite effectively. So did social reality in which women functioned well in labour and commerce; so did various theoreticians within the Church; so did the ordinary practice of many churchmen. In short, the viewpoint represented in the Wife of Bath's recital had to be chosen against others.

So, of course, did the action of individuals. A strongly persuasive circumstantial argument has been made by P.R. Watts, a historian of medieval law, that Chaucer did commit rape. The *raptus* from responsibility for which, in 1380, Cecily Chaumpaigne released the poet, is likely to have been a sexual assault, no abduction for a friend's marriage as Chaucerians have usually preferred to believe. That Chaucer was able to escape the serious legal consequences of this charge may well have been due to the lady's (for him) fortuitous pregnancy which – thanks to medieval sex lore – would have annihilated her legal case. According to medieval medicine, pregnancy followed from orgasm ('female semination') which in turn implied a consenting will and therefore obviated rape.

A similarly persuasive and similarly circumstantial argument has been made on the basis of heraldry. For Kraus, the heraldic reading of Thomas Chaucer's tomb, together with other information, suggests that Chaucer's jet-set wife, the French noblewoman and courtier Philippa

Payne de Roet, was mistress of John of Gaunt both before and during her marriage to the poet. Her son Thomas Chaucer may have been sired by John of Gaunt. The poet's own experience might therefore have posed rather clearly both the dilemma of the fair and faithless wife, and the question of attitudes toward rape.

In the absence of conclusive evidence, such speculation must remain hypothetical. It is certainly no more hypothetical than many other speculations about less distasteful matters of the poet's life, or about the dating and chronology of his works. The interest of the speculations made here is that they ask us to bring into play the experience and desires of the poet who stands behind the fiction, those of his culture, and those of the critics, ourselves, who stand before it.

The haunted work: politics and the paralysis of poetic imagination in *The Physician's Tale*

The fortunes of a single story surviving through radically different cultures can offer a clearly focused case-history in the reception and reproduction of tradition. *Translatio studii* – the carrying over of knowledge from classical to medieval times – is a central and fascinating phenomenon in medieval intellectual life, and in many cases a primary condition of literary production. The advantage of that condition is expressed in the oft-cited metaphor of Bernard of Chartres: 'If we see further than our ancestors did, it is because we are dwarves seated on the shoulders of giants.'[1] A self-conscious modernity is evident here despite the apparent modesty, as well as a certain self-congratulatory confidence in a strong, unbroken and supportive tradition.

Yet medieval intertextuality did not always or necessarily produce such confidence, nor did it necessarily produce a superior, more 'far-seeing' version of classical narrative. My case-study here will be *The Physician's Tale*, generally conceded to be one of Chaucer's least interesting and least successful efforts. The piece displays flat characters, a rather incompetent narrative flawed by irrelevant digressions, a plot exceedingly improbable, and – unlike *The Clerk's Tale* or *The Man of Law's Tale* – no redeeming symbolic depth. I want to propose that the collision of Chaucer's social views with those of his sources produced, in *The Physician's Tale*, an imaginative impasse manifested in the aesthetic inferiority of the tale.

What stands out in *The Physician's Tale*, setting it apart from Chaucer's sources and from other medieval versions of the Virginius legend accessible to him, is the virtually complete depoliticisation of a political anecdote.

The story of Virginius – who kills his daughter rather than see her coerced by legal fraud ino a life of fornication – was known to the Middle Ages in Livy's history of Rome (Titus Livius, *Ab Urbe Condita* III:44 ff.). Livy adapted it in turn from an older regional legend. Chaucer probably used Livy's history, at least as a supplement to his main source, the *Roman de la Rose* of Jean de Meun. Livy's theme was the degeneration of Rome from its great republican golden age: he sets the legend of Virginius in the mid-fifth century B.C., some 400 years in the past, during a period of intense conflict between plebs and patriciate.[2] The legend shows how tyrannical were the patrician rulers and how oppressed the plebs; it also serves to justify the 'Third Roman Revolution' of 449 B.C. which won important gains for the plebs. Appius Claudius, the judge who prevents justice in the interest of lust, is a patrician and decemvir. Virginius is a plebeian and military man. Virginia is engaged to marry Icilius, also a plebeian and a noted champion of his class. The other important *dramatis persona* in Livy's account is the Roman populace, who are present throughout the story. Virginia's arrest occurs in the crowded forum; the people foil the seizure and offer bail for her; the trial and sentence are public, as is the murder. Protesting the atrocity to which Virginius has been forced to save his daughter's honour, the people unite with the army to depose Appius and the rest of the decemvirate. They demand and win restoration of the people's tribunes – plebeian magistrates whose veto could protect the plebs against unjust patrician legislation. They also win the right to judicial appeal, and a series of measures is passed (the Valerian-Horatian laws) which increased plebeian powers. Appius kills himself in prison; his accomplice goes into exile; Roman popular liberties are restored.

Jean de Meun relied on Livy for his account of the story, but in several ways depoliticised it. Specific social classes are not named (except that Virginius is 'bons chevaliers bien renomez');[3] the populace enter only at the end to save Virginius from hanging; no insurrection follows although Appius is imprisoned, his witnesses condemned to death, and the accomplice sent into exile. Nonetheless, in its context Jean's version retains a clear social thrust; for Jean, exploring the conception of justice in general and specifically its relation to wealth, contrasts a golden age of primitive justice with the social stratification and oppression of his own epoch (5345-74). Indeed the tale of Virginius immediately follows Genius's vision of a classless and stateless society in which justice is no longer required to mediate right and wrong, nor is any special judicial, legislative, or repressive apparatus necessary, for

puis que Forfez s'en iroit,	since Crime would be gone,
Joutice, de quoi serviroit? (5523–4)	what use would Justice serve?

car se ne fust maus et pechiez,	for if there were no evil and sin,
dom li mondes est entechiez,	with which the world is infected,
l'en n'eust onques roi veu	you'd never have seen a king
ne juige en terre conneu. (5537-40)	nor would a judge be known on earth.

Of course Jean speaks here not as a utopian socialist but as a Christian humanist; the society Genius describes is presumably not to be attained on earth but only in heaven. This is a moral vision with a political effect: to expose and denounce the perversion of social justice by the rich. To this end Genius brings in the Roman exemplum.

Though there is no hard evidence that Chaucer borrowed from Boccaccio's version of the Virginius legend in *De Claris Mulieribus* (1:8), it was from that work that Chaucer drew material for the story of Zenobia (*The Monk's Tale*),and it seems reasonable to suppose that he at least skimmed the rest of the volume. Boccaccio began to compose his text in 1361, toward the end of a period of intense political activity when, as orator, counsellor, diplomat, and elected representative, he served the Florentine city-state in its complicated municipal and international affairs. The work is close in spirit to Livy, its source, for Boccaccio – an ardent partisan of republican rights in 'the good and holy Commune' – uses the legend of Virginius to advance his *haut bourgeois* republican ideals. Vittore Branca's comment about one of Boccaccio's letters could as well apply to his version of our legend: that it is 'the clear reflection of intensely mediated personal experience' (p. 129).[4] As in Livy, class lines are sharply drawn: decemvirs versus plebs. Virginius's deed is described as one that, despite its severity, secured Roman liberties; the populace plays a prominent role throughout. After the insurrection of army and people, Virginius is chosen tribune and sentences Appius to prison, where he commits suicide. There follows a long diatribe against unjust judges and a passionate denunciation of tyrants in general for their arrogance, violence, corruption, and licence. We recall that Boccaccio hated tyrannical feudal aristocrats and reproached his friend Petrarch for making his home at their courts.

Chaucer's close friend John Gower included the legend of Virginius as the penultimate exemplum in Book 7 of his *Confessio Amantis*. While the independence of Chaucer's text is generally acknowledged, he would certainly have had easy access to Gower's work after 1390, its publication date, and probably was aware of it before that date. Gower used the legend to an end at once moral and political: to exhort rulers to avoid vice and its socially disruptive consequences. Book 7 is a political treatise on the place of good governance in the universe – a mirror for magistrates in the broadest sense – and, as in the Roman de la Rose, the spokesman is Genius. As John H. Fisher shows, Gower did indeed have a political axe to grind: he was committed to the Lancastrian cause and in 1392 or 1393 changed the dedication of the Confessio from Richard II to Henry Bolingbroke, for Richard's intemperate financial policies had alienated many of Gower's – and Chaucer's – friends in the London business community. In the tale, Appius is referred to as 'king;' Virginius urges the army to correct domestic injustice before engaging in foreign wars; the people's revolt is vindicated because they do uphold justice and law; constantly we hear the phrases 'comun lawe', 'comun right', 'comun fere', 'comun counseil'. Gower's treatment of thm tale is very much at home in the social-protest tradition already sketched: its spirit is not a republican spirit, but it does reflect real partisanship in admonishing a tyrannical ruuler on behalf of his citizenry.

A certain consenus appears, then, among the four authors discussed so far. Whether lust or injustice is treated as the main theme, social criticism remains a key element in the story; the latter may be conveyed in dramatic action, in authorial comment, or in both. Turning to The Physician's Tale, we find that only it lacks a clear political thrust. Only Chaucer systematically obliterates the traditional social content of the legend of Virginius and fails to replace it with explicit social commentary in his own or a narrator's voice. In so doing, I suggest, he deprives the story of convincing dramatic motivation and his characters of plausible psychological and ethical motives. I want now to examine the changes Chaucer made in the tale, along with their aesthetic consequences.

The theme of class conflict is effaced in several ways. Virginius is a knight 'of greet richesse' (4) and Appius a local governor, so that they are more or less on the same social level. Icilius, Virginia's fiancé and champion of the people, is dropped from the story altogether (as in Jean), an omission which further obscures the theme of political struggle. Of course the elimination of Icilius also gives us a more saint-like and pathetic picture of Virginia. It intensifies her will to virginity, creating a more starkly moralistic counterposition to the lust of Appius.

The population, always so crucial to this tale, also disappears from Chaucer's story. Most of the action occurs in private, and, as in the Roman, the people intervene only to rescue Virginius – not one of their own class, as in Livy or Boccaccio, but one of the ruling class: Virginius must be a virtuous knight indeed to generate such loyalty among the masses.

However, the absence of the populace from the body of the tale introduces some narrative puzzles. If Virginia is 'strong of freendes' (135),
why is there no earlier protest or intervention? And how likely is it that
the people would intervene to save a knight, motivated only for 'routhe
and for pitee' (261), or, moreoever, depose their district governor merely
because 'They wisten wel that he was lecherus' (266), without perceiving
this crisis as an opportunity to present demands on their own behalf?
Such altruism scarcely corresponds to what Chaucer could observe of
'the people' in his own turbulent time. Nor does it correspond to the
role played by the general populace in The Clerk's Tale, who are present at
critical moments in the narrative and are shown to be fickle and
treacherous.[5] Thus in The Physician's Tale the people's intervention is devoid
of social motive, while their moral motive is unconvincing.

To reduce or eliminate the political dimension in a political anecdote
must alter the equilibrium of a narrative. Here it increases the relative
weight of the murder. In Livy, Virginia's death is provoked by an unjust
system of government and in turn provokes popular revolt. The social
component in Livy lets us share the plebs' view of the murder as a
desperate act by an intolerably victimised member of the oppressed
class. We can derive satisfaction, too, from the redress of grievances that
is achieved when that class forcefully asserts its rights. With Jean de
Meun, the murder justifies Genius's denunciation of the abuse of justice
by the rich. Even though Jean gives no social redress in the form of
rebellion, he expresses general indignation against the wicked wealthy
who provoke such extreme acts as the murder. Hence there is some
legitimation of rebellion, at least to the extent that the rebellion protests
tyranny.

Since Chaucer omits both the revolt and any commentary on social
injustice, there is neither dramatic nor thematic justification for the
atrocity. It becomes a more or less free-floating *acte gratuite*: it becomes
unnecessary. We must focus, then, on moral justification: 'outher deeth
or shame' (214). But this choice seems shallow. Virginius could consider
taking his daughter away; he could find a substitute for her, bribe his way
out of the dilemma, appeal the decision to higher authority (in Livy, of
course we know that the plebs could not do this; but Chaucer gives us no
reason why not). How much does the father want his daughter to survive
if he fails to consider these possibilities? We recall that escape with
Criseyde is one of the options that Chaucer makes available to Troilus;
further, that Troilus's rejection of such decisive action is presented as
consistent with his general deplorable passivity (35-6). Is the killing, then,

a monstrous, unnatural act, or the necessary sacrifice of a Christian martyr? The new Chaucerian context forces forward Virginius's determination to kill the girl. That determination now becomes the story's dramatic centre, displacing the social theme. But the motivation and literary consistency formerly provided in the social theme are not replaced in other material that might justify the sacrifice: praise of chastity, exemplary saints' lives, scriptural precedent, and so forth – material of the kind that allows us to see, for instance, the equally outrageous or offensive action of The Clerk's Tale as appropriate to Chaucer's aesthetic and moral purposes (explained quite lucidly by the Clerk at the end of his tale). The original material that Chaucer does add only compounds our discomfort since it seems so irrelevant and, unlike other Chaucerian 'irrelevancies', for no discernible reason.[6] The story falls between two stools: its 'realistic' (social) dimension is gone, but nothing propels it to a different level of fictional meaning.

Let me return to the list of alternatives available to Virginius. None of the possibilities that I mentioned above would be as realistic or as effective as another: Virginius could raise a popular revolt against Appius. (It is worth noting, again, that among the last-minute possibilities Troilus considers is to raise a riot on Criseyde's behalf: V, 43–6.) Clearly this is his best chance to save Virginia, and if the population can be aroused after the murder, surely they could be moved to prevent it. (We might make the same objection to Livy and versions close to him, except that there the death is dramatically necessary to justify the revolt or, later, invective.) But here precisely is Chaucer's double bind. Virginia cannot be saved without mass action; her death cannot be fully meaningful nor fully avenged without mass action; yet mass action is just what Chaucer excises from the legend.

In response to such criticism one could propose, as Middleton has done, that all of the foregoing problems are intentionally present as part of Chaucer's artful ironic vision; that they force us to 'examine, define and redefine ethical abstractions that are treated as given in his originals', that we are not supposed to fully suspend disbelief in the work because in that margin of discomfort we contemplate 'a world of wider and more emotionally complex choices than the source tale offers' (p. 15).

In my view there are deficiencies in such an apologia for The Physician's Tale. One is that the sources do not strike me as less complex or realistic than Chaucer's version but as more so. The given in the sources is not 'ethical abstraction' but the ongoing struggle for social justice; this, Chaucer scarcely 'chips away at' – he simply ignores it. He fails to encounter the sources on their own terrain, as he would have to do to undercut that terrain – the procedure in *Troilus*, for example. Thus if the argument is that Chaucer shows the inadequacy of both Livy (because nothing justifies murder, not even revolution) and the Physician (because he passes over the atrocity too easily), then surely Chaucer's case would be far stronger it if made some connection between republican politics and the notorious rationalism of physicians.

At a certain point critics arrive at irreducible opinion. While acknowledging that some of Chaucer's best work purposely distances the reader in the interest of moral judgement, I don't believe that *The Physician's Tale* occupies that category, but rather that it is, simply, a bad piece of work no matter how we read it. Professor Middleton has compiled an extensive list of flaws and problems in the tale – she agrees it is 'dull and inferior', 'a dull little tale' – yet she maintains that the piece is not inartistic. I take it this means it is not an aesthetic failure, but I should think such a list does amount to a statement of aesthetic failure: the test of artistic quality isn't only that 'the marks of making are there' but that they succeed in producing a work that is on some level coherent. The problem with *The Physician's Tale* is that we don't care enough about it to fall into the trap of suspending disbelief in the first place. If virtually every flaw and mediocrity in the tale is a deliberate distancing device, where's the good stuff – the tempting, persuasive material that we need to be distanced from? And what does the tale offer us that is better than the sources? Nothing, as far as I can see.

Another angle: any story of public maladministration must objectively pose the issue of social justice. How did the corrupt official attain his position? Has he too much power? Are others complicit in the abuse? Are only individuals, or is an entire system, at fault? One scarcely needs to be a revolutionary to ask such questions: our other authors are no flaming radicals. But Chaucer, unlike the others, is unwilling to draw out the question implicit in his plot. He deplores the corruption of Appius as an individual, but does not generalise from the incident: yet it is generalisation that confers on this story its more serious interest and importance.

The last creative stalemate I wish to discuss pertains to the people. Chaucer will not show the people as collective hero, cleansing society with purgative revolt. Yet in traditional versions of the tale, the people are precisely a collective hero. This function can be demonstrated by superimposing on Livy's tale a structural grid suggested by V. Propp's analysis of folktale, as follows: 1. One of the members of a family absents himself.

(Virginius is away in the army.) 4. The villain makes an attempt at reconnaissance. (Appius tries to seduce Virginia.) 6. The villain attempts to deceive his victim in order to take possession of him or his belongings. (Appius initiates a false court case in which his agent claims Virginia as his abducted servant.) 8. The villain causes harm or injury to a member of a family. (Appius is morally responsible for the murder of Virginia; he is able to consummate his plot because the plebs have no right of appeal.) 9. Misfortune or lack is made known; the hero is approached with a request or command; he is allowed to go or he is dispatched. (Virginius appeals to a mixed crowd of civilians and soldiers to defend him and themselves against the patriciate.) 10. The seeker agrees to or decides upon counteraction. (Civilians and soldiers march on Rome.) 16. The hero and the villain join in direct combat. (There is no actual war but the threat of imminent attack by the massed and armed population suffices to carry the day.) 18. The villain is defeated. (Appius and other decemvirs are deposed.) 19. Initial misfortune or lack is liquidated. (Virginia is not revived, as occurs in some tales, but the legislative power of the patriciate, morally the cause of her death, is eliminated in the new legislation: right of appeal – 'the one real safeguard of liberty' – is stressed.) 30. The villain is punished. (Appius is jailed and commits suicide before the trial; other decemvirs go into exile.) 31. The hero is married and ascends the throne. (The plebs eventually win the right to intermarry with patricians and to hold the highest civic offices; liberty and harmony are restored.)

In short, then, the role of the people is not merely a theme in our tale but part of its very morphology, its structure of relations. Chaucer reduces the real hero of his story, without providing another. Simultaneously, though, he cannot eliminate the people completely, nor deprecate them too far by showing them vicious or fickle, for they do after all side with the right person (and must do if injustice is not to flourish). So that 'the people', in The Physician's Tale, occupy a fictional never-never land. They are agents of justice and moral retribution, but must not be shown to act in their own legitimate interest, must not be allowed to 'go too far', above all must not emerge from the story as a genuinely sympathetic model for social action.

To glorify rebellion – the original aim of the Virginius legend – is utterly alien to Chaucer's world-view: our poet is a prosperous, socially conservative, prudent courtier and civil servant, directly dependent for his living upon the good will of kings and dukes. Whether despite or because of his position, throughout his creative life Chaucer struggled with the question of truth in art. It is curious, then, that here, where Chaucer's truth differs so sharply from that of the received tradition, the question is not raised. For Chaucer, more conservative than any of the other four writers discussed above, the challenge is to transform a political anecdote into a moral tale: to rework a tract for the times into a tract for all time. But in this case at least, the material is simply not that tractable, it is not infinitely receptive; as sculptors and wood-carvers know, the material sometimes suggests its own completed form. Remove social complexity from the legend of Virginius and you are left with insipid moralising and trite sentimentality, a protagonist of dubious character, an unjustified crime.

Yet the social function is cryingly there *because* of its exclusion, especially once we are aware of its role in other versions. The effaced trace remains a conspicuous absence, demanding recognition. In a sense the entire text could be read as a structure of absences: not only the absence of popular insurrection but of a hero, of resistance by the main characters, of convincing motives, of an ideological or aesthetic centre. In this way the text verges on a kind of pornographic or free-floating sadistic sensationalism, with the murder as its only real centre. The atypicality of the text emerges even more sharply when we compare Chaucer's procedure here with that in several other works.

Chaucer's exclusion of the social function in *The Physician Tale* is noteworthy because we have seen him revise some sources in the same direction, others in the opposite, and in both cases succeed brilliantly. With *The Reeve's Tale* and other *fabliaux*, social content is deliberately heightened in order to sharpen the ironic edge of the work by exposing pretentious social ambition (see Chapter 7 above). In *Troilus*, Chaucer adds a solid backdrop of social reality – war, parliament, the mechanics of seduction, ruling class dinners and flirtations, inconvenient conjectures about age and experience – which contributes to ironically undercutting romance convention and the courtly love ethos, and consequently to orchestrating the Christian ideology that is counterposed throughout, explicitly in the finale. In *The Clerk's Tale* Chaucer keeps the population as an important element in the story (adding to the Petrarchan source some strong vituperation against their unreliability), the better to create an allegory meaningful on the social as well as moral and doctrinal levels (people are to ruler as wife to husband and humanity to God).

So we know that Chaucer can augment the social content of his sources as a powerful instrument of exposure or commentary. But he is also able to diminish the social content of his source, or invert its social-satirical edge, with equal effect: *The Nun's Priest's Tale* illustrates this (see Chapter 10), as does *The Man of Law's Tale*.

What these samples indicate is that whether Chaucer augments or reduces the social dimension of his source, the net effect is to polarise moral issues more intensely than the source does, to dot the i's and cross the t's as it were, to provide a clearer ideological and aesthetic centre for the work as a platform from which the reader may be instructed and may judge: 'For oure book seith, "Al that is writen is writen for oure doctrine", and that is myn entente' (Retraction to *The Canterbury Tales*).

Two corollaries may now be posited. One is that social reality in art is not necessarily the hallmark of a 'progressive' world-view, but may constitute a stylistic element in the service of conservatism. Second, the degree of social content, or the political stance, in a given work is not correlated to its aesthetic success. *The Reeve's Tale* succeeds, as does *The Man of Law's Tale*, despite their very different levels of social reality. Most of Chaucer's works succeed, with (I deliberately avoid 'despite') their social conservatism. Indeed one might suggest that Chaucer succeeds not 'despite' his politics at all, but because of them, insofar as Augustinian orthodoxy gave him the certainty necessary to write effectively, laying to rest the earlier ambivalence manifest in *The House of Fame*. I am reminded here of Balzac's remarks from the Preface to *La Comédie Humaine*:

The law of the writer, by virtue of which he is a writer . . . is his judgment, whatever it may be, on human affairs, and his absolute devotion to certain principles . . . 'A writer ought to have settled opinions on morals and politics; he should regard himself as a tutor of men; for men need no masters to teach them to doubt,' says Bonald. I took these noble words as my guide long ago, they are the written law of the monarchical writer just as much as that of the democratic writer.

The immense creative energy of *The Wife of Bath's Tale* suggests that at some level Chaucer, like Balzac in contradiction to his actual social views, may have seen 'the men of the future where, for the time being, they alone were to be found', or that he at least sensed in the bourgeoisie that vitality and 'brainy opportunism' lacking in the decaying feudal aristocracy.[7] Perhaps it was that visceral sympathy (sympathy for the devil, as Blake hypothesised of Milton) that produced in Dame Alice one of the most vividly powerful characters in world literature. May we speculate about *The Physician's Tale* that the relevant social reality (insurrection) was simply too dangerous to write about for a courtier with everything to lose, or that it was not a topic appropriate to Chaucer's talent? Revolt is an absolute, not to be put in its place (like an 'uppity woman') with irony. It transcends rhetoric, or, as Leon Trotsky wrote of the Bolsheviks, 'They were adequate to the epoch and its tasks. Curses in plenty resounded in their direction, but irony would not stick to them – it had nothing to catch hold of.' One wonders if that is the real fear behind the multiple absences that constitute The Physician's Tale: that the tempestuous, ambitious bourgeoisie might after all prove adequate to the task, just as the plebs had done.

We do not know whether Chaucer thought, with his friend Gower and, later, the Tudor preachers, that rebels are beasts and the creatures of Satan: his silence on the rebellions of his own day is notorious.[8] In any case, the tale at hand permits no outright denunciation of rebellion, so that Chaucer is left in a narrative, structural, and ideological limbo, neither with the people nor against them.

If we know the 'Balade de Bon Conseyl' – also known as 'Truth' – we can hardly be surprised that the tradition of middle-class insurrection and republican rights evoked from Chaucer no energetic creative response. I doubt we can know what drew Chaucer to take up the story of Virginia in the first place, and am content to hazard a guess that if the project taught him something as an artist, it was the importance of choosing material more suitable to his own temperament. For us it suggests that poetic failure may be as instructive as poetic success, as productive a field for the play of criticism. All the more so when failure signals the history shaping a tradition that is as far from unbroken as the history itself. To attend to those connections is, as Pierre Macherey puts it, 'to trace the path which leads from the haunted work to that which haunts it' (p. 94). It is not, he adds, 'a question of redoubling the work with an unconscious, but a question of revealing in the very gestures of expression that which it is not. Then, the reverse side of what is written will be history itself.'

'Mulier est hominis confusio': the anti-popular Nun's Priest's Tale

The journal in which this article was first published – a special issue of *Mosaic* called 'For Better or Worse. Attitudes Toward Marriage in Literature' – featured on its cover a photograph of Grant Wood's famous 1930 painting 'American Gothic'. The title originally proposed for the special number was 'Discord in Marriage', and the reproduction was clearly intended to suggest something negative about marriage. In its austerity and in its religious reference (which is also, conveniently for my purpose, a medieval reference), we are evidently intended to see an icon of the institution of marriage, especially its repressive and oppressive power.

In fact, the models for the painting were not married nor even related. They were Wood's sister Nan and his dentist, Dr B.H. McKeeby. The house, with its nineteenth-century Gothic-revival window, stood in Eldon, Iowa. Moreover there is nothing in the painting itself to imply marriage as its special theme: the couple could be brother and sister or father and daughter, or either one could be the other's employer or employee: she housekeeper, he handyman. What relationship we read into the painting scarcely matters. What matters is that we do tend to read into the painting some relation of power, and the economic marginality represented in the painting seems to render any power-relation between the figures the only social power they do have.

Still, that the painting has achieved iconic status in North American culture, and that the editors of *Mosaic* relied upon its status to produce an automatic interpretation which would carry the import of their special issue, says something about how a work of art maintains popularity through continual reinterpretation, whether this is consistent with or at the expense of its original reality or intention. This chapter is about popularity and reinterpretation as displayed in the representation of marriage in several late-medieval texts.

When George Lyman Kittredge proposed his 'marriage group' for *The*

Canterbury Tales in 1912, he did not include *The Nun's Priest's Tale* as one in which Chaucer aimed to explore the marital relation. Kittredge's group consisted only of *The Wife of Bath's*, *Clerk's*, *Merchant's* and *Franklin's Tales*. Yet the couple relation is central to many of Chaucer's works from mid-career onward, and in most cases it is a marital relation he writes of. A list of tales in which the dynamic of a marriage shapes plot and moral would certainly add, to the four just listed, those of Miller, Man of Law, Shipman, Manciple, Nun's Priest and perhaps Melibee. Although some of the comedy of NPT does rely on parody of the conventions of courtly love, nonetheless it is clear that Chauntecleer and Pertelote are meant to be seen as a wedded pair. She is referred to as one of his 'wyves' (2883); she comments that women desire brave 'housbondes' (2914), not cowards; she cried 'louder than dide Hasdrubales wyf / Whan that hir housbonde hadde lost his lyf' (3363-4); the other hens are compared to 'senatoures wyves' (3371). The bond between the central characters in NPT is a sexual and long-term domestic one. It may not be a monogamous marriage, but it is a marriage.

Moreover, if we include couples linked by clandestine marriage (whether or not we consider that link a morally binding one, as H.A. Kelly does), then we may place Troilus and Criseyde on our list, along with most of the couples in *The Legend of Good Women*. It is clear, then, that Chaucer used the couple relationship as a kind of open field on which a number of battles might be fought: experience versus authority, rebellion versus submission, impetuosity versus prudence, determinism versus free will, passivity versus moral action, as well as conflicts centring on money, possessive jealousy or utopianism.

The facts and probabilities we possess about the poet's life suggest a marriage, and a subjective experience of marriage, far from the culturally projected ideal of his day – or, for that matter, of our day. (The ideals, alas, are not substantially different, despite widely variant practise in both epochs.) The young man was already married in his early twenties, by 1366. His wife, Philippa Payne de Roet, a French lady-in-waiting in the royal retinue, was of considerably higher social rank than the middle-class Londoner and civil servant she married. Throughout her career Philippa maintained an independent career, receiving in her own name gifts and pensions from her brother-in-law and chief patron John of Gaunt, arguably the most powerful man in Europe. Much of Philippa's time was spent away from Geoffrey's home, in attendance on her royal employers and patrons. During one of these absences, Geoffrey was involved in a scandalous affair – the *raptus* of a young woman, Cecily

Champaigne – which, as Watts shows, was most likely a sexual assault, and which may have produced the 'little Lewis' whom Chaucer refers to as his son in his *Treatise on the Astrolabe*. On Philippa's side, a strong circumstantial case has been made by Russell Krauss, using heraldry and other evidence, that her son Thomas Chaucer was fathered by John of Gaunt some years after Philippa's marriage to the young courtier-poet.

Whatever the eccentricity of Chaucer's own marital experience in the 'fast lane' of courtly life, the treatment of marriage in his work remained orthodox and traditional, to the point of obsolescence. The 'literature of sexual politics' was no new thing to Chaucer, for in several works – one thinks of *The Man of Law's* and *Clerk's Tales* – the subordination of wife to husband serves as emblem of natural, social and cosmic hierarchies. This was part of the intellectual baggage of late-medieval neoplatonism, and such, I shall argue, is the image of marriage in the NPT if we follow its narrator's advice:

> But ye that holden this tale a folye,
> As of a fox, or of a cok and hen,
> Taketh the moralite, goode men.
> For seint Paul seith that al that writen is,
> To oure doctrine it is ywrite, ywis;
> Taketh the fruyt, and lat the chaf be stille. (3438-43)

The 'fruyt' is a world-view so extremely traditional that by the fourteenth century it could properly be characterised, in its own cultural context, as reactionary. A modern vocabulary might describe it as anti-feminist, antipopular and anti-materialist – or (the other side of the coin) male supremacist, elitist, idealist.

But this is not a world-view that came ready-made in all the sources for NPT. On the contrary, a deliberate process of selection and alteration was required to transform the old cock-and-fox story into a vehicle for Chaucerian orthodoxy. The issues I have just named are most sharply posed in the protracted argument between Chauntecleer and Pertelote. The verbal collision of husband and wife, cock and hen, is the collision of two different but co-existing medieval cultural traditions. It was neither the first nor the last time these traditions would collide. The consequences in our poem are innocuous when compared with the tragic results that occurred when Pertelote and Chauntecleer spoke in historically real human voices, whose most drastically polarised institutional version would be the voices of heretic and inquisitor. Before turning to the nature of Chaucerian revision in the interest of 'oure doctrine', I want to consider the notion of popularity.

To write of popular literature or popular culture requires utmost clarity, for popularity may refer to authorship, audience, subject matter or ideological thrust.[1] A work may be 'popular' in one or several of its dimensions without being popular in all of them. There are plenty of illustrations from modern literature. Judith Krantz's *Princess Daisy* (1981) had a wide and doubtless popular readership, combined with elite authorship (the author attended an Ivy League women's college) and elite subject matter (the very wealthy) and a mixture of attitudes. The *Communist Manifesto* was genuinely popular in all but authorship (through a good argument could be made for authorship as well). In medieval literature, *The Second Shepherd's Play* is a work thoroughly popular in provenance, subject, audience and attitudes; guild production, local audience, public performance, and the present-ation of the lives of working people, their transgressions and complaints, their piety and humour. Yet all is finally in the service of an ideology that supports the feudal-hierarchal Catholic Church – itself, however, an institution that recruited democratically from all social classes from noble to villein. Similarly, the *Legenda Aurea* still exists in a phenomenal thousand manuscripts in Latin alone, yet these were not directly accessible to laity, and its lessons, as transmitted by clergy, were oppressive to 'popular' aspirations.

An especially interesting case of trans-class appeal is the Griselda story (the patient wife who withstands her husband's tests) and the complicated series of revisions that constitute its medieval history. Originating probably in a folk tale of the Psyche type, during the fourteenth and fifteenth centuries the story passed through the hands of several elite writers, some courtly, some bourgeois in their political sympathies: Petrarch, Boccaccio, Chaucer, Philippe de Mézières, Christine de Pizan. The tale was turned into Latin (hence distanced from a popular audience), then back again to the vernacular as poetry, prose and drama intended for consumption by differing social strata. With respect to meaning, the story can be received in two ways, either of which might explain its appeal to a broad and socially heterogeneous audience. In validating an ethos of unquestioning obedience, the story objectively supports the interest of oppressor classes whether aristocra-tic or bourgeois (an interpretation in no way altered by allegorical reading). On the other hand, in giving us a serf-heroine who rises to the highest social rank by her willingness to abide by nobility's rules, the story also offers an image of successful social mobility that does accurately represent contemporary social life, and that was duplicated in the life of many an upward-bound medieval bourgeois, artisan and churl. Nor is the referent of 'popular' the only problem to be considered. Among the others: 1) What is the social content of the word 'popular'? Who are 'the people'? During the late medieval period, serfs, villeins, rural and urban wage-workers, apprentices, servants, artisans and much of the bourgeoisie would constitute 'the people'. They might well unite on occasion against a feudal aristocrat or the aristocratic regime; at other times they might equally well rise up against one another. Then as now, the word 'popular' may efface important differences. 2) What is the origin of a 'folk' tale? Is it composed by a member of the folk, or by a member of the owning class – or by a professional poet – for the folk (or against the folk, for that matter)? 3) Much medieval literature had a cross-class audience: romance and fabliau were enjoyed by nobles and artisans alike. Moreover, Carlo Ginzburg has shown that the uses to which a given work – a travel book, for instance, or a saint's life – might be put by an 'uncultured' reader are not always those its 'cultured' author had in mind. In English literature, such complexities of author and audience have been noted in romance and lyric. Thus the Anglo-Norman ancestral romance, 'written by members of the regular clergy, inmates of houses founded or patronised by the [noble] family for whom these stories were concocted', gained 'widespread popularity' and 'had sufficient topical interest to become part of universal literature' (Legge, p. 175). And the lyric offers particularly labyrinthine relations of clerical elite and lay-popular composition, audience and materials as David Jeffrey demonstrates.

The NPT is certainly elite with respect to authorship and ideology, both elite and popular in audience (depending on how we rate the middle classes), wholly popular in material. I want now to turn to the relation of material and ideology.

Robert A. Pratt has shown that Chaucer drew on three Old French sources for his tale of the cock. They are the fable 'Del cok e del gupil' of Marie de France (c. 1180); an episode in the well-known fox-and-wolf cycle Le Roman de Renart – specifically Branch II by Pierre de St. Cloud (1176 or 77); and a redaction of the Roman, Renart le Contrefait, composed by an anonymous clerk of Troyes (c. 1320). Since Chaucer's indebtedness to Marie does not extend to that portion of his tale that centres on the dream I omit her contribution from my discussion.

Now Pratt points out that while the Nun's Priest's Tale differs from the Roman in reversing the attitudes of hen and cock, this reversal was already

anticipated in *Renart le Contrefait*. There the hen's scepticism about the
cock's dream is proven wrong – as in Chaucer's tale – whereas in the
Roman the hen offers a correct interpretation of the dream and is ridiculed
by the cock. That Chaucer's treatment of the relation of the cock and hen
is not wholly original should not, however, deter analysis of his version
of the story. The English poet's demonstrated familiarity with both
French sources offers a special opportunity to observe his selectivity at
work, and my purpose here will be to comment on some of the social
and ideological implications of his literary choice. To this end I shall use,
as foils to Chaucer's tale, both the *Roman* and a derivative German
analogue from the *Reinhart Fuchs* cycle by Heinrich der Glichezaere (about
1200). Both texts can be defined as 'popular' works, certainly with
respect to audience, but more particularly – my main interest here – with
respect to social attitudes, and nowhere more pronouncedly than in
their portrait of woman's role in marriage.[2]

Both the German (RF) and the earlier French version (RR) open by
establishing marital discord between the human characters, the peasant
couple who own the chickens. It is the wife who spots possible or actual
danger to the farmyard; she nags her man to build a better fence (RF) or to
chase the fox (RR); the husband is arrogant (RR) or incompetent (RF) and
his response is insulting in the French version, inadequate in the German
(for Reinhart easily spoils the new fence).

The peasant wife's role is echoed in that of Pinte the hen, who correctly
interprets Chauntecleer's dream of the fox, only to be ridiculed and then
ignored. Pinte's interpretation is justified in advance, for she had already
glimpsed the fox while Chauntecleer slept on a sandpile (RR, 75-84; RF,
51-58). Thus her fear is entirely rational, while the cock's dismissal of it is
exposed as a piece of typical, and in this case potentially fatal, masculine
arrogance. The moral with which the cock summarises his adventure
surely applies to the foolish peasant and his careful wife, as well as to
chickens:

La male gote li cret l'oil	Bad judgement blinds his eye
Qui s'entremet de someller	Who devotes himself to sleep
A l'ore que il doit veillier. (RR, 450-52)	At the moment when he should wake.
Er were	He would be,
Weiz Got nuht alwere,	God knows, no fool
Swer sich behutete ze aller zit.	Who is always on guard.
(RF, 167-9)	

In the ancient battle of sexes, then, the wife on both animal and human
levels is superior to her man in perception and foresight. In this sense we

can characterise both texts as supporting a 'feminist' viewpoint clearly opposed to the clerical antifeminist tradition which maintained the subordination of wife and husband. According to the antifeminist theory, the masculine monopoly on moral intellectual capacity makes the husband leader or 'head' of that most fundamental social organism, the family. Our texts subvert this tradition by vindicating the wife.

But beyond this outcome, it is also important to note the methodology that is validated in the pre-Chaucerian texts. It is a materialist and empirical methodology, counterposed to the male's frivolous abstractions. The fox is a material reality, and the female's dream truly reflects that reality; it is no mere invention (fable, RR, 275) or image (erscheinen, RF, 87) of dubious meaning. Pinte's personal experience, then, is entirely valid as epistemology and interpretive principle; it is entirely adequate to the real situation.

Now the Renart literature is above all a literature of parody; that is in large part the source of its humour. It parodies chanson de geste and courtly romance, clerical pretensions and clerical corruption, ecclesiastical proceedings and ecclesiastical rhetoric. The validation of woman's counsel and of a materialist epistemology constitutes another dimension in the 'popular' critique advanced in these texts. It is a critique which, for all its geniality, is often cruelly ironic. The butt of its satire is the lay and clerical ruling classes, and I would suggest that this satire forms part of what Ginzburg has called 'the autonomous current of peasant radicalism' (p. 21) in late-medieval and Renaissance culture: that steady current of materialist, rationalist and sceptical ideas that makes itself felt throughout the period.[3] In the episode at hand, the target is not the ruling class per se but rather their trans-class analogue, the husband-as-institution or instrument of oppression in the smallest possible social organisation, the family. When Engels wrote that 'Within the family [the husband] is the bourgeois and the wife represents the proletariat', (p. 65) he was paraphrasing a perfectly traditional medieval topos: the system of correspondence which privileged God, king, husband and reason over nature, populace, wife and passion. (In neither case, of course, is the idea merely metaphorical, for the institutional structures of religion, state, family and education did and do reinforce one another's hierarchies.)

The Chaucerian version of the fowl and fox story offers an interesting example of how a single plot can be made to serve quite different values. To begin with, Chaucer alters the human situation which frames the animal fable. There is no prosperous peasant couple. Instead the chickens are owned by a virtuous old widow who lives in penury with her two daughters, three sows, three cows and a sheep in a kind of

F

miniature Amazonia, a little community of females. The widow is a model of moderated desire and goodnatured acceptance 'of swich as God hir sente', for the widow,

> Syn thilke day that she was last a wyf,
> In pacience ladde a ful symple lyf. . . .
> No deyntee morsel passed thurgh hir throte;
> Hir diete was accordant to hir cote.
> Repleccion ne made hire nevere sik;
> Attempree diete was al hir phisik,
> And exercise, and hertes suffisaunce. . . .
> No wyn ne drank she, neither whit ne reed. (2825-42)

Neither ambition, lust, pride nor greed is part of the widow's temperament; she is as diametrically opposed to Alison of Bath as another widow could possibly be. This widow operates as a kind of moral exemplum or touchstone of female behaviour – not, as in the analogues, in parallel to the hen but rather in contrast.

Next, Chaucer (following *Renart le Contrefait*) has reversed the roles of cock and hen with respect to dream-interpretation. It is Pertelote who trivialises the dream, denying it any genuine reflective or predictive value, while Chauntecleer insists on oneiric truth. (Neither of them, in Chaucer's version, has seen the fox.) True to her prototype in the *Roman*, Pertelote remains a materialist, relying on her knowledge of the natural world, that is, of herbal medicine, the tradition of popular healing or folk medicine which, moreover, was frequently practised by women. She prides herself on requiring 'noon apothecarie' (2948): no chemicals, no elaborate preparations, no arduous training, nothing but the natural or experiential backyard medicine available to virtually anyone by observation and oral tradition. But with Chaucer the value attached to such pragmatism is negative, and Pertelote's materialism becomes a reductive methodology. Dreams, she argues, are merely the effect of physical humors; 'nothyng . . . but vanitee in sweven is' (2922), and the remedy is a laxative!

It falls to Chauntecleer, therefore, to defend the truth-value of dreams, and he does so on the basis of a scholarly idealism embroidered with many a comical *amplificatio* and *exemplum* along the way. His confidence in the stories he cites is also confidence in the mysterious process by which a future event makes itself known in dream, with no antecedent material cause: thus murder is revealed, shipwreck predicted, defeats, disasters and other events foretold. It is all as mysterious as the working of Providence, and equally demanding of faith. Indeed, Chauntecleer's attitude toward dream is analogous to the correct Christian attitude toward Providence, a miniature barnyard version of it. It is no accident, therefore, that the next section of the tale takes up the topic of free will and determinism in relation to Divine Providence (3234-50): the 'real' referent, we may deduce, of all the talk about dreams.

Despite Pertelote's attractive practicality, and Chauntecleer's absurd pomposity, she is presented as wrong, he as right. Can we see their debate as another version of the Chaucerian experience-versus-authority topos? I think we can, though not without some qualification, for Pertelote – like the Wife of Bath – cites authority, and her theories are quite in accord with certain respected medical texts. Yet it is important to note the kind of authority each party cites. Chauntecleer uses classical philosophy, saints' lives, the Old Testament and ancient history – authorities far superior to Pertelote's merely medical references (as he does not fail to point out (2970-83)). In Walter Clyde Curry's view, Pertelote

is a scientist, who has peered into many strange corners of medical lore. That egotist, Chauntecleer . . . would like to pass as a philosopher and a deep student of the occult . . . Pertelote's contentions are well founded when the dream is a *somnium naturale*; Chauntecleer's claims are undeniable when the vision is a true *somnium coeleste*. . . .

Against Pertelote's presentation of scientifically accurate facts and sound medical theory, Chauntecleer has nothing to oppose but his colossal conceit and a few stories gleaned from old authorities. (pp. 219-20, 227)

Yet it is these 'stories gleaned from old authorities' that carry the day as far as Chaucer is concerned, for all their rhetorical overkill. We must recall, in this connection, Chaucer's wariness about medicine. The limit and even the danger of medicine is precisely its materialism. 'His studie was but litel on the Bible' (I, 438) remarks Chaucer of his Doctour of Phisik, and F.N. Robinson cites, in his note to this line, the proverb *Ubi tres medici, duo athei*. For a Christian, faith is ultimately the best medicine, for 'Goddes worthy forwityng' (3243) must eventually prevail. Ostensibly the marital argument is a debate of authorities. Yet inasmuch as one set of authorities propounds a naturalistic or materialistic approach, while the other stresses faith in mysterious processes, the vindication of Chauntecleer does represent a vindication of authority over experience, clerical-intellectual tradition over popular tradition, idealism over materialism, as well as husband over wife.

'In principio / Mulier est hominis confusio', concludes Chauntecleer, dissolving the debate in love-play and food. He mistranslates (whether purposely or not, we do not know) this commonplace as 'Womman is mannes joy and al his blis' (3166). Later the Narrator provides as it were a gloss on Chauntecleer's ambivalent motto:

> Wommennes conseils been ful ofte colde;
> Wommannes conseil broghte us first to wo,
> And made Adam fro Paradys to go,
> Ther as he was ful myrie and wel at ese.
> But for I noot to whom it myght displese,
> If I conseil of wommen wolde blame,
> Passe over, for I seyde it in my game.
> Rede auctors, where they trete of swich mateere,
> And what they seyn of wommen ye may heere.
> Thise been the cokkes wordes, and nat myne;
> I kan noon harm of no womman divyne. (3256-66)

Here experience and authority again collide: clerical authority versus the Narrator's personal knowledge of women. But again, authority is given far the greater weight, as the Nun's Priest likely intends. One need not interpret the tale as an allegory of the fall (Spiers, p. 190) to detect in this passage the implication that Pertelote, or any woman, carries something of the old Eve in her nature.

In Chauntecleer's mistranslation we may see either ignorance masquerading as erudition, or deliberate condescension intended to placate a mistaken but beloved spouse. About Chaucer's *translatio* there is no such uncertainty, for in carrying his story across the gulf of language the English poet also rescued it for a social ideology alien to the original. It is the hierarchical and dualistic Pauline/Augustinian ideology whose aesthetic is commended at the end of the tale and again in the maker's Retraction. Still, given the sentiments in the Retraction, and given the Parson's resolute, austere rejection beforehand of fable and rhyme, it is likely that even The Nun's Priest's Tale would be consigned to silence as one of those 'that sownen into synne'. If so, it would be because of the parodistic images of human will and desire, marriage and discord which, despite the anti-popular ethos of the tale, and despite the poet's pious retraction, continue perversely to ensure its 'popularity' in our own time.

Women, nature and language: Chaucer's *Legend of Good Women*

Why should a poet choose, as the test or praxis of his aesthetic theory, the literary representation of women? What makes woman the most suitable object of representation, among the poet's wide range of choices, for a text so evidently about nature and language as Chaucer's *Legend of Good Women*? These are the questions I shall address in this chapter, and it behooves me to dispatch at once the answer closest to hand: Chaucer chose the literary representation of women as the test case of his aesthetics for generic and genealogical reasons; it is what some of his favourite authors had done. The trouble with answers closest to hand is that they often do little more than defer the question. In this case, that there were antecedents is no sufficient answer, for we should then have to interrogate Ovid's *Heroides* about its representational choices and strategies, and likewise Boccaccio's collection *De Mulieribus Claris*. Moreover, the answers would probably differ from case to case, for we cannot assume identity of purpose among exemplars in a diachronically dispersed generic or representational tradition. My aim, therefore, is to problematise the obvious, which always seems less problematic than the obscure, but which – as Roland Barthes showed in *Mythologies* and elsewhere – constitutes the ideology-laden language of a culture.

That *Legend of Good Women* is above all a collection of stories, Robert Frank reminded us nearly two decades ago. The reminder has served as a useful warning against an approach to the poem which is particularly tempting in a period of renewed interest in literary theory and Chaucerian poetics. This is, moreover, a temptation to which numerous scholars have succumbed: I mean the temptation to concentrate on the Prologue as a poetic credo while ignoring or minimising the legends themselves. The Prologue is a poetic credo, but not a free-standing one. It not only introduces the legends that follow, but its fiction motivates their production. If that fiction constitutes a statement of poetic principles, then the poetry it generates can legitimately be seen as the manifestation of those principles. This is why Prologue and legends are related as theory and practice. The legends exemplify a poetic that is defined in the Prologue in a variety of indirect ways, to be analysed below. That poetic, or aesthetic – it is, in any case, a great deal more than what we now consider proper to either aesthetics or poetics – I have called an aesthetic of nature. Yet it is necessary to add to Frank's reminder the further observation that the Legend is a collection of stories about women, and it is this fact that has informed my investigation of the text and its context.

Language, nature, women

I shall begin in res medias, with a passage from the Prologue, a mise en abîme which, like so many of Chaucer's rhetorical flights, condenses issues and meanings of the whole work. I have in mind the description of the spring season, lines 125–52 in F-text. The passage opens with a short dramatic scene or enargia: the warfare of winter against earth, and the rescue of earth by the sun.

> Forgeten hadde the erthe his pore estat
> Of wynter, that hym naked made and mat,
> And with his swerd of cold so sore greved;
> Now hath th' atempre sonne all that releved,
> That naked was, and clad him new agayn. (F, 125–9)

The struggle of personified seasons here recalls the wonderful passage in Gawain and the Green Knight (Fitt 2, stanzas 1–2) describing the progress of the seasonal cycle. In both places, personification conveys a sense of dynamic purposiveness in nature. But personification of natural process is a rhetorical device fraught with ideological implications. It carries a sense of that 'commerce twixt heaven and earth', that 'traffique' whose loss John Donne would lament some two and a quarter centuries later in 'The First Anniversary'. It is a kind of mutual transferrability that lets us believe we observe ourselves writ large in nature, and nature writ small in our human selves. The trope is a rhetorical consequence, one might say, of the theory of correspondence between microcosm and macrocosm, that series of interlocking metaphorical registers that was the foundation of traditional political theory, natural philosophy and medicine. This ideology found perhaps its clearest practical expression in the Etymologies of Isidore of Seville (560–636) with their intense desire for connection between word and meaning, word and thing. Some of Isidore's etymologies are perfectly correct because of the metaphorical nature of many words; others are more fanciful. *Amor* (love) is derived from *amus* (hook) because love entraps us like a hook. The spider's name, *aranea*, is derived from *aer* because it is an aerial worm, nourished on air. And so forth. The history of correspondence as a basis for language-theory or sign-theory extends from Plato (especially the *Cratylus*) through Augustine, Anselm and Aquinas.

The pun, or *paranomasia*, in the penultimate line of the passage – relieved-releaved – is more obvious in G's version, where the mention of greenery in the last line ('And clothed hym in grene all newe ageyn' G, 117) becomes a fairly blatant signal of it.[1] Pun does in small what allegory does on a larger scale: it holds in equilibrium two systems of interpretation. Here, the pun duplicates linguistically the two-level operation of the little allegorical scene to which it belongs. It also operates thematically, restating in linguistic example the stable instability of nature, the perpetual alternation of opposites held in equilibrium in the seasonal cycle. In this way, equivocal language imitates equivocal reality. Finally, the polysemous word – the signifier with multiple signifieds – represents a condition of plenitude. It does not destroy the relation of words with things but rather fulfils it, literally: fills it full, as do Isidore's multiple etymologies to a single word. In doing so, language is once again true to nature, for nature was created as full as it possibly could have been. We may observe the principle of plenitude of work in both microcosm and macrocosm (Lovejoy, Chapter 2). Through these uses of language, then, we begin to notice that the Prologue is developing a concept of language as itself resembling nature, language perhaps as an aspect of nature. The consequences of such a notion for the poem as a whole, and its relation to the literary representation of women, will become evident further on.

So that the nature of language and of the linguistic sign is inscribed already as a sub-text in some of the rhetoric Chaucer has used in the short passage quoted above. It was a problem that also occupied philosophers of language throughout the Middle Ages. Is language a natural phenomenon or is it arbitrarily consensual? Is a word *signa Dei*, *flatus vocis*, or some compromise? The controversy – already recorded in Plato's *Cratylus* – was carried, during the thirteenth and fourteenth centuries, in competing theories of the modist and the terminist or nominalist grammarians. Jan Pinborg describes the modist approach as follows: it assumed

that language, thought, and things are isomorphic with one another: the elements of any one of these three systems correspond to the elements of both the others in their internal relations.

... According to this 'modistic' analysis words are endowed with an immutable meaning, derived from the original imposition of words to signify something specific, which can be influenced by context not at all, or only to a strictly limited degree. . . . The modistae tried to bridge the gap between words and objects by various kinds of entities . . . partaking both in the nature of signs and the nature of objects. And so, unavoidably, they ran into the trouble of all picture-theories: the construction of 'bridging' entities could go on ad infinitum since there is no real tertium comparationis between objects, concepts and words. In the years after 1300 these difficulties caused considerable tension which gradually undermined the theory.[2]

The work of terminist or nominalist opponents of this approach – scholars like Jean Buridan, William of Ockham, Pierre d'Ailly and Johannes Aurifaber – has received far less attention than that of the modists. Nonetheless from what has been done it is possible to deduce that the essence of the anti-modist position was to emphasise the truth-value of propositions, and to reject the existence of 'modes of signification' as something distinct from signifier or signified. Terminist theory 'therefore displayed what has been called a contextual approach, that is, it attended to the precise function and reference the term actually had in the proposition analysed.'[3]

   That Chaucer was no scholastic was, once again, no bar to his awareness of the general problem. It would be futile to try to label Chaucer either 'nominalist' or 'realist' – not least because these terms are themselves so contested, but also because the poet is too complex. I suppose one might hazard the formulation that Chaucer is, or would like to be, philosophically realist, but that he is aesthetically nominalist. That division in consciousness, that fissure, is by no means inconsistent with the Augustinian orthodoxy which I ascribe to Chaucer in this and other essays. In any case, as a practising poet and as a reader of Augustine, Chaucer would have had to confront the nature of signification. Moreover, one of the most important works of medieval literature and one of Chaucer's most fertile sources – the Roman de la Rose – poses the problem of signification both implicitly and explicitly. The implicit method occurs, as Daniel Poirion points out, in the first part: Guillaume's use of codified courtly language, and his use of dream (which signifies the allegory, which signifies a truth). Jean de Meun, on the other hand, uncomfortable with both allegory and courtly love, exemplifies the 'crise de signification' that French literature would experience during the thirteenth century. This is accomplished most obviously in the famous discussion of Reason's use of the word 'coilles' (testicles) in her account of Saturn's fall (RR, 6871 ff.). 'Voilà une souriante leçon de philosophie de langage!' comments Poirion, a lesson in which is evident 'ce courant nominaliste qui se caracterise par l'opposition entre *res* et *vox*.'

The poetic proposed in the Prologue and exemplified in the legends plays with notions of language and meaning, as I want to show in my exegesis of the passage at hand. That the text of the poem hovers in the space of what Jacques Derrida has called 'différance' may account for the difficulty scholars have had in reading and interpreting it. One finds in the poem the play of differing/deferring/deference between and among – on one hand – the ideals of a pristine, stable, absolute and paradigmatic *langue*, and – on the other – the realities of fallen, contingent, infinitely variable *parole*. The signifying system or code in which this occurs both can be and is language, ethics, literature, love, beauty, nature or the human body. This play of differance destabilises the poem, producing an aura of uncertainty about meaning and the status of language which affects content and structure, narrative and rhetoric.

For the text resists classification. It is hard to pin down, unusually hard even for a text within a corpus well known for its ambiguities. On one hand it expresses a longing for 'the naked text' (G, 86), whether that means a text bare of rhetoric, a text faithfully translated, a text devoid of gloss, or a text completely transparent to meaning. On the other hand, its linguistic surface could scarcely be more elaborately draped, incorporating as it does the techniques of classical rhetoric, metaphysical speculation, formulas of courtly love, and a range of ironic devices including pun and obscenity. A puzzling text, then, as rich and as self-contradictory as the three entities, the ones named in my title, that it unites. Let us return now to nature, women and language.

The passage I have chosen continues with another *enargia*, also a scene of conflict, this time between the little birds and their old enemy the fowler.

> The smale foules, of the sesoun fayn,
> That from the panter and the net ben scaped,
> Upon the foweler, that hem made awhaped
> In wynter, and distroyed hadde hire brood,
> In his dispit hem thoghte yt did hem good
> To synge of hym, and in hir song despise
> The foule cherl that, for his coveytise,
> Had hem betrayed with his sophistrye. (130–7)

Here the oppoments are types of rational and non-rational life: or, to replace that Aristotelian formulation with a Christian one, creatures with and without a soul. We know how fond Chaucer was of dovetailing the activities of avian and human species: The Parliament of Fowls reminds us of it, and The Nun's Priest's Tale, as does the opening of The Canterbury Tales. The present birds have escaped the fowler's nets and traps, though he has frightened them all winter long and destroyed their young. We would scarcely expect a Chaucerian bird to turn the other cheek, and indeed these gloat in triumphant self-assertion, for their survival is the trapper's failure.

Who, or what, is this fowler? Satan, B.G. Koonce proposed, basing his interpretation on scriptural exegesis. The art historian Meyer Schapiro, though, writing on the bowman and bird mofit in the plastic arts, grouped it with a 'large class of medieval images of the hunter and the beast', many of which have secular rather than religious significance. I consider a secular source for Chaucer's fowler more likely than a scriptural or patristic one: specifically, the well-known story of the churl and the bird, in which a greedy churl tries to outwit the bird but is himself outwitted. This story is told in the Disciplina Clericalis, in several French tales, and in a short poem, 'The Churl and the Bird', attributed to John Lydgate. But whatever his origin, the fowler can be understood only contextually and therefore diacritically: what he is and what he is not, what he is for and what he is set against. The latter is, of course, the birds.

The simplest relation of fowler to birds is that of hunter to victims. If hunting is natural to humanity; if rapacity is part of the natural order, as The Parliament of Fowls suggests it is; if the sexual power-struggle is a principle of nature, as the presence of Pluto and Proserpina indicates in The Merchant's Tale, then the Prologue's relation between fowler and prey forecasts what is to come. It invites us to see the battle of sexes waged in the legends as a permanent condition of post-lapsarian life: men will victimise women.

Yet our birds are no silent victims. They turn the tables in derogatory song, as surely as May turns the tables on January with the ready reply guaranteed her and all women by Proserpina. It is through language the word, that – Proserpina assures us – women will always triumph. It is through language that the victimised women in the Legend also finally triumph, their suffering memorialised and perhaps transcended through the works of art that tell their stories and renew their lives to posterity. That it is not their own language that does so but someone else's – many others, Virgil, Ovid, Chaucer among them – suggests again the necessary intermediacy that is art or tradition, namely language itself. Alceste is female motivator of the language that commemorates these female lives,

Proserpina female motivator of the language women use to facilitate their real lives. Is it sheer coincidence that these figures, linked in a similar relation to women by way of language, also share several other elements in their stories? Both travel to hell, and both are companion to a powerful god who represents a force of nature (Eros and Thanatos respectively). In both cases the female companion has to mitigate the punitive force of the deity she attends. Here, then, is another permutation on the woman/nature/language triangulation: the language of art, inspired by women (particularly if the art is poetry about love), as a means to moderate the effects of nature.

There is more to our birds, though, for these are poet-birds. They have a natural song based on experience and instinctual desire, with which they are able to insult the fowler. The fowler, on the other hand, has technology: the panter and the net. He also has a complicated moral life which attests his insertion in a complicated social life: he is impelled by 'coveytise', the profit motive. The fowler does not trap birds to eat, but to sell. His relation to the birds is neither aesthetic, therefore, nor strictly natural: he is neither appreciating their song nor hunting them for biological sustenance. From the fowler's position, the birds are a commodity. They have no immediate use-value but rather exchange-value on the market, where they may be bought as food, as pets, as bait for larger birds, as a source for feathers, etc. The birds are, for the fowler, mediated and distanced by a socially-determined system of value within which they are signs and therefore to be exchanged. We will return to this notion of signs and exchange later on in connection with women.

If such is the fowler's view of the birds, they too have their special view of him. From a bird's-eye view, the fowler has 'sophistrie' and 'craft'. Now these are curious qualities with which to endow a 'cherl', an undereducated rural working man, for they are linked to advanced verbal skills both oral and written: sophistry to philosophical argumentation, craft to poetic making. That Chaucer has chosen these heavily-freighted words for his fowler should alert us to the language theme. If the birds can be read as natural singers, what sort of wordsmith might the fowler represent? Is he perhaps a hostile critic or censorious patron, or a heavyhanded ideological poet, or simply an abuser of verbality in any genre? Louis Marin has written, in Récit, of narrative itself as a trap, though this is not a trail I want to follow here. Nonetheless, the vocabulary of sophistry and craft bespeaks a long-standing mistrust of the rhetor, and of rhetoric as techniques of disguise, hence entrapment. If we can see the fowler's technology as snares of rhetoric, this offers a direct connection to the stories to follow, where a male lover lays verbal traps for his 'bridde' (ME: woman/bird).

However we read the fowler, he is as much a philistine as the God of Love will shortly prove to be with his critical sophistry and all his craft of love. And the fowler is as cleverly defied in birdsong as Eros is defied in the ironical legendary whose making escapes his control. Are they, Eros and the fowler, to be condemned? Yes and no, depending on what view we take. In their defence it can be observed that, from a normative medieval perspective, neither erotic nor economic compulsion is entirely avoidable in the world as we have it: such is Jahweh's curse on Adam and Eve. We might therefore want to see fowler and birds as a necessary dialectic in nature – much like men and women. We might want to see them as two kinds of artist in confrontation: the trained, sophisticated/sophistical rhetor with his elaborate nets, limes and traps, versus the intuitive, naif, spontaneous singer who blurts out its love and its hate. We might even want to see fowler and birds as two aspects of the same artist, like the two brothers in Sam Shepard's play *True West*. One of them, a professional and well-paid script-writer in suburban Los Angeles, hasn't a compelling story to tell; the other, an ill-educated wanderer, can recount his fascinating experience in the desert but can't write it up. Eventually the two change places: the script-writer abandons his house and typewriter to go on pilgrimage to the desert in search of material, inspiration and his 'real self'; while the wanderer moves into the house, learns to type, and sells scripts. It is, in short, about the integration of book, experience and dream in a writer's work: a theme familiar to Chaucerians.

It remains only to add that the birds do not only produce a song of hatred. They are also capable of 'clere / Layes of love, that joye it was to here' (F, 139–40), songs in praise of springtime and Saint Valentine, who lets them choose their mate (F, 145–7). These simple, contrasting songs reflect the double reality of the birds' merely instinctual lives. As nature is dual and contradictory, so is our experience of it, and so must art be if it is faithful to nature and to life. But how much more ambivalent and nuanced must be the *lais* of the human artist if he or she is to maintain a similar 'troth' with nature. Nature is the given – and yet nature is not all, for the opening lines of the Prologue have already warned us that there is more than meets the senses. Nonetheless, fidelity to nature is at least where one starts to tell the truth, and part of the truth is the 'troth', the connections, bonds or promises that are present but invisible, possible but unachieved, or originary but lost.

The power, and the danger, of the God of Love, is that he aims precisely to break a representational troth, the bond between signifier and signified. Demanding an unbalanced representation of women which is really misrepresentation, Eros requires Geffrey to falsify experience in the name of a specialised literary tradition. Much like the discourse of Pandarus, though in another register, the god's command can only cut language off from its mooring in reality. He will effect a divorce rather than a marriage. The image of woman that Eros proposes is simply a massive synechdoche, taking the part for the whole. It substitutes a rhetorical device for reality. Of course there are good, faithful and true women, but there are also bad and faithless women, and then there are most women, whose goodness is mixed with error of various kinds and degrees. To let the individual stand for the sex is a standard tactic of misogyny which some twenty years later Christine de Pizan would denounce in her *Livre de la Cité des Dames*. As a defence of women, essentialism destroys itself. To argue that women are by nature good is to accept the conceptual foundation for the opposite view: that they are by nature bad. Either position is reductive, therefore false. Chaucer's intent, I suggest, is to occupy the orthodox middle ground, neither misogyny nor courtly adulation.

To return to my exegesis, here are the last lines of the passage at hand:

And therewithalle hire bekes gonnen meete,
Yeldyng honour and humble obeysaunces
To love, and diden hire other observaunces
That longeth onto love and to nature;
Construeth that as yow lyst, I do no cure. (148–52)

The last three lines contain a favourite Chaucerian device, the 'deliberate mystification' as Talbot Donaldson christened it, or coy evasion that tells all. Sexuality belongs to nature and therefore to love. No love-poetry that omits it can claim to be realistic or complete. The coy remark above hints at this perspective, and we ought not to expect that the tales to follow will be purged of lust or sexuality. The steady current of sexual wordplay in the legends keeps this dimension of natural experience firmly before us (Delany, 'Logic').

Finally, a curious thing happens in the very last line of the passage. We the audience are suddenly transformed into the subject of poetry, for the author reaches out in the imperative mood to collar us into judgement. In addressing us directly, the poet forces us to realise that there is an author, who now separates himself from what he has just written and designates his composition as 'that'. Moreover, the author literally orders us to interpret his composition: 'Construeth that!' We are not to lose ourselves in delight at the marvellous poetry we have just read. On the contrary, we must now contemplate this fabrication with critical intelligence. And how exactly do we wish to construe it? This is no mere rhetorical question, for the problem of construal will soon be raised by Eros and Alceste. It will motivate the production of the work itself, a penalty for Eros's negative construal of the Narrator's previous work. Is the Narrator a misogynistic lout, as Eros asserts? Or is he merely a gullible fool, as Alceste replies? Do we interpret the legends as ironic? Are these women to be pitied, or condemned, or both? The history of *Legend* scholarship in this century shows how live a problem construal has remained.

Though the imbrication of women, nature and language is especially strong in the passage we have just examined, it is prominent everywhere in the Prologue. Most centrally this is so of the daisy which is at once flower, object of erotic devotion, (female poetic) muse, poetic subject, linguistic equivalent to Margaret, and 'remembraunce' (F, 530) of Alceste. Nothing distracts the bookish narrator from his studies, he says, except devotion to the daisy. Though his protestations of inadequacy undercut themselves in their virtuosity, what one can believe is the Narrator's lament for his own belatedness, addressed to his famous precursors the great love-poets:

> For wel I wot that ye han her-biforn
> Of makyng ropen, and lad awey the corn,
> And I come after, glenyng here and there,
> And am ful glad yf I may fynde an ere
> Of any goodly word that ye han left. (F, 73–7)

The central conceit is of reaping and gleaning grain. This agricultural image also evokes the figure of a woman, the scriptural Ruth, which in turn evokes the question of literary tradition and authority already addressed in the opening lines of the Prologue. And there is the triple pun in line 76 on the word 'ear', again uniting nature, language and woman as ear of corn, audience's ear, lover's ear.

Lastly I would mention the courtly fad of leaf and flower, twice cited as an occasion for poetic making:

> In this cas oghte ye [lover-poets] be diligent
> To forthren me somwhat in my labour,
> Whethir ye ben with the leef or with the flour. (F, 70–2)

But natheles, ne wene nat that I make
In preysing of the flour agayn the leef,
No more than of the corn agayn the sheef;
For, as to me, nys lever noon ne lother.
I nam withholden yit with never nother;
Ne I not who serveth leef, ne who the flour. (F, 188–93)

Furthering the language-nature connection, Jesse Gellrich has noted the possible play on 'leaf' as page of a book, and 'flower' as flower of rhetoric (p. 212). Beyond rhetoric though, there is an underlying idea, or even ideology. Flower and leaf, corn and sheaf: courtiers may set them in competition, but in nature they are part of a single organism. To insist on one or the other is at best an innocuous pastime. At worst, though, it might indicate a taste for verbal or intellectual structures that are unnaturally rigid, unnecessarily divisive. This idea allows us to look forward to the legends to come. Good women or bad women, dark or fair, slim or plump: should the one be 'lever or lother' than the other? Is any woman all bad or all good, or do the two aspects of personality coexist as closely as corn and sheaf?

Nature, women, language

A piece is missing. It is a piece of rhetoric, a metaphor so deeply embedded in western culture, so absolutely taken for granted, that it is virtually invisible. Nonetheless it is this missing piece which enables the connection of theory to practise – that is, of Prologue to legends – and of the aesthetic of nature to the literary representation of women. This link is the equivalency of women with nature. This is so ancient and omnipresent a turn of thought and of language that only with difficulty can it be treated simply as metaphor. It has become what Medvedev and Bakhtin called an 'ideologeme' (pp. 17, 21–25). 'Is female to male as nature is to culture?' Anthropologist Sherry Ortner asked this question in the title of her well-known essay, and the answer, she claims, in most cultures is 'Yes.' She cites three reasons for this phenomenon. First, women's reproductive capacity; second, women's social role as family nurturer and socializer of children; third, the 'feminine' personality structure that is a consequence of social arrangements, particularly division of labour and family structures.

While Ortner's evidence comes mainly from the tribal societies that constitute her field of specialisation, the idea itself is by no means limited to these societies. In ancient Greece, gender difference was intimately

linked with agriculture and with writing: 'For the Greeks, writing is like
plowing is like sexual intercourse', and women are 'tablets for
inscription, fields for sowing and writing, assuring the scriptural, agricultural and sexual reproduction of the polis' (duBois). Since my interest
here is the analogy itself rather than its socio-economic determinants, I
will confine myself to noting its amazing longevity through the most
drastic metamorphoses of social life. Wolfram's *Parzival* gives us the start-
ing image of earth as a virgin grandmother raped by her grandson Cain
(IX, 464), while the feminity of nature was an accepted topos among the
Chartrian humanists of the same period. We learn from Annette
Kolodny that 'Mother Earth' – a slogan in the Battle for People's Park in
Berkeley, 1969 – was a recurrence of the 'land-as-woman symbolisation
in American life and letters' (Kolodny, *Lay*) and Susan Gubar brings the
metaphors full circle with her discussion of places in modern and contemporary literature where woman is likened to text. I choose these
moments – classical, medieval and modern – as representative of what
would otherwise be an unwieldly list of references. To transfer these
data, then, to *The Legend of Good Women*: the literary representation of
women can serve as test case for an aesthetic of nature because woman
has traditionally been thought to bear a far more intimate relation to
nature than man does, a relation so close as to border on equivalency.

Women and nature, then; but where does language fit, the third
component of my argument? Here anthropology can help again, for it
is Claude Lévi-Strauss's exposition of the exchange of women that links
women to language through the notion of the sign.[4] Insofar as women
present value, they become signs. It is not, however, simply as 'a thing of
worth' that Lévi-Strauss uses the term 'value', though women's reproductive capacity certainly renders them valuable in this sense. Like language they are full of 'meaning' in their ability to generate other signs,
more people, the wealth of the tribe. But the value represented by
women, according to Lévi-Strauss, is rather a social function, the prohi-
bition of incest. This rule has the same purpose as language: communication and integration with others. Rules governing marriage and
non-marriage are 'a means of binding others through alliance', so that
'The relations between the sexes can be conceived as one of the modali-
ties of a great "communication function" which also includes language.'
Thus 'Women themselves are treated as signs, which are misused when
not put to the use reserved to signs, which is to be communicated.'
Though the exchange of women is no longer as important as it was, the
remnants survive, as testified in these words to an old jazz classic: 'As a

silver dollar goes from hand to hand, – So a woman goes from man to man.'

In the Middle Ages, though, the exchange function of women was still a very prominent aspect of marriage mores: witness dowries, property-settlements, and family or political alliances made by marriage. Chaucer himself, as guardian of marriageable young aristocrats and bourgeois, personally profited from the marriage market of his day. The socio-economic realities of marriage, especially the exchange-value of women, are an important theme in *The Canterbury Tales*. Obvious examples are the Merchant's sardonic praise of a wife as a more durable gift than 'londes, rentes, pasture, or comune, / Or moebles' (IV, 1313–14), and Alison of Bath's commodification of her own sexuality as a response to society's commodification of women. Less obvious, perhaps, is Chaucer's description of the other Alison, the young wife of *The Miller's Tale*. In a long series of natural images – animal, avian and botanical (I, 3233–70) – there intrudes the following dissonant couplet:

Ful brighter was the shynyng of hir hewe
Than in the Tour the noble yforged newe. (3255–6)

Why an intrusive money image – social, urban, manmade, technological – to disrupt this otherwise consistent set, if not to make the point that woman, like the coin, has exchange value: she does go 'from hand to hand'. In one sense, of course, she ought not do to so; that is, in the adulterous or promiscuous sense represented in the narrative. Yet in another sense she must, for such are the demands of marriage as a social institution when a woman goes from her father's hand to that of her husband, her exchange value dependent on her father's income and status. Of this perspective we are reminded in the last lines of the descriptive passage:

She was a prymerole, a piggesnye,
For any lord to leggen in his bedde,
Or yet for any good yeman to wedde.

Intertextually, though, the money-image was related to nature in the Chartrian discourse familiar to Chaucer. In a passage he had already used as a source for *The Parliament of Fowls*, Natura defines herself as God's vicar using the imagery of numismatics:

He appointed me as his substitute, his vice-regent, the mistress of his mint, to put the stamp on the different classes of things. . . . I obeyed the commander's orders in my work and I, to use a metaphor, striking various coins of things according to

G

the mould of the exemplar, and producing copies of my original by fashioning like out of like gave to my imprints the appearance of things imaged. (Prosa 4)

By way of Alanus's De Planctu Naturae, then, the coin-and-mint image came to Chaucer already integrated into a doctrine of nature, already spoken by a female figure whose fertility links woman, nature and language in the metaphor of exchange.

It might be objected here that men as well as women were exchanged in medieval marriage; in fact both of Chaucer's wards were young men. Yet this would be a superficial judgement. One needs to ask with whom exchange is made, and for what. To the extent that men hold positions of social power (government, clergy, administration) and, in the main, own capital, land and other means of production, to that extent it is men with whom political alliances or property settlements are made. Hence woman remains, structurally, the exchanged item. Had women equal power and status with men, we would then be able to speak of exchange of men and women, though this power and status would have to be general rather than exceptional. Two centuries after Chaucer wrote The Legend of Good Women, even Queen Elizabeth knew full well that her best strategy to retain 'maistrie', both personal and political, was precisely to maintain her single state.

Returning now to language, I note that an interesting feature of Chaucer's rhetoric in the Legend is an absence. Nowhere in any legend does the poet describe the lady who is its protagonist. This absence of physical description is especially striking because the blason of female charms was so prominent a convention in the courtly literature that the Narrator has been ordered to imitate. In Troilus the deferral of physical description invests those descriptions with special force when they do finally appear in Book V. Here, the omission of physical description seems a clue to the poet's subversive intention. He refuses to titillate the reader with a conventional catalogue of female charms, or to fragment the natural human body and hand it over, in fetishised form, on a silver platter of rhetoric.

Yet if this refusal of the catalogue signals a poetic practise that Chaucer means to reject, it simultaneously implies what he wishes to endorse. I mean that sense of the proper use of goods that came to Chaucer from numerous late-classical and medieval sources. Here is one formulation, taken from Augustine's discussion in The City of God (22:17) whether women's bodies will retain their own sex in the resurrection.

For may part, they seem to be wiser who make no doubt that both sexes shall rise.

For there shall be no lust, which is now the cause of confusion. From those bodies, then, vice shall be withdrawn, while nature shall be preserved. And the sex of a woman is not a vice, but nature. It shall then indeed be superior to carnal intercourse and child-bearing; nevertheless the female members shall remain adapted not to the old uses but to a new beauty, which, so far from provoking lust, now extinct, shall excite praise to the wisdom and clemency of God, who both made what was not and delivered from corruption what He made.

If the poet Jack Spicer is right that the desire for meaning is the desire for love, then the medieval poet's wish for 'the naked text' (G, 86) is a utopian wish for the naked body too. Text-as-language becomes analogous to woman, the two linked as versions of temporality (Vance). It is a wish infinitely deferred, as Augustine writes, to the time or non-time beyond nature, when we will see naked bodies with no ill effect; when we will interpret everything aright and meaning be redeemed in the transcendent signifier. This, I propose, is what Chaucer too considers the best use of signs whether these are female beauty, nature or language: as good coin in the exchange between this world and the next. That his text juggles these registers of meaning may explain not only the silence of scholars but that of the text itself: unfinished, after all, like The House of Fame before it, which also dealt with the nature of language, textuality and communication. To end where I began, with Barthes: 'The disintegration of language can only lead to the silence of writing' (Writing, p. 75). It is no coincidence, therefore, that I find a fit ending in the last chapter of Writing Degree Zero, entitled 'The Utopia of Language':

Feeling permanently guilty of its own solitude, [literary language] is none the less an imagination eagerly desiring a felicity of words, it hastens toward a dreamed-of language whose freshness, by a kind of ideal anticipation, might portray the perfection of some new Adamic world where language would no longer be alienated. The proliferation of modes of writing brings a new mode of Literature into being in so far as the latter invents its language only in order to be a project: Literature becomes the Utopia of Language.

For the medieval writer, necessarily mistrustful of utopia, literature could not be the site of utopia outright, not while there remained, in Catholic ideology, a 'mystical society of universality' which did hold forth the ultimate possibility of transparent signification, of 'naked text'. At best, literary language could acknowledge the utopian wish together with its natural failure, so that only in this restricted sense can one add to Barthes's conclusion the rejoinder: it always has been.

Notes

Chapter 1, 'Run silent'

1 Frank and Fritzie Manuel's *Utopian Thought* omits feminist utopias of the early and later twentieth century; for the medieval period it briefly mentions such incarnations of 'the utopian propensity' as 'paradisaical, apocalyptic, and millenarian fantasies . . . heretical and some orthodox movements of reformation . . . [and] a cokaygne utopia' (p. 16). My reasons for excluding millenialism and Cokaygne are discussed below. Ernst Bloch's survey in volume 2 of *The Principle of Hope* gives such a diffuse definition of utopianism as 'the Not-Yet-Conscious' that utopia is discerned everywhere. I became aware of Bloch's discussion of alchemy (2; 634–46) after this chapter was completed: his focus is on alchemy of the seventeenth century and later, and his approach is quite different from mine.

   The Manuels remark that 'To most observers utopianism seemed a corpse by the 1920s and 1930s;' in 1947 Parrington deplored the scepticism, fear and insecurity which had produced the dystopian sensibility (p. 218). On feminist utopias of the seventies, see Khanna and Kunar.

2 LeClair, p. 45. Sister Ida shows that St. Thomas was even more anti-utopian than normative theology required, for he argued that social class and permanent monogamous union would have existed even before the fall (p. 87).

3 Marin, *Utopics*, p. 198. The thesis quoted, along with its supporting argument, seems, in its focus on precisely the possible, to negate Marin's general attempt to strip utopia of its possibilism. On Marx's concept of ideology, see McCarney, *The Real World of Ideology*.

4 On Cokaygne, see Cocchiara and Vaananen.

5 On Joachism, see Kestenberg-Gladstein and Marjorie Reeves.

6 The information in this section is drawn from numerous sources, among them Werner, Koch, Russell, Thomson, Leff, Le Goff, ed., *Hérésies et Sociétés*; McDonnell, Stephens, Loos, Lourdaux, Lambert, Moore, Orioli, Aston and Hudson.

7 Doiron, also McDonnell, 492–6. A modern translation of the text has been published in the Spiritual Classics series ed. John Griffiths (New York, 1981), though the Introduction nowhere mentions the author.

8 Ladurie, p. 171; see also pp. 157, 159 and passim, and Noonan, *Contraception*.

9 LeGoff, 'The Historian and the Ordinary Man', in *Time*, p. 230; Duby, *Le Chevalier, La Femme et le Prêtre*, p. 119 (my translation); Stock, p. 88. As Koch and Moore point out, the Cathars became considerably more conservative on the role of women in the later thirteenth century, and the number of *perfectae* declined. Abels and Harrison argue that Cathar *perfectae* rarely performed the functions they theoretically could. It seems to me nonetheless that the possibility itself would have been a decisive factor in attracting women.

10 Breton, 'Second Manifeste', quoted in Browder, p. 71. Max Ernst and Giorgio Dechirico also drew (other) analogies with alchemy: see Lippard, pp. 77, 130. Also Carl Jung, *Mysterium Conjunctionis* and *Psychology and Alchemy*; Silberer.

11 *Philosophical Notebooks* in *Collected Works* 38, p. 43.

12 My sources on alchemy include Atwood, Brunet (Chapter 49), Read, Ganzenmuller, Eliade (*The Forge and the Crucible*), Anon., *Alchemy and Chemistry*, van Lennep, Trinick, Duncan and Fabricius. Medieval texts, consulted at the library of Columbia University and the

New York Public Library, include *Arnaldi di Villanova Speculum Alchimiae* (Francofurti MDCIII); Bacon, *The Mirror of Alchemy* (London, 1597), a volume which includes 'The Smaragdine Table of Hermes Trismegistus' and Bonus of Ferrara, *The New Pearl of Great Price*.

13 Burland, p. 22. See also Patai; however, the study contains no hard evidence that Maria actually existed. 'An Alchemical Tract Ascribed to Mary the Copt' has been translated by E.J. Holmyard.

14 On Flamel, see Gagnon, *Description* and 'Les alchimistes et les speculateurs'; Le Villain.

15 See Dahmer and Pike.

Chapter 2, 'Undoing substantial connection'

1 In some of his work Chaucer uses allegorical personifications in a decorative way, or inserts allegorical episodes. Nonetheless, I am in basic agreement with C.S. Lewis's statement that 'Nowhere in Chaucer do we find what can be called a radically allegorical poem' (p. 166). In saying this I don't wish to commit myself to defending Lewis's position on everything else. The distinction between allegory and symbol, for example, is usually less clear-cut than Lewis suggests; and, as Rosamund Tuve points out, it is 'born of nineteenth-century German critical theory, not medieval usage' (p. 3). Tuve's *caveat* doesn't invalidate the distinction though it should be applied cautiously (as I hope I have done later on).
   I do want to distinguish between allegory as a creative mode and allegorical exegesis of the Bible or the classics. I am not, in this essay, concerned with the latter.

2 Many 'allegories' are less consistent or continuously allegorical than those I have mentioned, e.g. *Piers Plowman* and *The Faerie Queene*. Other works (such as Boethius's *De Consolatione Philosophiae*, *Pearl*, and Thomas Usk's *Testament of Love*) establish an allegorical situation which frames a straightforward instructional dialogue. Such mixture of modes does not invalidate a discussion of allegory in its purer forms – or, more accurately, of allegory in those works wherein the mode is more rigorously sustained.

3 The purpose of *Timaeus*, like that of Plato's other dialogues, is to disengage our attention from the physical world in order to focus it upon the 'true reality' of abstract Forms. Plato's anti-scientific bias has been discussed by Ste-Croix in Crombie, *Scientific Change*, pp. 83–4; Crowther, pp. 103–6, 134–5; and Winspear, pp. 156–60. *Timaeus* was known to medieval scholars through the fourth-century translation and commentary of Chalcidius.

4 I *Sent.* 4, 2. Although Aquinas wrote no separate treatise on analogy, it is a recurrent topic in his writing. The *loci* are collected and analysed in Klubertanz.

5 Aristotle's debt to Plato is acknowledged by most scholars, though its exact extent is debated. See, for example, Taylor (pp. 44–5), Owen, and Jaeger.

6 The 'impetus' theory was not original with Buridan, but had been proposed as early as the sixth century by John Philoponus, a Greek commentator of Aristotle. Philoponus's theory was transmitted to European scholars through the work of Arabic Aristotelians.

7 The excerpt, from Buridan's *Questions on Aristotle's Physics*, is translated from the French version given in Duhem, vol. 3, p. 52. See also Clagett, pp. 536, 561.

8 Oresme refused to commit himself to this position, though, concluding his demonstration with an assertion of faith in the doctrinal teaching that 'Deus enim firmavit orbem terrae, qui non commovetur' (*Livre*, 144B). Also see Grant.

9 Buridan's arguments are stated in his *Questions . . . on the Heavens and the World*, book II, 9, 12. The relevant excerpt appears in Clagett, pp. 557–62.

10 A discussion of the theoretical basis of papalist analogies and an exhaustive list of references are found in the text and notes of Gierke.

11 'History, after all, is the memory of a nation. Just as memory enables the individual to learn . . . so history is the means by which a nation establishes its sense of identity and purpose': John Kennedy, 'On History', forward to *The American Heritage . . . History of the United States* (New York: American Heritage, 1963).

12 That mode is figural representation. Its development and its use in *The Divine Comedy* are
     studied by Erich Auerbach in 'Figura', pp. 11–76. Figura is of course allegorical in the
     widest sense, but Auerbach distinguishes it from allegory 'by the historicity both of the
     sign and what it signifies'. The characters in the *Comedy* are not personified abstractions,
     they do not simply represent 'an attribute, virtue, capacity, power or historical institu-
     tion'; they are actual historical figures who have 'become the truth' – figures whose
     historical reality is itself representative.
13 It is not agreed by Ockham scholars whether the philosopher ought to be called
     nominalist, conceptualist or terminist; see, e.g., Menges and Boehner, 'The Realistic
     Conceptualism of William Ockham'. However, Tornay's defence of the term nominalist
     seems valid to me (pp. 1–28).
14 On Gottschalk, see Raby (pp. 189–92), and Jolivet.
15 *Sent.* I, dist. 2, q. 8f, in Tornay, p. 132. Ockham's notion of the universal evolved over a
     period of several years, though this development does not seem to have entailed any
     major alteration in his thought. The development of Ockham's universals theory is
     discussed in Boehner, *Ockham*, p. xxix and in Maurer, p. 281.
16 This is perhaps a too-simple way of stating the principle of 'Ockham's razor', which was
     not in any case original with Ockham. For a more detailed discussion of the formulation,
     meaning and application of the principle, see Boehner, *Ockham*, p. xx and Maurer, p. 284;
     also Maurer, 'Ockham's Razor'.
17 Such questions as these were anticipated by Ockham, and against them he could make no
     other defence than pure faith. In *Sent.* I, xxx, 1 (Whether a relation is a thing distinct from
     absolutes), Ockham says of the mystery of the trinity: 'One who wishes to be supported
     only by the reason possible to him and who did not wish to accept any authority
     whatsoever would say that it is impossible for three persons distinct in reality to be one
     supremely simple thing. Likewise such a one would say that God is not man . . .' (Hyman,
     p. 635; and see p. 637). For Ockham, of course, the truth of Christian doctrine was
     necessary and inevitable, while that of natural reason was contingent, hence of an inferior
     order. Even Ockham's own fideism does not, however, suffice to resolve the problems
     raised by his logic. Despite its sincerity, it served as a means of avoiding the direct
     confrontation of faith and reason, as it had similarly served such thirteenth-century
     philosophers as Siger de Brabant and Boetius of Dacia.
         The problem of 'humanity' is treated in the *Summa Totius Logicae*; see especially Ock-
     ham's demonstration that the proposition 'humanity is in Socrates' is false (Boehner, pp.
     76–79). On shared essence, *Summa*, I, xv (Boehner, pp. 35–37).
18 In *Sent.* II, 12, for example, speaking of sins of commission, Ockham writes that 'the
     created will is not alone the efficient cause of that act, but God himself, who causes
     immediately every act. . . . And so He is the positve cause of deformity in such an act, just
     as of the substance itself of the act. . . . And if you say that God would then sin in causing
     such a deformed act . . . I reply that God is under obligation to no one; and hence He is
     neither bound to cause that act, nor the opposite act, nor not to cause it.' Likewise Jean
     Buridan, *Questions on Aristotle's Physics*, II, i (Hyman, p. 704); and Nicholas Autrecourt (d. after
     1350), letters to Bernard of Arezzo, trans. Ernest Moody and printed in Herman Shapiro,
     Medieval Philosophy. Both Buridan and Nicholas argue against total skepticism, claiming that
     even in a contingent universe we can know some truths, even if those truths are limited to
     'the common course of nature'. I don't think that this argument diminishes the impact of
     their vision of ultimate contingency.

Chapter 3, 'The politics of allegory'

1 Karl Marx, *Contribution*, pp. 11–12. The concept of substructure and superstructure has
    been revised by Althusser: see 'Contradiction and Overdetermination' and 'On the
    Materialist Dialectic' in *For Marx*; 'Ideology and Ideological State Apparatuses' in *Lenin and*

Philosophy. Though this is not the place for a detailed critique of Althusser, I am in substantial agreement with essays by Simon Clarke, Victor Seidler, Kevin McDonnell, Kevin Robbins and Terry Lovell in Clarke, and see Raymond Williams, 'Base and Superstructure'.

2 Thus C.S. Lewis admits that at one end of the medieval period, the Dark Ages produced very little original allegory, so that the twelfth-century efflorescence of the mode was 'a genuinely new creation' (pp. 84–7). At the other, there was in the fourteenth and fifteenth centuries a serious 'weakening of the genuinely allegorical impulse' (pp. 234–59). Yet none of these phenomena are accounted for, and the unevenness in production is glossed over for the sake of continuity.

Paul Piehler notes that 'Allegory as a serious genre waned in the fifteenth century owing to the growing inability of allegorical poets to continue to achieve imaginative comprehension of the symbolical and mythical elements of the form', p. 20; but their inability is not explained.

Northrop Frye admits the class uses of culture generally (p. 346); he hints at the social function of allegory in connecting it with 'the habitual or customary ideas fostered by education and ritual' (p. 90). But he recoils from these perceptions, all the way back to the idealistic Arnoldian notion that true culture transcends social class (pp. 347–8).

D.W. Robertson, attempting to trace what he sees as a nearly monolithic Augustinian tradition of allegorical thought over a thousand years of history, writes of 'the medieval world with its quiet hierarchies', 'a world without dynamically interacting polarities', which knew nothing of 'class struggles, balances of power, or . . . conflicts between economic realities and traditional ideals' (p. 51). With such statements (by now notorious among medievalists) wishful thinking becomes outright fiction. See also Fletcher for a deliberately unhistorical treatment.

Probably the most compatible with my approach, among recent work, is Maureen Quilligan's theory of allegory as related to a shift in language theory from 'suprarealist' to 'merely arbitrary'; although – following Foucault in *The Order of Things* – she places 'the vast epistemological shift' at the end of the seventeenth century (Chapter 3). Though the epistemic shift may have taken that long to become culturally dominant, its beginnings – as this paper shows – are in the fourteenth century, as are some of its early literary consequences. Foucault has, I believe, a very inadequate sense of medieval intellectual life, perhaps a consequence of his general and rather idealising focus on virtually monolithic discourses of power. See, among others, the essays by Taylor and Said in Hoy.

3 Lovejoy notes this use of medieval cosmic theory (p. 122). He adds that Renaissance astronomy would only have intensified the sense of humility, in emphasising man's littleness.

4 For this section on painting and sculpture I am indebted to Bunim, Antal, Hauser, and Kidson.

5 In Kula, p. 20, citing A. Sapori in *Annali* I (1960), p. 6. Kula adds that 'one must regard [these words] as an assertion born in the fever of polemics', not as a literal expression of methodology.

6 The paradox in the piece is to maintain a crude empiricism in its recommendations, along with idealism in its frustrated or disillusioned expectations: for the underlying premise seems to be disappointment in the lack of pure univocity in historical terms. As Marc Bloch stressed in 'Historical Analysis', the section on 'Nomenclature': 'History receives its vocabulary . . . already worn out and deformed by long usage; frequently, moreover, ambiguous from the very beginning. . . . Neither this variety of origins, nor these deviations of meaning are an inconvenience . . . if "Feudal" currently serves to characterise societies in which the fief was certainly not the most significant feature, that in no way contradicts the universal practise of all sciences, which as soon as they are no longer content with pure algebraic symbols are obliged to draw upon the confused vocabulary of daily life': *The Historian's Craft*, pp. 158, 170. To which Guy Bois adds: 'It is no

longer possible to ignore the fact that the economic life of a society, even a medieval
society, has a real coherence, and that one can and must discover the rules according to
which it functions. It is even less admissible that we should avoid this task by hiding
behind scholastic criticism of the term feudalism.' His note here reads: 'If the word is
objectionable, one can choose another. But the problem will not disappear in this way'
(p. 391).

7 These debates are taken up in Bois, Hindess and Hirst, Wolfe, and the *Past & Present*
symposium in response to Brenner. Replies from G. Bois, M. Postan, R. Hilton, E. Leroy
Ladurie and others appear in issues 78, 79 and 80 (1978), with Brenner's rebuttal in 97
(1982). See also Leach, Dobb, Bloch, *French Rural History*, Hilton in Carus-Wilson, Génicot,
and McFarlane.

8 The estate was not, of course, absolutely self-sufficient. Some luxury items were
imported; there were some merchants and peddlers; some surplus products were sold in
small local markets. But these factors were too limited to affect significantly the manorial
economy.

9 See Bloch, 'Medieval Inventions' and 'The Advent and Triumph of the Watermill', *Land
and Work*; also Carus-Wilson, 'An Industrial Revolution'.

10 These developments can perhaps be traced in turn to an influx of Arab gold to Europe,
though on the dating and precise effect of this there is some controversy. M. Lombard
argues that the gold-hoards of Egypt and the Orient, discovered and re-circulated by
Muslim conquerors during the ninth century, began from that time to revive the
European economy via the importation of European slaves, furs, wood and metal. With
the general thesis Robert Latouche substantially agrees, though arguing for a delayed
effect of the Muslim trade. Bloch (*Feudal Society*, p. 71) adduces repopulation, better
communications and the end of the Scandinavian invasions as partial causes of the revival
of commerce. For more general surveys of money and gold, see Bloch, 'The Problem of
Gold in the Middle Ages' in *Land and Work*; and M.M. Postan, 'The Rise of a Money
Economy' in Carus-Wilson, *Essays*, vol. 1.

11 For an illuminating discussion of labour and capital in the medieval period, see Marx,
Pre-Capitalist Economic Formations. The Florentine woollen industry of the fourteenth century
offers an interesting example of reverse commutation – what might almost be called wage
serfdom if not wage slavery: by a law of 1371 the worker was forbidden to repay in money
his debts to his employer, but had to repay all debts in the form of work. Cited in Mandel,
vol. I, p. 115.

12 On the meaning of liberty, see Caudwell, 'Liberty: A Study in Bourgeois Illusion', *Studies
and Further Studies*. It is no coincidence that Lagarde compares William of Ockham to
Rousseau with respect to individualism, for Rousseau fulfils what Ockham anticipated. Of
course medieval industry and trade were not absolutely 'free' but were closely regulated,
especially in the fifteenth century. But this sort of internal control does not affect my
argument about the relation of the bourgeoisie to the landed ruling classes.

13 From Quaestiones in Lib. I Physicorum, Q. cxxxvi; in Boehner, *Ockham*, p. 124.

Chapter 4, 'Havelok'

1 See Power and, for a convenient summary of scholarship on medieval English government and social structure, Wickson.

2 Text in McKechnie. Article 61, McKechnie notes, was 'nothing more nor less than
legalised rebellion' (p. 153); and though it was scarcely a feasible concession, it is
nonetheless a significant one.

3 Bracton, *De Leg.*, f. 5b, in the edition of Woodbine, vol. 2, p. 33; quoted in Kantorowiz, p.
156. See also Schulz, Pollock, and Maitland, vol. I; and McIlwain, Chapter 4.

4 The later limit is generally taken to be 1303, the date of composition of Robert Mannyng's
Handlyng Synne, which seems to imitate parts of *Havelok*. Skeat's discussion of final -e

suggests that the poem was originally written before 1300, and other internal evidence points to a date after 1296. See 'Introduction' (revised by K. Sisam) to W. Skeat's edition (Oxford, 2nd ed. 1915). All quotations in my text are from the edition of Sands. The two earlier versions of the Havelok story are Geoffrey Gaimer's Anglo-Norman *Estorie des engles*, and the Old French *Lai d'Havelok*, both twelfth century.

5 Thus Bede's *History* (2:16) praises the great peace in Britain under King Edwin, commenting on the king's special care for travellers. The *Anglo-Saxon Chronicle* for 1087 commends the righteousness and piety of William the Conqueror, his mildness to good men and severity to bad; his reign is described as a time when 'a man might go over the kingdom unhurt, with his bosom full of gold'. The Peterborough continuation of the *Chronicle* claims that under Henry I a man could carry treasure anywhere without being molested. For some details in my account of the religious theme, I am indebted to a paper by V. Ishkanian, my graduate student at Simon Fraser University.

6 The reduction of free men to servile status was not in itself unheard of in the later thirteenth century, for it was a widely debated legal question whether performance of base services over several generations could make free stock servile (Pollock and Maitland, p. 410). Opinion generally ran that it could not. As applied to magnates the threat can have had no real social analogue, and is meant to show the hyperbolic viciousness of Godrich's nature, as well as his contempt for the law of the land.

7 This may allude to Edward's special campaign against robbery, embodied in the Statute of Winchester (1285). The Statute specifies the duties of towns and hundreds, lords, sheriffs and bailiffs in expanding roads, cutting forests, guarding estates, and general surveillance against strangers: see *Records of the Borough of Northampton* (Northampton, 1889) vol. I, pp. 416–19. This was only one of Edward's many attempts to investigate and correct the bureaucratic abuses of the previous regime and his own; the results of his official inquiries appear in the Hundred Rolls and in various county assize rolls.

8 Pollock and Maitland add that the same law applied to serfs who escaped to the king's domain. As a borough privilege, the law of year and day helped to create a pool of free labour required by the bourgeoisie. Encouraged partly by this law, serfs and villeins deserted the manors in considerable numbers; see Dobb, Chapter 2.

9 See Richardson. A convenient guide to scholarship on the coronation ceremonies and oaths is the bibliography in Hoyt. Schramm provides a full study of the ceremony and its tradition.

10 The relation of rank and character is a familiar theme in the literature of the twelfth through fourteenth centuries. It is debated in *De Arte Honesti Amandi* of Andreas Capellanus (Dialogues two and three). In Jean de Meun's continuation of the *Roman de la Rose*, Reason shows that the nobleman who seeks only pleasure becomes Satan's serf (4396–8). Chaucer, following Jean, would take up the question of true 'gentilesse' in his *Wife of Bath's Tale*, and it would be illustrated (through from a different angle) by Langland in the person of Piers Plowman.

11 While I admire Halvorsen's wish to place *Havelok* in its social context, his concept of class is vague and inaccurate. He suggests, for instance, that 'middle class' is preferable to 'bourgeois' as a designation for this type of literature, because the former term is more inclusive, ranging from 'the villager and peasant at one end [of the social spectrum] and powerful burgher and even petty nobility at the other'. But it is just this inclusiveness that produces imprecision: witness Halvoren's inclusion of peasants in the middle class with no specification as to rich or poor peasant, servile or free, etc. My argument is that *Havelok* is by no means as diffuse in its ideology as Halvorsen implies: its range of social consciousness does not include that of villagers and peasants but is limited to that of burgesses and barons. One would be surprised to find a work of literature so false to social reality that it could claim identity of values among classes so divergent in their interests.

Such, however, appears to be the vision of David Staines, whose discussion of *Havelok* is hopelessly confused as far as class and class ideology are concerned. For Staines, the poem expresses social ideas suitable to royalty and 'the lower classes' alike. This would be quite a juggling act, even if Staines had enlightened us as to the referent of 'lower classes' and explained what they are lower than: lower than the king? lower than the bourgeoisie? lower than the artisanate? The article beautifully illustrates the need for precision in class terminology.

Susan Crane rightly rejects the peasant view, arguing that *Havelok* 'attends to some interests that the barony shared with the emerging professional and mercantile class' (p. 44); she characterises the poem as 'a utopian vision of harmony and happiness' (p. 44), 'a romance of the law' (p. 48).

Chapter 5, 'Rewriting woman good'

1 I don't endorse Cixous's exhortation to women writers to 'write the body' and agree in this with critiques offered by Homans (pp. 3–4), Ann Jones and Hélène Wenzel.
2 There is no evidence that Chaucer and Christine met, or used one another's works, but it is likely that they knew of one another. They inhabited the same international courtly and intellectual community, read the same books (ranging from Boethius to Matheolus, Boccaccio, and Deschamps), shared a patron in Henry IV, who liked Christine's poetry and invited her to England. Christine was a close friend of the Earl of Salisbury who took her son to England in 1937. When Salisbury was beheaded two years later as a supporter of Richard II, Henry became the boy's protector. Chaucer died in 1400, Christine about 1430.
3 An instance of such juxtaposition from another period would be the Gilgamesh epic (c. 2500 B.C.) and the more or less contemporaneous *Exaltation of Inanna* (ed. Hallo). The first text shows the depreciation of the goddess Ishtar and her cult by the (male) monarch, in favor of the sun-god Shamash. The second – composed by the poet/priestess/princess Enkeduanna – asserts the supremacy of Ishtar (Inanna). The problem with this pair of texts is that we do not unequivocally know the Gilgamesh epic to be the work of male authors, even though it seems to celebrate male supremacy in rule.
4 On Chaucer's general use of sceptical fideism, see my *Chaucer's House of Fame*.
5 The Prologue to *LGW* exists in two texts, designated F and G. On differences between F and G, see David and Leonard. I have used the F-text as the somewhat fuller version, but my reading of the Prologue would not be substantially different had I used G.
6 It is a telling clue to Chaucer's ironic intention that he omits from his collection the story of Penelope: surely the most absolute and unambiguous exemplum of female virtue that a genuine vindicator of the sex could use, and one that Chaucer uses in numerous other places (*BD* 1081, *Frank T*, V, 1443–44 and elsewhere).
7 Working women were the norm in late-medieval society for every class except the aristocracy. Certainly the peasantry, artisans and urban bourgeoisie took female labour for granted: Shahar, and my *Writing Woman*, Chapters 2 and 5. The writing woman was a far more threatening, and far less typical, phenomenon than the working woman; cf. King ('Retreat').
8 Quotations are from the extremely thorough critical edition, with Introduction and Notes, by Maureen Curnow. I have also consulted a microfilm of the 1521 English translation of Bryan Anslay. My translations are done from Curnow's edition, since this chapter was written before the appearance of Jeffrey Richards's translation.
9 Matheolus was also an important immediate source for some of Chaucer's best-known work; cf. Thundy. So it is possible that Chaucer's and Christine's crises were triggered by the same source: Matheolus as a relatively recent clerical *auctor* defining the misogynist tradition. The *Lamentations* were written about 1280 and translated into French about 1370. Matheolus (or his narrator) reveals that he was prompted to write by an unhappy marriage to a much younger woman whom he was unable to satisfy sexually. Jill Mann refers frequently to Matheolus as social satirist. Katharine M. Rogers provides further

references but not a particularly illuminating discussion of the misogynistic tradition. See
also Utley, and Ferrante, *Woman as Image.*

10 Pierre-Yves Badel points out that Christine's use of 'certaine science' as opposed to mere
opinion is taken ultimately from Aristotle's *Metaphysics* and was discussed by other
medieval writers, including Thomas Aquinas (pp. 439–40). Susan Schibanoff also stresses
that experience (rather than literacy) is the real source of wisdom for Christine.

11 Christine knew Boccaccio's text through a French translation, *Des Cleres et Nobles Femmes*, as
Curnow demonstrates. For several stories she also used the *Decameron* in the original
Italian, and, also in French translation, *De Casibus Virorum Illustrium*. For a modern transla-
tion see Guarini.

12 Annette Kolodny takes up this problem in 'A Map for Rereading', offering as a 'fictive
rendering of the dilemma of the woman writer' an interesting short story (1917), by Susan
K. Glaspell. See also Feit-Diehl and Homans.

Chapter 6, 'Mothers to think back through'

1 Haight, K.M. Wilson, Bogin, LaBalme, King and Rabil, Rabil, Jones, Richards and Willard.

2 Earlier versions of Richards's position were put forward by Rigaud, who writes of 'cette
femme "moderne," féministe convaincue . . . "précurseur" ' (p. 25 and of 'la théori-
cienne du féminisme moderne' (p. 142); also by Abensour, who claims that Christine
'élabore un corps de doctrine féministe . . . avec la même méthode que les modernes
défenseurs des droits de la femme' (p. v.). Though Lulu M. Richardson began her book
with a chapter on Christine, she nonetheless concluded that there is nothing in
Christine's work that 'could give anyone any grounds for calling Christine a radical
feminist' (p. 33); and even Rigaud is circumspect enough to place Christine 'à la droite du
mouvement actuel' (p. 143).
    More recently, Lucas sees Christine as 'dedicated to championing women's interests in
her society;' Joan Kelly characterises Christine as a feminist who 'defined what was to
become the modern feminist sensibility'. Rabant describes her as 'la première féministe
connue', p. 19; and two militants of the French women's movement have taken the
names of two women whom they obviously consider precursors and role models; cf.
Annie de Pisan and Anne Tristan. The irony is that neither Christine nor Flora Tristan was
a feminist, if by feminist we mean someone who draws the sex line before the class (or
race) line. Christine was loyal first and foremost to the French aristocracy, Flora Tristan to
the international proletariat.
    Recent scholars who have seen Christine as conservative or even reactionary include
Douglass Kelly, Baird and Kane (p. 18), and Davis. In 1975 Willard warned against using
Christine for ideas that she did not really express, observing that Christine's role in the
Roman quarrel does not bear out the recent view of her as forerunner of modern feminists:
'A Fifteenth-Century View'. This reverses an earlier opinion, for in the Introduction to her
edition of the *Livre de la Paix*, Willard had urged us to see Christine as 'precursor . . . of the
whole feminist movement' (p. 14).

3 See Curnow, vol. 1, chap. 5. For a different perspective on Christine's style, Richards,
'Christine de Pizan and the Question of Feminist Rhetoric'.

4 There is autobiographical material in *Cité des Dames*, in the *Mutacion*, and in *Lavision.*

5 Tuchman, William C. Jordan, Lagarde, *Naissance* and Crombie, *Medieval and Early Modern
Science*, vol. 2, offer helpful discussion and bibliography.

6 In 'Le débat du heraut, du vassault et du villain' (ed. Laidlaw), the villein interrupts the
other two to present the views of the peasantry on the state of society. Kenneth Varty
makes the point about criticism of government in his edition of Christine's *Ballades,
Rondeaux and Virelais*, p. 164. Sandra Hindman fine-tunes our sense of Christine at court in
her impressive study of the illuminations to several mss. of Christine's work.

7 For information in this paragraph, see Gies, Abram, Green, Thrupp, Renard, Kanner, ed.,

and Shahar. On the Italian women scholars see LaBalme, King and Rabil. Gervase Mathew lists at leasts a half-dozen well-educated romance heroines (p. 193).

8 As for the urban poor, her treatment is equally literary. Brian Woledge calls attention to passages in the *Mutacion* in which Christine writes vividly of the suffering of city dwellers who have been reduced to poverty by misfortune. See Lis and Soly, Mollat, and Aers.

9 Christine's failure to recommend advanced learning to her contemporaries is addressed by Bell who seems to agree with Christine's view that 'it is woman's work to keep the fabric of society intact'. The three reasons she offers for Christine's limited educational policy did not convince me. Bell claims that Christine had in mind the necessity of repopulation during a period of war; that she realised most women had insufficient time to study anyway; that as a writer – an isolated woman doing 'man's work' – Christine 'outgrew her female friends and became estranged from the essential female network of her society'. These strike me more as excuses than as reasons. See also Astrik L. Gabriel, 'The Educational Ideas of Christine de Pisan'.

10 See Duby. I am not suggesting that Jean de Meun advocated fornication. I tend to agree with Fleming's interpretation of the work, though Fleming ignores the social context of sexual politics which Duby illuminates and which surely affected response to the *Roman*. This lack is plentifully made good by Payen, who writes, in *La Rose et l'Utopie*, of 'révolution sexuelle et communisme nostalgique chez Jean de Meung'. It seems to me that while Payen bends the stick too far the other way, his polarisation is a salutary one in context of a perhaps too-conservative modern approach.

11 See the collection of riddles and jokes in Roy; also Muscatine (*Fabliaux*), Bowden, and Menard.

12 On homosexuality and the evolution of ecclesiastical attitudes toward it, see Boswell; for methods of and attitudes toward contraception, Noonan, *Contraception*.

13 *Mutacion*, 8413–42. For this reference I am indebted to the unpublished dissertation of Nadia Margolis (Stanford, 1977). Though Margolis claims Christine 'was no more anti-semitic than any other Christian living in France or Italy at that time' (p. 205), see Richard Schoeck.

14 My thanks for this comment to Sandra Gilbert, who heard an earlier version of this chapter.

Chapter 7, 'Clerks and quiting'

1 The notion of quiting extends through the Cook's prologue as well: 'But er we part, ywis, thou shalt be quit' (I,4362), are the Cook's words to Harry Bailey. This suggests that *The Cooks Tale* might have been a nasty 'quiting' (retaliation), based on professional hostility, to the Host's jocular exposure of Roger's dubious practices (4346–52), and the trio of tales a set united by varying interpretations of the word 'quit'. But since *The Cook's Tale* is hardly begun, it is possible only to speculate on structural relations among the three *fabliaux*.

2 In *The Old French Fabliaux*, Charles Muscatine adjusts Nykrog's overall theory of the social origins and viewpoint of the *fabliaux* in general. Though Muscatine does not refer to the role of the university student, it is one point that tends to support his remarks. On the whole I think Muscatine protests too much against a social reading, as his own conclud-ing paragraphs suggest: so that the book provides an instance of what Paul de Man has called 'blindness and insight', a shying away from its own fissures, contradictions and larger implications.

3 For the following summary of medieval academic privileges I have used Rashdall, Kibre, Gabriel, and Cobban.

4 Brewer suggests the (rather slender) possibility that the original reading might have been 'Scolers' or 'Scoler' rather than 'Soler' Hall.

5 On priests' offspring, see Schimmelpfennig; on millers, Jones.

Chapter 8, 'Strategies of silence'

1 For the Wife's treatment of Scripture, see Robertson, *Preface*; on the classics, Allen and Gallacher, and Robertson, 'The Wife of Bath and Midas'.

2 No. 23 in Ewert and Johnston; No. 37 in Warnke. Chaucer used another of Marie's fables as a source for *The Nun's Priest's Tale*.

3 An intriguing illustration of the persistence of psychologism is H. Marshall Leicester's 'Of a fire in the dark: Public and private feminism in the *Wife of Bath's Tale*', *Women's Studies* 11 (1984), 157–78. The piece displays on oddly unselfconscious slippage away from its opening premises. 'Of course there is no Wife of Bath. What there is is an impersonation' (175). Nonetheless this impersonation 'remains a mystery to herself', while Chaucer tries to 'sustain her mystery, her possibility and her independence . . . respect her privacy' (176). By the end it's the character who takes over, dictates the author's strategy: she *has* a real psychology, it's just that she won't reveal it!

4 See my 'Sexual Economics, the Wife of Bath, and *The Book of Margery Kempe*' in *Writing Woman*.

5 Shapiro concentrates on the Wife's suppression of her own suffering in marriage. Shapiro too takes a psychologistic approach, assuming the omissions tell us something about the kind of 'person' Alison 'really was'; she sees Alison as one who 'avoids speaking of things that deeply move her' (p. 135).

6 Christine de Pizan devotes several chapter in *Cité des Dames* to rape and to the slander that women enjoy rape: Book 2, chapter 43–46. She believes that rape should be a capital offence.

7 In 'Male Fantasy', Ferrante similarly problematises the figure of the 'real' woman who sometimes appears in courtly lyric to debunk the conventions of courtly love. 'The poet uses the fiction of the "real" woman precisely to express his own doubts and to ridicule his own fantasies. In other words, the woman as realist is as much a projection of the man's self-image as the woman who is symbol of the ideal.' Bec confirms this tendency in his discussion of certain cynical, naturalistic or obscene troubador lyrics which fail to extinguish 'la misogynie ambiante qui retrouve son émergence, et cela dans une textualité pseudo-féminine qui est en fait, encore une fois, un contre-texte masculin': pp. 8–9. Also see Felman, and Irigaray's deconstruction of Freud's theories of femininity in *Speculum*.

Chapter 9, 'The haunted work'

1 On Bernard see Dutton; on the image, Jeauneau. I have given the passage a more aphoristic character than it has in the original.

2 During the period 500–300 B.C., 'plebs' meant a section of the population that could loosely be termed 'the middle classes': that is, between noble patricians and the poor, or, as the *Oxford Companion to Classical Literature* puts it, 'the Roman burgesses other than the patricians'. Their struggle, a gradual but eventually successful one, was to win full civil rights: e.g., the right to intermarry with patricians and to hold all political and priestly offices. Once these rights were won, the name 'plebs' passed over to the working population, the Roman masses of artisans, shopkeepers, day labourers, servants, etc. See Cowell and P.G. Walsh.

3 'Chevalier' is the obvious equivalent for the Latin 'milites', but this leaves an inconsistency between the medieval knight's priviledged status as a member of the lower feudal nobility, and, on the other hand, the erstwhile exclusion of the plebs from such privileged status. Perhaps Boccaccio acknowledges this inconsistency in describing Virginius as 'plebian but honest' (*plebs sed honestus*). Of course the really radical innovation in a medieval treatment of this legend would have been to present Virginius as a wealthy and virtuous bourgeois, Applius as a representative or ally of the feudal aristocracy. While that

would have been a more accurate analogy to the political struggle recounted in Livy, it would have required a crystallised class consciousness that the bourgeoisie would develop only over the next few centuries. During the high Middle Ages the upper bourgeoisie aspired to emulate aristocrats and ally with kings – not depose or expropriate them.

4 The phrase about the commune is Boccaccio's. For a clear outline of economic and political struggle in Florence, see also Antal, Chapters 1 and 2. Antal notes, interestingly for my purpose here, that in the Ordinamenti di Giustizia – the constitution of 1293, in which the upper bourgeoisie won a decisive victory in obtaining political power for their guilds – 'the revolutionary bourgeoisie had still proudly called themselves "plebians" (p. 33, n. 38). The Roman tradition remained rhetorically viable well into our own period: witness Karl Marx's comment from *The Eighteenth Brumaire*: '. . . the heroes as well as the parties and the masses of the old French Revolution performed the task of their time in Roman costume and with Roman phrases, the task of unchaining and setting up modern *bourgeois* society . . .' (his italics).

5 For Chaucer's usually unflattering view of 'the people', we may also adduce *Troilus*, 5:141–217, where it is the majority of parliament who unscrupulously vote to exchange Criseyde for Antenor, despite Hector's well-taken objection that she is no prisoner of war. The assembly in *The Parliament of Fowls* offers an obvious parody of the greed of the lower orders (as well, to be sure, of the theatricality of the upper) for those who are inclined to take that scene as a social fable.

6 The 'digressions' are often attributed to the Physician's dubious character, as are the manifold aesthetic and moral inadequacies of the tale. This approach doesn't, I believe, stand up to two objections. First: usually when a tale is a failure and intended as such (e.g. *The Squire's Tale* or *The Tale of Sir Thopas*) or when narrative inconsistencies or quirks further characterise a narrator (Wife of Bath, Prioress, Merchant) those intentions are fairly obvious: the audience reacts to the former, or in the latter case, we can pretty clearly demonstrate the relation between tale and teller. Second, there is no necessary relation between a narrator's moral character and the quality of his or her tale (Pardoner, Summoner, even Wife of Bath). Some critics have found ways of relating the digressions to a central theme, but not, in my view, convincingly. For example, Middleton finds that the added material shows artists and parents functioning as 'secondary creators', and that it poses the problem of who finally controls the disposition of human life.

7 The first phrase comes from F. Engels's letter of November 26, 1895, to Minna Kautsky. The second is from Langer (p. 331).

8 Although Stephen Knight argues convincingly that the 1381 revolt is present to *The Canterbury Tales* in subtler ways (pp. 67 ff.).

Chapter 10, 'Mulier est hominis confusio'

1 Gurevich also emphasises the various angles from which it is possible to discuss the 'popular' (pp. xv–xvi).

2 Both texts published in *Sources and Analogues*. Foulet shows that Glichezaere's version is not merely a translation but a blending and reordering – not without originality – of material from several branches of the *Renart* (Chapter 17).

3 Wakefield suggests that this current was not necessarily the residue of heretical thought, but 'may well have arisen spontaneously from the cogitations of men and women searching for explanations that accorded with the realities of the life in which they were enmeshed' (p. 33).

Chapter 11, 'Women, nature and language'

1 Spearing notes of this pun that we can't be absolutely certain it is one because 're-leave'

isn't attested in the OED until the seventeenth century, and the vowel sounds in the two 'releve's would be slightly different (pp. 9–10). I think we can press our dependence on OED too far: words circulate orally long before they are canonised into writing, and many a pun depends on neologism which may or may not eventually enter the mainstream. As for differing vowel sounds, Ahl shows that this was no obstacle to Latin poets in their word-play, and I doubt it was to medievals either (p. 55).

2 'The English Contribution to Logic Before Ockham.' On the *modistae* (so called because of their stress on modes of signification), also see Bursill-Hall and Rosier. One might look at the Stoic tradition as an unacknowledged influence on the modistae: see Colish.

3 Pinborg, 'English Contribution', p. 25. Howard Bloch's treatment of late-medieval linguistics collapses the modist/terminist opposition, Chapter 4. In light of Pinborg's work, Bloch's claim that 'Both the nominalists and the *modistae* . . . disrupt the assumed continuity of words and things characteristic of early medieval linguistics' (p. 153) seems inaccurate.

4 Lévi-Strauss, *Structures*; quotations and paraphrases from pages 493–6. See also *Structural Anthropology*, Chapters 3, 5 and 15 especially. In adducing Lévi-Strauss, I don't wish to imply complete solidarity with his approach, which omits sexual division of labour as a necessary precondition to the exchange of women. See critique by Rubin, Cowie, deLauretis (pp. 18–20); and Irigaray, 'Women on the Market', in *This Sex*.

Texts cited

Abels, Richard and Ellen Harrison, 'The Participation of Women in Languedocian Catharism', *Mediaeval Studies* 41 (1979), pp. 215-51.

Abram, A., 'Women Traders in Medieval London', *The Economic Journal* 26 (1916), pp. 276-85.

Abensour, Leon, *La Femme et le Féminisme avant la Révolution* (Paris, 1923).

Aers, David, 'Piers Plowman and Problems in the Perception of Poverty: A Culture in Transition', *Leeds Studies in English* n.s. 14 (1983), pp. 5-25.

Ahl, Frederick, *Metaformations. Soundplay and Wordplay in Ovid and Other Classical Poets* (Ithaca, 1985).

Alanus de Insulis, *The Plaint of Nature*, trans. James J. Sheridan (Toronto, 1980).

Alighieri, Dante, *On World-Government*, trans. Herbert W. Schneider (New York, 1957).

Allen, Judson B. and Patrick Gallacher, 'Alisoun Through the Looking Glass: or Every Man His Own Midas', *The Chaucer Review* 4 (1970), pp. 99-105.

——, *The Ethical Poetic of the Later Middle Ages* (Toronto, 1982).

Alpers, Svetlana, *The Art of Describing* (Chicago, 1983).

Althusser, Louis, *Lenin and Philosophy and other essays* (London, 1971).

——, *For Marx* (London, 1979).

Anderson, Perry, *Passages From Antiquity to Feudalism* (London, 1974).

Andreas Capellanus, *The Art of Courtly Love*, trans. John Jay Parry (New York, 1941).

Anon., *Alchemy and Chemistry in the Seventeenth Century* (Los Angeles, 1966).

——, trans., *Nicholas Flammel His Exposition* (London, 1624).

Antal, Frederick, *Florentine Painting and Its Social Background* (London, 1948).

Aston, Margaret, *Lollards and Reformers* (London, 1984).

Atwood, Mary Anne, *A Suggestive Inquiry into the Hermetic Mystery* (1850; rev. 3rd ed. Belfaast, 1920; repr. Salem, N.H., 1976).

Auerbach, Erich, 'Figura' in *Scenes from the Drama of European Literature* (New York, 1959).

Baczko, Bronislaw, *Lumières de l'Utopie* (Paris, 1978).

Badel, Pierre-Yves, *Le Roman de la Rose au XIVe Siècle, Etude de la Réception de l'Oeuvre* (Geneva, 1980).

Baird, Joseph L. and John R. Kane, *La Querelle de la Rose. Letters and Documents* (Chapel Hill, 1978).

Barker, Francis, *The Tremulous Private Body* (London, 1984).

Barthes, Roland, *Writing Degree Zero* (Paris, 1953; New York, 1968).

——, *Mythologies* (1957; New York, 1972).

Bec, Pierre, *Burlesque et Obscenité Chez les Troubadours* (Paris, 1984).

Bell, Susan Groag, 'Christine de Pizan (1364-1430): Humanism and the Problem of a Studious Woman', *Feminist Studies* (1976), pp. 173-84.

Bigongiari, Dino, ed., *The Political Ideas of St. Thomas Aquinas* (New York, 1965).

Bloch, Ernst, The Principle of Hope (1938; English trans. Cambridge, Mass., 1986), 3 vols.

Bloch, Marc, The Historian's Craft (New York, 1953).

——, Feudal Society (London, 1961).

——, French Rural History (Berkeley, 1966).

——, Land and Work in Medieval Europe: Selected Papers (New York, 1969).

Bloch, R. Howard, Etymologies and Genealogies. A Literary Anthropology of the Middle Ages (Chicago, 1983).

Bloom, Harold, The Anxiety of Influence (New York, 1973).

Boehner, Philotheus, 'The Realistic Conceptualism of William Ockham', Traditio 4 (1946), 307-35 and reprinted in Collected Articles on Ockham (St. Bonaventura, N.Y., 1958).

——, ed., Ockham, Philosophical Writings (London, 1957).

Bogin, Meg, The Woman Troubadours (Scarsborough, 1976).

Bois, Guy, The Crisis of Feudalism. Economy and Society in Eastern Normandy c. 1300-1550 (Cambridge, 1984).

Bonaventura, Saint, The Mind's Road to God, trans. George Boas (New York, 1953).

Bonus of Ferrara, The New Pearl of Great Price, trans. A. Waite (London, 1894; repr. Salem, N.H., 1974).

Boren, James L., 'Alysoun of Bath and the Vulgate "Perfect Wife" ', Neuphilologische Mitteilungen 76 (1975), pp. 247-56.

Boswell, John, Christianity, Social Tolerance, and Homosexuality (Chicago, 1980).

Bowden, Betsy, 'The Art of Courtly Copulation', Medievalia et Humanistica n.s.9 (1979), pp. 67-86.

Branca, Vittore, Boccaccio: The Man and His Works (New York, 1976).

Brewer, Derek, 'The Reeve's Tale and the King's Hall, Cambridge', Chaucer Review 5 (1971), pp. 311-17; repr. in Tradition and Innovation in Chaucer (London, 1982).

Browder, Clifford, André Breton, Arbiter of Surrealism (Geneva, 1967).

Brown, Elizabeth A.R., 'The Tyranny of a Construct: Feudalism and Historians of Medieval Europe', American Historical Review 79 (1974), pp. 1063-88.

Brunet, P., ed., Histoire des Sciences (Paris, 1935).

Bryan, W.R. and Germaine Dempster, eds., Sources and Analogues of Chaucer's Canterbury Tales (New York, 1941).

Bunim, Miriam Schild, Space in Medieval Painting and the Forerunners of Perspective (New York, 1940).

Burland, C.A., The Arts of the Alchemists (London, 1967).

Bursill-Hall, G.L., Speculative Grammars of the Middle Ages (Hague, 1971).

Carruthers, Mary, 'The Wife of Bath and the Painting of Lions', PMLA 94 (1979), pp. 209-22.

Carus-Wilson, E.M., 'An Industrial Revolution of the Thirteenth Century' in Medieval Merchant Venturers (London, 1954).

——, ed., Essays in Economic History, 2 vols. (London, 1962).

Cassirer, Ernst, The Philosophy of Symbolic Forms, 3 vols. (New Haven, 1953-57).

Caudwell, Christopher, Studies and Further Studies in A Dying Culture (New York, 1971).

Chicago, Judy, The Dinner Party. A Symbol of our Heritage (New York, 1979).

Cixous, Hélène, 'The Laugh of the Medusa', Signs 1 (1976), pp. 875-93 and reprinted in New French Feminisms, ed. Elaine Marks and Isabelle de Courtivron (New York, 1981).

Clagett, Marshall, ed., *The Science of Mechanics in the Middle Ages* (Madison, 1959).

Clarke, Simon, ed., *One-Dimensional Marxism. Althusser and the Politics of Culture* (London, 1980).

Cobban, Alan B., *The Medieval Universities, their development and organization* (London, 1978).

Cocchiara, Giuseppe, *Il Paese di Cuccagna e altri studi di folklore* (Turin, 1950).

Colish, Marcia L., 'The Stoic Theory of Verbal Signification' in *Archéologie du Signe*, ed. Lucie Brind'amour and Eugene Vance (Toronto, 1983).

Cornford, F.M., trans., *Plato's Cosmology* (London and New York, 1937).

Coville, Alfred, *Les Cabochiens et l'Ordonnance de 1413* (Paris, 1888).

Cowell, F.R.., *The Revolutions of Ancient Rome* (London, 1962).

Cowie, Elizabeth, 'Woman as sign', m/f 1 (1978), pp. 49-63.

Crane, Susan, *Insular Romance. Politics, Faith and Culture in Anglo-Norman and Middle English Literature* (Berkeley, 1986).

Crombie, A.C., *Medieval and Early Modern Science*, 2 vols. (New York, 1959).

——, ed., *Scientific Change* (New York, 1963).

Crowther, J.G., *The Social Relations of Science* (London, 1939; New York, 1966).

Curnow, Maureen, *The Livre de la Cité des Dames of Christine de Pisan: A Critical Edition*, 2 vols. (Ph.D. dissertation, Vanderbilt University, 1975).

Curry, Walter Clyde, *Chaucer and the Medieval Sciences* (Oxford, 1926; 2nd ed., London, 1960).

Dahmer, Helmut, 'Bertolt Brecht and Stalinism', *Telos* 22 (1974/75), pp. 96-105.

David, Alfred, *The Strumpet Muse* (Bloomington, 1976).

Davis, Judith M., 'Christine de Pisan and Chauvinist Diplomacy', *Female Studies* 6 (Old Westbury, N.Y., 1973).

Dawson, J.G., trans. *De Regimine Principium in Aquinas: Selected Political Writings*, ed A.P. D'Entrèves (Oxford, 1959).

de Boer, Cornelis, ed., *Ovide Moralisé* (Amsterdam, 1915-38).

Delany, Sheila, *Chaucer's House of Fame: the Poetics of Skeptical Fideism* (Chicago, 1972).

——, *Writing Woman. Women Writers and Women in Literature, Medieval to Modern* (New York, 1983).

——, 'The Logic of Obscenity in Chaucer's *Legend of Good Women*', *Florilegium* 7 (1987 for 1985), pp. 189-205.

de Lauretis, Teresa, *Alice Doesn't: Feminism, Semiotics, Cinema* (Bloomington, 1981).

Diamond, Arlyn and Lee R. Edwards, eds., *The Authority of Experience* (Amherst, 1977).

Dobb, Maurice, *Studies in the Development of Capitalism* (New York, 1947).

Doiron, Sister Marilyn, 'The Middle English Translation of Le Mirouer des Simples Ames' in *Dr. L. Reypens-Album*, ed. Dr. Alb. Ampe, S.J. (Antwerp, 1964).

duBois, Page, 'Sexual Difference: Ancient and Modern', *Pacific Coast Philology* (November, 1984), pp. 43-49.

Duby, Georges, *Le Chevalier, La Femme et le Prêtre. Le Mariage dans la France Féodale* (Paris, 1981).

Duhem, Pierre, *Etudes sur Léonardo da Vinci*, 3 vols. (Paris, 1906).

Duncan, Edgar H., 'The Literature of Alchemy and Chaucer's *Canon's Yeoman's Tale*', *Speculum* 43 (1968), pp. 633-56.

Dutton, Paul, 'The Uncovering of the *Glosae Super Platonem* of Bernard of Chartres', *Mediaeval Studies* 46 (1984), pp. 192-221.

Eagleton, Terry, *Literary Theory. An Introduction* (Oxford, 1983).

Eliade, Mircea, *Cosmos and History* (New York, 1954).

——, *The Forge and the Crucible. The Origins and Structures of Alchemy* (Chicago, 1962).

Erdman, David, *The Poetry and Prose of William Blake* (Garden City, N.Y., 1965).

Fabricius, Johannes, *Alchemy: The Medieval Alchemists and Their Royal Art* (Copenhagen, 1976).

Feit-Diehl, Joanne, ' "Come Slowly – Eden": An Exploration of Women Poets and their Muse', *Signs* 3 (1978), pp. 572-87.

Felman, Shoshana, 'Rereading Femininity', *Yale French Studies* 62 (1981), pp. 19-44.

Ferrante, Joan, *Woman as Image in Medieval Literature* (New York, 1975).

——, 'Male fantasy and female reality in courtly literature', *Women's Studies* 11 (1984), pp. 67-97.

Fetterley, Judith, *The Resisting Reader. A Feminist Approach to American Fiction* (Indiana, 1978).

Finke, Laurie, 'The Rhetoric of Marginality: Why I do Feminist Theory', *Tulsa Studies in Women's Literature* 5 (1986), pp. 251-72.

Fisher, Bernice, 'Review', *Feminist Studies* (1981), pp. 100-12.

Fisher, John H. *John Gower: Moral Philosopher and Friend of Chaucer* (New York, 1964).

Fleming, John V., *The Roman de la Rose. A Study in Allegory and Iconography* (Princeton, 1969).

Fletcher, Angus, *Allegory: The Theory of a Symbolic Mode* (Ithaca, 1964).

Foucault, Michel, 'What Is An Author?' in *Textual Strategies*, ed. Josué Harari (Ithaca, 1979).

Foulet, Lucien, *Le Roman de Renard* (Paris, 1914).

Frank, Robert W., Jr., *Chaucer and the Legend of Good Women* (Cambridge, Mass., 1972).

Frye, Northrop, *Anatomy of Criticism* (Princeton, 1957).

Gabriel, Astrik L., 'The Educational Ideas of Christine de Pisan', *Journal of the History of Ideas* 16 (1955), pp. 3-21.

——, 'The College System in the Fourteenth Century Universities', in *The Forward Movement of the Fourteenth Century* ed., Francis Lee Utley (Columbus, 1961).

Gagnon, Claude, 'Les alchimistes et les spéculateurs' in *Aspects de la marginalité au Moyen Age*, ed. Guy-H. Allard (Montreal, 1975).

——, *Description du Livre des Figures . . . attribué a Nicolas Flamel* (Montreal, 1977).

Ganzenmuller, Wilhelm, *L'Alchimie au Moyen Age* (Paris, 1939).

Garbaty, Thomas J., 'Studies in the Franciscan "The Land of Cokaygne" in the Kildare Ms.', *Franziskanische Studien* 45 (1963).

Gellrich, Jesse, *The Idea of the Book in the Middle Ages. Language Theory, Mythology and Fiction* (Ithaca, 1985).

Génicot, Leopold, 'Crisis: From the Middle Ages to Modern Times', in *The Cambridge Economic History of Europe*, vol. 1.

Gewirth, Alan, trans., *Marsilius of Padua. The Defender of Peace*, 2 vols. (New York, 1967).

Gierke, Otto, *Political Thought of the Middle Ages*, trans. F.W. Maitland (Cambridge, 1900, 1958).

Gies, Frances and Joseph, *Women in the Middle Ages* (New York, 1978).

Gilbert, Sandra and Susan Gubar, *The Madwoman in the Attic. The Woman Writer and the Nineteenth-Century Literary Imagination* (New Haven, 1979).

Ginzberg, Carlo, *The Cheese and the Worms. The Cosmos of a Sixteenth-Century Miller* (Baltimore, 1980).

Grant, Edward, 'Late Medieval Thought, Copernicus, and the Scientific Revolution', *Journal of the History of Ideas* 23 (1962), pp. 197-220.

Green, Alice S., *Town Life in the Fifteenth Century*, 2 vols. (Boston, 1894; repr. New York, 1971).

Guarini, Guido A., trans. *Concerning Famous Women* (New Brunswick, 1963).

Gubar, Susan, ' "The Blank Page" and Female Creativity', in *Writing and Sexual Difference*, ed. Elizabeth Abel (Chicago, 1982).

Gurevitch, Aron, *Medieval Popular Culture* (Cambridge, 1988).

Haight, Ann L., ed., *Hroswitha of Gandersheim: Her Life, Times and Works* (New York, 1965).

Hallo, W.W. and J. van Dijk eds., *The Exaltation of Inanna* (New Haven, 1968).

Halvorsen, John, 'Havelok the Dane and Society', *Chaucer Review* 6 (1971), pp. 142-51.

Hauser, Arnold, *The Social History of Art*, 4 vols. (New York, 1957).

Henderson, Ernest J., ed. and trans., *Select Historical Documents of the Middle Ages* (London, 1910).

Hicks, Eric, *Le Débat sur le Roman de la Rose* (Paris, 1977).

Hilka, Alfons and Werner Soderhjelm, eds., *Petri Alfonsi Disciplina Clericalis* (Helsingfors, 1919).

Hindess, Barry and Paul Hirst, *Pre-Capitalist Modes of Production* (London, 1975).

Hindman, Sandra, *Christine de Pizan's 'Epistre Othea.' Painting and Politics at the Court of Charles VI* (Toronto, 1986).

Holmyard, E.J., trans., 'An Alchemical Tract Ascribed to Mary the Copt', *Archivo dei storia della scienza* 8 (1927), pp. 161-68.

Homans, Margaret, *Woman Writers and Poetic Identity* (Princeton, 1980).

Hoy, David, *Foucault. A Critical Reader* (Oxford, 1986).

Hoyt, Robert S., 'The Coronation oath of 1308', *Traditio* 11 (1955), pp. 235-57.

Hudson, Anne, *Lollards and Their Books* (London, 1985).

Hyman, Arthur and James J. Walsh, eds., *Philosophy in the Middle Ages* (New York, 1967).

Irigaray, Luce, *Speculum of the Other Woman* (Ithaca, 1985).

——, *This Sex Which is Not One* (Ithaca, 1985).

Jaeger, Werner, *Aristotle* (Oxford, 1923).

Jeauneau, Edouard, 'Nains et Geants', in *Entretiens sur la Renaissance du 12e Siècle* (Hague, 1968), pp. 21-52 (including discussion).

Jeffrey, David L., *The Early English Lyric and Franciscan Spirituality* (Lincoln, Neb., 1975).

Johnstone, H., Chapter 14, vol. 7 in *The Cambridge Medieval History*, 8 vols. (Cambridge, repr. 1964-67).

Jolivet, Jean, *Godescalc d'Orbais et la Trinité* (Paris, 1958).

Jones, Ann, 'Writing the Body: Toward an Understanding of l'Ecriture Feminine', in *Feminist Studies* 7 (1981), pp. 247-63.

——, 'Two Renaissance Poets', *Yale French Studies* 62 (1981), pp. 135-53.

Jones, George F., 'Chaucer and the Medieval Miller', *Modern Language Quarterly* 16 (1955), pp. 3-15.

Jordan, Robert M., letter in 'Forum', *PMLA* 96 (1979), pp. 950-52.

Jordan, William C. et al., eds., *Order and Innovation in the Middle Ages* (Princeton, 1976).

Jung, Carl, *Psychology and Alchemy* (Princeton, 1968).

——, *Mysterium Conjunctionis* (Princeton, 1970).

Kanner, Barbara, ed. *The Women of England from Anglo-Saxon Times to the Present*,

Interpretive Bibliographical Essays (Hamden, 1979).

Kantorowicz, Ernst, *The King's Two Bodies* (Princeton, 1957).

Kelly, F. Douglass, 'Reflections on the Role of Christine de Pisan as a Feminist Writer', *sub-stance* 2 (1972),pp. 63-72.

Kelly, Henry Ansgar, *Love and Marriage in the Age of Chaucer* (Ithaca, 1975).

Kelly, Joan, 'Early Feminist Theory and the Querelle des Femmes', *Signs* 8 (1972), pp. 4-28.

Kestenberg-Gladstein, Ruth, ' "The Third Reich." A fifteenth century polemic against Joachism, and its background', *Journal of the Warburg and Courtauld Institutes* 18 (1955), pp. 245-95.

Khanna, Lee C., 'Women's Worlds: New Directions in Utopian Fiction', *Alternative Futures* 4 (1981), pp. 47-60.

Kibre, Pearl, *Scholarly Privileges in the Middle Ages* (Cambridge, Mass., 1962).

Kidson, Peter, *The Medieval World* (Toronto, 1967).

King, Margaret L., 'The Religious Retreat of Isotta Nogarola (1418-1466): Sexism and Its Consequences in the Fifteenth Century', *Signs* 3 (1978), pp. 807-22.

—— and Albert Rabil, eds., *Her Immaculate Hand. The Women Humanists of Quattrocento Italy* (Binghamton, 1983).

Kittredge, George Lyman, 'Chaucer's Discussion of Marriage', *Modern Philology* 9 (1911-12), 435-67; reprinted in *Chaucer: Modern Essays in Criticism*, ed. Edward Wagenknecht (New York, 1959).

Klubertanz, George P., *St. Thomas on Analogy* (Chicago, 1960).

Knight, Stephen, *Geoffrey Chaucer* (Oxford, 1986).

Koch, Gottfried, *Frauenfrage und Ketzertum im Mittelalter* (Berlin, 1962).

Kolodny, Annette, *The Lay of the Land. Metaphor as Experience and History in American Life and Letters* (Chapel Hill, 1975).

——, 'A Map for Rereading: Or, Gender and the Interpretation of Literary texts', *NLH* 11 (1980), pp. 451-68.

Koonce, B.G., 'Satan the Fowler', *Mediaeval Studies* 21 (1959), pp. 176-84.

Krauss, Russell, in *Three Chaucer Studies*, ed. Carleton Brown (London, 1932).

Kula, Witold, *An Economic theory of the Feudal System. Towards a model of the Polish economy 1500-1800* (London, 1976).

Kunar, Kristian, 'Primitivism in Feminist Utopias', *Alternative Futures* 4 (1981), pp. 61-6.

LaBalme, Patricia, ed., *Beyond Their Sex: Learned Women of the European Past* (New York, 1980).

Ladurie, E.LeRoy, *Montaillou. The Promised Land of Error* (New York, 1978).

Lagarde, G. de, 'L'idée de la représentation dans les oeuvres de Guillaume d'Ockham', *International Committee of Historical Sciences Bulletin* 9 (1937), pp. 425-51.

——, *La naissance de l'esprit laïque au déclin du moyen âge*, 6 vols. (Paris, 1934-46).

Laidlaw, J.C., ed., *The Poetic Works of Alain Chartier* (Cambridge, 1974).

Lambert, M.D., *Medieval Heresy. Popular Movements from Bogomil to Hus* (New York, 1977).

Langer, Suzanne, *Feeling and Form* (New York, 1953).

Latouche, Robert, *The Birth of the Western Economy* (Paris, 1956, New York, 1966).

Leach, Edmund, ed., *Feudalism: Comparative Studies* (Sydney, 1985).

LeClair, Sister M. Ida, *Utopias and the Philosophy of Saint Thomas* (Washington, D.C., 1941).

Leclerq, Jean, *Jean de Paris et l'Ecclésiologie du XIIIe Siècle* (Paris, 1942).
Leff, Gordon, *Heresy in the Later Middle Ages* (Manchester, 1967).
Legge, M. Dominica, *Anglo-Norman Literature and Its Background* (Oxford, 1963).
LeGoff, Jacques, ed., *Hérésies et Sociétés dans l'Europe pré-industrielle* (Paris, 1968).
——, 'The Historian and the Ordinary Man' in LeGoff, *Time, Work and Culture in the Middle Ages* (Chicago, 1980).
Leicester, H. Marshall, 'Of a fire in the dark: Public and private feminism in *The Wife of Bath's Tale*', *Women's Studies* 11 (1984), pp. 157-78.
Lenin, V.I., *Philosophical Notebooks* in *Collected Works* 38 (Moscow, 1972).
Leonard, Frances M., *Laughter in the Courts of Love* (Norman, 1981).
Le Villain, M., *Histoire Critique de Nicholas Flamel et de Pernelle sa Femme* (Paris, 1761).
Levi-Strauss, Claude, *The Elementary Structures of Kinship* (Paris, 1949; Boston, 1969).
——, *Structural Anthropology* (Paris, 1958; New York, 1963).
Lewis, C.S., *The Allegory of Love* (New York, 1936).
Lippard, Lucy, ed., *Surrealists on Art* (Englewood Cliffs. N.J., 1970).
Lis, C. and H. Soly, *Poverty and Capitalism in Pre-Industrial Europe* (London, 1979).
Lombard, M., 'L'Or Musulman du VIIe au XIe Siècle', *Annales* 2 (1947).
Loos, Milan, *Dualist Heresy in the Middle Ages* (Prague, 1974).
Lovejoy, Arthur O., *The Great Chain of Being* (Cambridge, Mass., 1936).
Lourdaux, W. and D. Verkels, eds., *The Concept of Heresy in the Middle Ages* (Louvain, 1976).
Lucas, Angela, *Women in the Middle Ages* (Norfolk, 1983).
MacPherson, C.B., *The Political Theory of Possessive Individualism* (Oxford, 1962).
Macherey, Pierre, *A Theory of Literary Production* (London, 1978).
Malvern, Marjorie, ' "Who peyntede the leon, tel me who?": Rhetorical and Didactic Roles Played by an Aesopic Fable in *The Wife of Bath's Prologue*', *Studies in Philology* 80 (1983), pp. 238-52.
Mandel, Ernest, *Marxist Economic Theory* (New York, 1962).
Mann, Jill, *Chaucer and Medieval Estates Satire* (Cambridge, 1973).
Manuel, Frank and Fritzie, eds., *Utopian Thought in the Western World* (Cambridge, Mass., 1979).
Margolis, Nadia, *The Poetics of History: An Analysis of Christine de Pizan's 'Livre de la Mutacion de Fortune'* (Ph.D. dissertation, Stanford University, 1977).
Marie de France, *Die Fabeln*, ed. Karl Warnke (Halle, 1898). ——, *Fables*, ed. A. Ewert and R.C. Johnston (Oxford, 1942; repr. 1966).
Marin, Louis, *Le Récit est un Piège* (Paris, 1978).
——, *Utopics: Spatial Play* (Atlantic Highlands, N.J., 1984).
Markus, R.A., ed., *Augustine, A Collection of Critical Essays* (Garden City, N.Y., 1972).
Marx, Karl, *A Contribution to the Critique of Political Economy* (Chicago, 1904).
——, *Pre-Capitalist Economic Formations*, ed. Eric J. Hobsbawm (New York, 1964).
Mathew, Gervase, *The Court of Richard II* (London, 1968).
Maurer, Armand A., *Medieval Philosophy* (New York, 1969).
——, 'Ockham's Razor and Chatton's Anti-Razor', *Medieval Studies* 46 (1984), pp. 463-75.
May, William H., 'The confession of Prous Boneta, Heretic and Heresiarch', in *Essays in Medieval Life and Thought*, ed. John H. Mundy (New York, 1955).
McCall, John P., *Chaucer Among the Gods* (University Park, Pa., 1979).
McCarney, Joe, *The Real World of Ideology* (Sussex and Atlantic Highlands, N.J., 1980).

McDonnell, Ernest W., *The Beguines and Beghards in Medieval Culture* (New York, 1969).
McFarlane, K.B., 'Bastard Feudalism', in *England in the Fifteenth Century. Collected Essays* (London, 1981).
McIlwain, C.H., *Constitutionalism Ancient and Modern* (Ithaca, rev. ed. 1947).
Medvedev, P.N. and M.M. Bakhtin, *The Formal Method in Literary Scholarship* (Leningrad, 1928; Baltimore, 1978).
Menard, Philippe, *Le Rire et le Sourire dans la Littérature Courtoise* (Geneva, 1969).
Menges, M.C., *The Concept of Univocity* (St. Bonaventura, N.Y., 1952).
Menut, Albert and Alexander J. Denomy, eds., *Le Livre du Ciel et du Monde* (Toronto, 1943).
Middleton, Anne, 'The *Physician's Tale* and Love's Martyrs: "Ensamples mo than ten" as a method in *The Canterbury Tales*', *The Chaucer Review* 8 (1973), pp. 9-32.
Mollat, M., *Les Pauvres au Moyen Age* (Paris, 1978).
Mombello, Gianni, 'Per un'edizione critica dell' "Epistre Othea" di Christine de Pizan', *Studi Francesi* 8 (1964), pp. 401-17 and 9 (1965), pp. 1-12.
Molnar, Thomas, *Utopia, the Perennial Heresy* (New York, 1967).
Moody, Ernest A., ed., *Johannis Buridani Quaestiones super libris quattuor de Caelo et Mundo* (Cambridge, Mass., 1942).
Moore, R.I., *The Origins of European Dissent* (London, 1977).
Morris, William, 'How I became a Socialist', in *Selected Writings*, ed. G.D.H. Cole (London, 1948).
Morton, A.L., *The English Utopia* (London, 1952).
Muscatine, Charles, 'Courtly Literature and Vulgar Language', in *Court and Poet*, ed. Glyn S. Burgess (Liverpool, 1981).
——, *The Old French Fabliaux* (New Haven, 1986).
Noonan, John T., Jr., *Contraception. A History of Its Treatment by the Catholic Theologians* (Cambridge, Mass., 1966).
——, 'Power to Choose', *Viator* 4 (1973), pp. 419-34.
Nykrog, Per, *Les Fabliaux* (Copenhagen, 1957).
Ockham, William, *Octo Quaestiones de Potestate Papae*, ed. J.G. Sikes in *Guillelmi de Ockham Opera Politica* (Manchester, 1940).
Orioli, Raniero, *L'eresia a Bologna fra XIII e XIV secolo*, vol. 2: *L'eresia dolciniana* (Rome, 1975).
Ortner, Sherry, 'Is female to male as nature is to culture?' in *Women, Culture and Society*, ed. Michelle Z. Rosaldo and Louise Lamphere (Stanford, 1974).
Owen, G.E.L., 'The Platonism of Aristotle', in *Proceedings of the British Academy* 51 (1965).
Parrington, Vern L., *American Dreams. A Study of American Utopias* (Providence, 1947).
Patai, Raphael, 'Maria the Jewess – Founding Mother of Alchemy', *Ambix* 29 (1982).
Payen, Jean-Charles, 'Genèse et finalités de la pensée allégorique au Moyen Age', *Revue de Métaphysique et de Morale* 19 (1973), pp. 466-79.
——, *La Rose et l'Utopie* (Paris, 1976).
Piehler, Paul, *The Visionary Landscape* (London, 1971).
Pike, David, 'Brecht and Stalin's Russia', in *Beyond Brecht. The Brecht Yearbook* 11 (1982), ed. John Fuegi (Detroit, 1983).
Pinborg, Jan, *Die Entwicklung der Sprachtheorie im Mittelalter* (Copenhagen, 1967).
——, 'The English Contribution to Logic Before Ockham', *Synthèse* 40 (1979), pp. 19-42.

Pisan, Annie de and Anne Tristan, *Histoires du M.L.F.* (Paris, 1977).

Pisan, Christine de, *Livre de la Paix*, ed. Charity C. Willard (Hague, 1958).

——, *La Mutacion de Fortune*, ed. Suzanne Solente, SATF, 4 vols. (Paris, 1959-66).

——, *Ballades, Rondeaux and Virelais*, ed. Kenneth Varty (Leicester, 1965).

——, *Le Livre du Corps de Policie*, ed. Robert H. Lucas (Geneva, 1967).

——, *Lavision Christine*, ed. Sister Mary L. Towner (New York, 1969).

——, 'Ditie de Jehanne d'Arc', ed. Angus J. Kennedy and Kenneth Varty in *Nottingham Mediaeval Studies* 18 (1974), pp. 29-55 and 19 (1975), pp. 53-79.

Poirion, Daniel, 'De la signification selon Jean de Meun' in *Archéologie du Signe*, ed. Lucie Brind-amour and Eugene Vance (Toronto, 1983).

Pollock F. and F.W. Maitland, 'The Age of Bracton' in *The History of English Law* (Cambridge, 1895).

Power, Eileen, *The Wool Trade in Medieval English History* (Oxford, 1941).

Pratt, Robert A., 'Three Old French Sources of the Nonnes Preestes Tale', *Speculum* 47 (1972), pp. 422-44, 646-68.

Propp, Vladimir, *Morphology of the Folktale* (Austin, 1968).

Quilligan, Maureen, *The Language of Allegory* (Ithaca, 1979).

Rabant, Jean, *Histoire des Féminismes Français* (Paris, 1978).

Rabil, Albert, *Laura Cereta, Quattrocento Humanist* (Binghamton, 1981).

Raby, F.J.E., *A History of Christian-Latin Poetry* (Oxford, 1927).

Rashdall, Hastings *The Universities of Europe in the Middle Ages*, 3 vols. (Oxford, 1895; rev. ed. 1936).

Read, John, *Prelude to Chemistry* (Cambridge, Mass., 1936).

Reeves, Marjorie, *The Influence of Prophecy in the Later Middle Ages. A Study in Joachism* (Oxford, 1969).

Renard, Georges, *Guilds in the Middle Ages* (London, 1918; repr. New York, 1968).

Richards, E. Jeffrey, trans., *The Book of the City of Ladies. Christine de Pizan* (New York, 1982).

——, 'Christine de Pizan and the Question of Feminist Rhetoric', *Teaching Language Through Literature* 22 (1983), pp. 15-24.

Richardson, H.G., 'The Coronation of Edward I', *Bulletin of the Institute for Historical Research* 15 (1937-8).

Richardson, Lulu M., *The Forerunners of Feminism in French Literature of the Renaissance* (Baltimore, 1929).

Rigaud, Rose, *Les Idées Féministes de Christine de Pisan* (Neuchatel, 1911; repr. Geneva, 1973).

Robertson, D.W., Jr., *A Preface to Chaucer* (Princeton 1962).

——, 'The Wife of Bath and Midas', *The Chaucer Review* 6 (1984), pp. 1-20.

Rogers, Katharine M., *The Troublesome Helpmate. A History of Misogyny in Literature* (Seattle, 1966).

Rosier, Irene, *La Grammaire Spéculative des Modistes* (Lille, 1983).

Roy, Bruno, ed., *L'Erotisme au Moyen Age* (Montreal, 1977).

Rubin, Gayle, 'The Traffic in Women: Notes on the "Political Economy" of Sex', in *Toward an Anthropology of Women*, ed. Raina Reiter (New York, 1975).

Russell, Jeffrey, 'Interpretations of the Origins of Medieval Heresy', *Mediaeval Studies* 25 (1963).

Salisbury, John, *The Statesman's Book of John of Salisbury*, trans. John Dickinson (New York, 1927).

Sands, Donald B., *Middle English Verse Romances* (New York, 1966).

Schapiro, Meyer, 'The Bowman and the Bird on the Ruthwell Cross', *Art Bulletin* 45 (1963), pp.351-4.

Schibanoff, Susan, 'Comment', *Signs* 9 (1983), pp. 320-26.

Schramm, P.E., *A History of the English Coronation* (Oxford, 1937).

Schimmelpfennig, Bernard, '*Ex fornicatione nati*: Studies in the Position of Priests' Sons from the Twelfth to the Fourteenth Century', *Studies in Medieval and Renaissance History* 2 (1979), pp. 1-50.

Schoeck, Richard, 'Chaucer's Prioress: Mercy and Tender Heart' in *The Bridge, A Yearbook of Judaeo-Christian Studies* 2 (New York, 1956) and reprinted in *Chaucer Criticism* vol. 2 (Notre Dame, 1960).

Schulz, F., 'Bracton on Kingship', *English Historical Review* 60 (1945), pp. 136-75.

Shahar, Shulamith, *The Fourth Estate: a history of women in the Middle Ages, 500-1500* (London, 1983).

Shapiro, Gloria, 'Dame Alice as Deceptive Narrator', *The Chaucer Review* 6 (1971), pp. 130-41.

Shapiro, Herman, *Medieval Philosophy* (New York, 1964).

Silberer, Herbert, *Probleme der Mystik und ihrer Symbolik* (Vienna, 1914).

Spearing, A.C., *Criticism and Medieval Poetry* (London, 1964).

Spiers, John, *Chaucer the Maker* (London, 1951).

Staines, David, '*Havelok the Dane*: A Thirteenth-Century Handbook for Princes', *Speculum* 51 (1976), pp. 602-23.

Steinberg, Leo, *The Sexuality of Christ in Renaissance Art and in Modern Oblivion* (New York, 1983).

Stephens, John N. 'Heresy in Medieval and Renaissance Florence', *Past & Present* 54 (1972), pp. 25-60.

Stock, Brian, *The Implications of Literacy* (Princeton, 1983).

Taylor, A.E., *Aristotle* (London, 1943).

Thomson, John A.F., *The Later Lollards, 1414-1520* (Oxford, 1965).

Thrupp, Sylvia, *The Merchant Class of Medieval London* (Ann Arbor, 1948).

Thundy, Zacharias P., 'Matheolus, Chaucer and the Wife of Bath', in *Chaucerian Problems and Perspectives*, ed. E. Vasta (Notre Dame, 1979).

Tornay, Stephen Chak, *Ockham: Studies and Selections* (La Salle, Pa., 1938).

Tout, T.F., *Edward the First* (London, 1913).

Trinick, John, *The Fire-Tried Stone* (Cornwall, 1967).

Vaananen, Vekko, 'Le *fabliau* de Cocagne', *Neuphilologische Mitteilungen* 48 (1947), pp. 3-36.

Tuchman, Barbara, *A Distant Mirror. The Calamitous Fourteenth Century* (New York, 1978).

Tuve, Rosamund, *Allegorical Imagery: Some Medieval Books and Their Posterity* (Princeton, 1966).

Ullman, Walter, *A History of Political Thought: The Middle Ages* (Harmondsworth, 1965).

Utley, Francis L. *The Crooked Rib, an analytical index to the argument about women* (Columbus, 1944).

van Lennep, J., *Art et Alchimie* (Brussels, 1966).

Vance, Eugene, 'Saint Augustine: Language as Temporality', in *Mervelous Signals. Poetics and Sign Theory in the Middle Ages* (Lincoln, 1986).

Wakefield, Walter, 'Some Unorthodox Popular Ideas of the Thirteenth Century',

Medievalia et Humanistica n.s.4 (1973), pp. 25-35.

Walsh, P.G., *Livy* (Cambridge, 1961).

Watts, P.R., 'The Strange Case of Geoffrey Chaucer and Cecily Chaumpaigne', *The Law Quarterly Review* 63 (1947), pp. 491-515.

Wenzel, Hélène, 'The Text as Body/Politics: On Appreciating Monique Wittig's Writings in Context', *Feminist Studies* 7 (1981), pp. 264-87.

Werner, Ernst, 'Die Stellung der Katharer zur Frau', *Studi Medievali* ser.3/2 (1961), pp. 295-301.

Wessley, Stephen E., 'The Thirteenth-Century Guglielmites: Salvation through Women', in *Medieval Women*, ed. Derek Baker (Oxford, 1978).

Wickson, Roger, *The Community of the Realm in Thirteenth Century England* (London, 1970).

Wilkinson, B., 'The "Political Revolution" of the Thirteenth and Fourteenth Centuries in England', *Speculum* 24 (1949), pp. 502-9.

Willard, Charity C., 'A Fifteenth-Century View of Women's Role in Medieval Society: Christine de Pizan's *Livre des Trois Vertus*' in *The Role of Women in the Middle Ages*, ed. Rosemary T. Morewedge (Albany, 1975).

——, *Christine de Pizan. Her Life and Works* (New York, 1984).

Williams, Raymond, 'Base and Superstructure in Marxist Cultural Theory', in *Problems in Materialism and Culture* (London, 1980).

Wilson, K.M., ed., *The Dramas of Hrotsvit of Gandersheim* (Saskatoon, 1985).

Winspear, Alban D. *The Genesis of Plato's Thought* (New York, 1940).

Woledge, Brian, 'Le Theme de la Pauvreté dans la Mutacion de Fortune de Christine de Pisan', in *Fin du Moyen Age et Renaissance. Mélanges . . . offerts a Robert Guiette* (Anvers, 1961).

Wolfe, Eric, *Europe and the People Without History* (Berkeley, 1982).

Woolf, Virginia, 'A Scribbling Dame', in *Virginia Woolf. Women and Writing*, ed. Michele Barrett (New York, 1979).

——, *A Room of One's Own* (1929, London, 1977).

Zink, Michel, 'The Allegorical Poem as Interior Memoir', *Yale French Studies* 70 (1986), pp. 100-126.

Index